James John Hissey

Through ten English counties

James John Hissey

Through ten English counties

ISBN/EAN: 9783744741651

Printed in Europe, USA, Canada, Australia, Japan

Cover: Foto ©Andreas Hilbeck / pixelio.de

More available books at **www.hansebooks.com**

PRIEST'S TOWER, STOKESAY CASTLE.

See page 284.

Through
Ten English Counties

BY

JAMES JOHN HISSEY

AUTHOR OF 'ON THE BOX SEAT,' 'A HOLIDAY ON THE ROAD,'
'ACROSS ENGLAND IN A DOG-CART,' ETC.

> The lost art of travelling
> in one's own country.
> LINNÆUS.

WITH SIXTEEN FULL-PAGE ILLUSTRATIONS BY THE AUTHOR
AND A MAP OF THE ROUTE

LONDON
RICHARD BENTLEY & SON, NEW BURLINGTON STREET
Publishers in Ordinary to Her Majesty the Queen
1894

All rights reserved

THE LIES COMING OUT OF JUDGE JEFFREYS' MOUTH.
See page 313.

PREFACE

THE following pages contain the chronicle of a journey by road taken through ten English counties. To the writer it seems that there can hardly be a pleasanter mode of spending a summer holiday than by driving about our own beautiful country, beyond the customary tourist's haunts, and out of the beaten track of travel, resting at the homely and homelike old-fashioned inns on the way, that still, the fates be praised, may be found scattered over the land, and what is more to the point, make the wayfarer exceedingly comfortable.

To those in search of a quiet holiday without dulness, and who object to crowded watering-places and the bustle of ordinary travel, a driving tour offers manifold advantages; the constant change of scene it provides keeps the attention always pleasantly occupied, whilst there is ever a feeling of delightful expectancy as to what each fresh bend of the road may reveal, so that anything approaching to *ennui* is impossible. And the rural folk one meets with from time to time are an interesting study in themselves.

In the pre-railway age the Briton who travelled

by post-chaise or by coach, of necessity saw, what his descendants seldom do, the rural beauties of his native land. The peaceful progress of a driving tour is the very antithesis of the haste, bustle, and clamour of the railway, and combines change of air and scene with the least possible amount of annoyance or fatigue. In such a storied land as Britain, so abounding in past memories, one can hardly drive anywhere without coming upon some interesting relic of departed days. It may be an old abbey, a ruined castle, a moated manor-house, a historic home, an ancient church, a sleepy medieval market town, or even a picturesque roadside. hostelry with its weather-toned front and traditions of the coaching times. And as for the country, away from large towns, the beauty of England is a dream of loveliness, gentle, mellow, and peace-bestowing; there is no scenery like it in the world. It is something to leave one's commonplace everyday surroundings behind, to blot them out from memory, and to travel for a time in this true Arcadia.

The illustrations, engraved by Mr. Pearson from a selection of my sketches made during the journey, may, I trust, add to the interest of the text. In an age of cheap and hasty process work, I further trust that the employment of good old-fashioned woodcuts may prove not unacceptable.

J. J. HISSEY.

1894.

CONTENTS

CHAPTER I

PAGE

The pleasures of travelling by road—Various ways of spending a holiday—Planning our tour—The start—Richmond Park — Kingston—"An old-fashioned inn with old-fashioned ways"—The Coronation Stone of the Saxon kings—Facts *versus* traditions—A fine prospect—A new pleasure—Bolder Mere—Pine woods—English scenery . 1

CHAPTER II

Ripley—The tyrants of the road—An old coaching inn—Old folk-lore—Guildford—Ancient buildings—A picturesque street—Past and present—A ruined fane—Godalming—A "thoroughfare" town—Gorse and heather—A lonely hostel—A gipsy encampment—At the sign of the Red Lion—Hindhead Hill—The highlands of Surrey . 16

CHAPTER III

A wayside monument—The Devil's Punch Bowl—A bit of primeval England—A legendary inn—A story of the road—The "Anchor" at Liphook—A misty day—Inn signs—Petersfield—Chats with country folk—A Hampshire "Hanger"—A railless land—Homes of the people—A pseudo Druids' Circle—A joke by the way . 35

CHAPTER IV

A country inn—An ancient poster—Changed times—A new mode of spending a holiday—A barren upland—Winchester—A hostelry with a history—A fifteenth-century half-timbered house—Winchester cathedral—Izaak Walton's tomb—A bit of eleventh-century ironwork—Ancient builders and modern restorers—A quaint conceit in words—Where Jane Austen lived and died . . 54

CHAPTER V

An ancient dole—A wonderful jump of a horse—Hursley—The grave of John Keble—Romsey and its Norman abbey—A beautiful monument—A ghastly relic—An evening walk—A curious mistake—The wrong use of words—An amateur angler—"Merrie England"—A lighthouse for land travellers—The finest view in England—Salisbury . 75

CHAPTER VI

Old Sarum—A windy spot—Gigantic earthworks—Salisbury Plain—Amesbury—Vespasian's Camp—Stonehenge—A chat with a caravanist—Over the downs—An ancient home—Old houses and new ones—Where Charles II. secreted himself for five days—"Hiding holes"—Woodford—A second Stratford-on-Avon—Old inscriptions . 94

CHAPTER VII

Salisbury Cathedral—Wilton—Good roads—A church and a museum—The flag of the ill-fated *Captain*—The valley of the Wylye—Wishford—A curious incised slab—Codford—A chat with an old villager—How the poor live—Legendary inns—Warminster, past and present . . 116

CHAPTER VIII

A breezy day—A chartless cruise—Westbury White Horse—Turner's Tower—Beckington—Old English gardens—A quaint village—A fifteenth-century inn with a history—A great "hiding-hole"—Ancient chambers—Vanished curiosities—"The twin maidens of Foscote"—A horrible tradition—A haunted room—Cider-making—Farleigh Castle—A picturesque spot—Storm-overtaken . . 133

CHAPTER IX

Two old manor-houses—An ancient Saxon church—Unexplored England!—An old monastic tithe barn—A stately Jacobean home—A mass chapel on a bridge—Great Chaldfield manor—A curious inscription on a window pane—A quaint church tower—A fifteenth-century mansion—Sir Walter Raleigh's smoke room—An interesting interior—Places and pictures—The legend of the lady with the white hand—A well in a living room 151

CHAPTER X

A land of stone—Corsham—Chippenham—A story of the road—Chance company at one's inn—Corston—Malmesbury—An ancient market cross—An ideal landlord—Trespassing—A "watching chamber"—Stories in stone—The Thames head—Cirencester—A misadventure . . 173

CHAPTER XI

The Cotswold Hills—"Posting" miles—A chat with a farmer—A twelfth-century churchyard cross—Old windows—A wooded valley—A picnic by the way—Cheltenham—Carriers' carts—Tewkesbury—Half-timbered inns—The Ideal *versus* the Real—Upton-on-Severn—A quaint church tower 197

CHAPTER XII

An ancient home — Old customs — A haunted room — A "Powder Chamber"—An old coach bill—The Malvern Hills—A country of orchards—Worcester—Old sayings —Knightsford—A picturesque spot—Inn yards—A quaintly-clipped yew tree—"Far from the madding crowd" 220

CHAPTER XIII

An old-fashioned garden—Amongst the hills—A steep bit of road—Storm and sunshine—Bromyard—Prosperous farmers—Twelve miles from Anywhere—Epitaph-hunting —Country life—Leominster—A quaint old home—A curious inscription—Nature's many moods . . . 242

CHAPTER XIV

The Teme valley—A romantic town—A quaint old hostelry— Round about Ludlow—The Whitcliff—Ludlow Castle— We come upon a character—A round chapel—"Buried history"— Old proverbs — A huge fireplace — Ludlow church—An ancient dole—Tales in carving—A pleasant land 260

CHAPTER XV

Bromfield Priory Gateway—Craven Arms—A flourishing village —Stokesay Castle—Relics of a forgotten fight—A medieval hall—A fortified manor-house—Corve Dale—A quiet corner of England—A curious church tower—Munslow —A picturesque church—A ghastly tomb—A seller of tracts 279

CHAPTER XVI

The Wrekin—A Shropshire toast—Bridgenorth—A leaning tower—Thirsty souls—Abbreviation of names—Romantic

and picturesque towns—Quatford—A curious effect—
Kidderminster—Round about an old coaching inn—
Hills and clouds—Droitwich—Satire in stone—Buildings
with characters—Pleasant company—On the road . . 298

CHAPTER XVII

Salwarp House—A paragon of perfection—Droitwich brine
baths—Up and down hill—Alcester—Changeful weather
—Histories in monuments—A veritable Arcadia—
"Shakespeare's Town"—Beneath the sign of the Red
Horse—Washington Irving's Parlour—Geoffrey Crayon's
Sceptre—A storied chamber. 317

CHAPTER XVIII

Stratford-on-Avon from the old coach road—Charlecote Park
—On the wrong track—Nature's music—Driving for
health—An old Roman fossway—The unexpected in
scenery—Kineton—Architectural details—A puzzling date
—Edgehill and battle-ground—A stiff ascent—An evening drive—Banbury cross—Horses on the road . . 335

CHAPTER XIX

A pleasant road—A morning drive—Railways and roads—
Aynho—Village stocks—A sketch—Old associations in
buildings—A trysting-place—A curious dispute—A crop
of Indian corn—Buckingham—The finest tonic in the
world—Bell-ringing—A tramp at prayer—Sunsets—
Winslow—A curious window—An amusing conversation. 354

CHAPTER XX

Mist and rain—An evening effect—Aylesbury—Notice to
trespassers—Exploring—Old-fashioned hospitality—
The building material of the country—Wayside inns—A

peaceful progress—The Chiltern Hills—Tring—Life at a country hostelry—Commercial travellers—" Nothing new under the sun "—Quaint gargoyles . . 373

CHAPTER XXI

A late drive—The hour of romance—The peace of evening—Berkhampstead—The last day of a holiday—Chance acquaintances on the road—A puzzling problem and a possible explanation—An ancient gabled house—The contrast of the old and new—A picturesque waterway—Watford—Bushey—A retrospect—Back again in London   387

CHAPTER XXII

Concerning driving tours   397

APPENDIX .   . 403

INDEX   . 405

ILLUSTRATIONS

Priest's Tower, Stokesay Castle	. *Frontispiece*	
Hindhead Hill . .	. *To face page*	32
In the Heart of Hampshire .	,, ,,	58
An English Common . .	,, ,,	88
Stonehenge . .	,, ,,	110
George Inn, Norton St. Philips .	,, ,,	138
Mass House on Bridge, Bradford-on-Avon	,, ,,	156
Malmesbury Abbey . . .	,, ,,	184
Old Bell Inn, Tewkesbury .	,, ,,	213
Talbot Inn, Knightsford . .	,, ,,	236
Ludlow Castle . .	,, ,,	265
Stokesay Castle . .	,, ,,	282
Roadside England . .	,, ,,	306
Salwarp House near Droitwich .	,, ,,	318
The View from Edgehill .	,, ,,	348
An old English Farmstead	,, ,,	376
Map of Route .	*End of Book*	

THROUGH TEN ENGLISH COUNTIES

CHAPTER I

The pleasures of travelling by road—Various ways of spending a holiday—Planning our tour—The start—Richmond Park—Kingston—"An old-fashioned inn with old-fashioned ways "—The Coronation Stone of the Saxon kings—Facts *versus* traditions—A fine prospect—A new pleasure—Bolder Mere—Pine woods—English scenery.

WHAT a pleasant thing it is to drive through a pretty country in the summer time; and granted this, how much more enjoyable must it be when—as in the case of an old-fashioned journey by road—a drive is extended to weeks through some portion of rural England, than which if there exists a more beautiful country it has yet to be discovered! Given a horse and carriage (owned or hired), a suitable companion, and a sufficiency of time, what can be more delightful than to start upon a lengthened driving tour with the whole of fair England before one and all sorts of pleasant possibilities in prospect?

It is of itself a novel and agreeable sensation to be able to leave home without even having to consult a time-table or to call a cab! It is a relief also to avoid the rush and crush of crowds, to know that your belongings cannot go astray (as these are always with you), and to escape wholly from the many petty and frequent annoyances that beset the ordinary tourist.

There is, too, a charming feeling of independence about this wandering mode of life. Travelling thus, you can rise early or late as the mood inclines; having no train to catch, you can breakfast at your leisure, and can start on the day's journey without consulting any one's convenience but your own: you can stop on the way, when and where you please, diverge therefrom, or even change your route altogether at any point should you be so minded. Such freedom is altogether delightful; and a holiday so spent in the midst of beautiful and changeful scenery is certainly not more expensive, and—to me at any rate—is infinitely more interesting and enjoyable than the ordinary sojourn at a crowded hotel, or at the dear and dull lodgings of a fashionable sea-side resort, with the usual accompaniments of shadeless sands or shingle, gritty and glaring promenades, the everlasting iron pier, and inevitable German band; all most inspiring—especially the German band!

Having elected to take our holiday thus, as had been our wont for years now past, and the time for our annual outing having once more arrived, the only matter to be arranged was, what portion of England we would select to explore. Sundry county maps, and our treasured copy of *Paterson's*

Roads, last edition of 1829 (the Bradshaw of the pre-railway days), were consulted, and a long evening was spent in discussing the programme of our proposed tour.

In former expeditions of a like nature we had fixed upon some distant point to drive to, such as the Land's End, or some spot in Scotland or Wales, and had set off thither by one line of country, returning by another. This time, however, we concluded that we would not aim for any special point or place, only roughly determining that we would first steer a southerly course for Romsey Abbey, and so by Salisbury and Stonehenge find our way to the west of England, striking from thence northward up to Ludlow and the Welsh border, and so see something of a part of England that we had not hitherto visited, returning home by another route to be arranged in due course.

But we did not bind ourselves in any way to even this somewhat broad programme. Our tour was solely one of pleasure, and open to change in accordance with our latest fancy; all that we really agreed upon was to spend a month or so driving about England—as far from railways as might be, in an age when the land is gridironed all over with them—simply in the search of healthful relaxation, such being the very essence of a real holiday. For the nonce we made pleasure-seeking our sole business, we would take our ease on the road, at our inn, and suffer no guide-book dictation as to what we should or should not see. Guide-books are, to a certain extent, tyrants, and on such an expedition best left at home, then you do not feel any compulsion to visit this or that spot because they make special mention of it,—we preferred to make our own discoveries. We had no intention of completing any definite itinerary; a restless desire to see everything turns holiday-making into genuine hard work.

We set forth upon our wanderings one fine autumn afternoon, having during the morning carefully packed our roomy dog-cart with all necessary belongings for the journey, including some warm wraps in case of need, waterproofs, maps, sketch-books, and photographic paraphernalia. It is a wise precaution, and one that we always take upon the eve of such an expedition, to make out a list of everything down even to the smallest trifle that is likely to be required; such articles as matches, a spare pair of brake blocks, also driving gloves, candles for carriage-lamps should one by chance be benighted, writing materials, a small flask of brandy (which we always take but luckily have never needed), a plentiful supply of tobacco, and sundry minor trifles likely to be forgotten at the last moment without such a list. It is a pleasant satisfaction on starting to feel certain that you have got everything with you that can possibly be required, from the absolutely needful down to little luxuries.

Having said our farewells and mounted our dog-cart we set off from Kensington at a brisk trot and soon reached Hammersmith, where we crossed the Thames, and presently found ourselves on Barnes

Common, which bit of open gorse-dotted space gave us our first savour of the country. Thence we proceeded by Sheen into Richmond Park, where the grand sweeps of green sward stretching down to dark woods, the tall waving bracken all around, and the great gnarled oaks beneath whose spreading branches the deer were resting, imbued us at the very outset of our journey with a feeling of the real country.

Richmond Park has in parts a genuine look of wild nature about it, in such pleasing contrast with the nature trimmed and tamed of town parks. So much indeed did its wildness impress us, that as we drove along a curious feeling of being far away from everywhere came over us, a very real feeling, yet one wholly beyond analysis. It seemed almost as though it must have been an illusion of our senses that so short a time ago we had been threading our way through the thronged and noisy streets of the greatest city in the world.

Richmond Park was strangely deserted that gloriously sunny afternoon, not a living thing was to be seen, excepting the quiet deer under the trees and the restless birds above. It is surprising how comparatively few Londoners find their way to the more secluded portions of this fine demesne; for there is nothing, as far as I am aware, within anything like the same distance of town, to at all approach it for wild beauty and for the restful impression it affords of remoteness from "the busy haunts of men." For ourselves, until we neared Kingston Gate, we did not see a single human creature; we might indeed have been in some distant Midland or Western shire, for all that our eyes could tell.

So we drove on through this woodland solitude towards the golden sunset and the ancient market town of Kingston, where we sought accommodation for the night beneath the sign of the Griffin, an old-time coaching house, duly mentioned in our *Paterson's Roads*. Driving under the low archway, that gives entrance to the inn, we discovered the waiter at the side door very successfully occupied in doing nothing. In answer to our inquiry he replied, "Certainly we can put you up, if you don't mind an old-fashioned inn with old-fashioned ways." Why he made such a reservation we could not exactly comprehend, but we hastened to assure him that such an inn and such ways was just what we especially liked; and certainly the old-fashioned mellow light of candles on our table, and the chops, cooked to perfection, which we had with our evening meal, made us gladly pardon the absence of the flare of gas, or the glare of electricity, and the long-drawn-out *table d'hôte* of the grander modern hotel. Old stagers by road as we are, we have learnt infinitely to prefer the comfortable homely inn, whereat our port-wine-loving, hail-fellow-well-met forefathers made merry, to the dearer showiness of the more pretentious nineteenth-century hotel,—the product of the railway age.

Next morning, following the example of the famous and entertaining Samuel Pepys of Diary renown, we "awoke betimes" to a beautifully fine day which made us all the more eager to commence our journey in earnest; for we only looked upon our short drive of the previous afternoon as a sort of preliminary affair, like as one regards the preface to a book,—an introduction rather than an integral part of it.

As we drove out of Kingston we passed by the famous Coronation Stone of the early Saxon kings that gives to the town its name (*i.e.* King's stone abbreviated to Kingston). This stone is carefully enclosed by railings, and to prove its genuineness has it not the names of several Saxon kings engraved thereon in quaint antique lettering, and after that who would dispute its authenticity? Not we, at any rate! Moreover, in spite of certain learned and hard-headed antiquaries the stone may really have served the purpose which tradition credits it with having done: there is no special reason why it should not,—and after all tradition is sometimes right! A too matter-of-fact spirit ruins a good deal of pleasant old-world romance, and spoils many an ancient legend that does no one any harm to believe, and that has been accepted by our uncritical ancestors for generations past as Gospel true.

Modern historians, with no sense of poetry in their compositions, have even dared to call in question the truth of the story of Lady Godiva and her famous ride through the streets of Coventry, "for the all-sufficient reason that at the date of her celebrated escapade there was no town of Coventry in existence through which to ride." In like manner amongst a number of other pretty traditions the one of King Canute struggling with the tide, and that of King Alfred letting the cakes burn in the neatherd's cottage, have also been declared on the same hard-hearted, but, I fear, unimpeachable authority to be apocryphal, and oh the pity of it! What a lot of romance is lost to one by living in an over-critical age! It was, doubtless, this feeling of loss that caused a modern American poet (Russell Lowell) to sing thus regretfully of the unsophisticated past—

> O days endeared to every muse,
> When nobody had any views. . . .
> O happy days, when men received
> From sire to son what all believed,
> And left the other world in bliss,
> Too busy with bedevilling this!

Leaving the Coronation Stone, that has caused this over-long digression, we skirted the side of the Thames for a while. The river, as we drove by, was gay with sailing boats; amongst the number a small yacht with a huge red sail looked exceedingly and pronouncedly eccentric,—attractive I cannot add, one wants to get used to such novelties to admire them! Sails of red and blue and yellow, if such should ever be fashion's decree, would certainly enliven the river with a pageant of moving colour—crossing, passing, and intermingling—that might cause frequented stretches of the Thames to out colour-rival even Turner's dream of Venice. Across the water we caught a glimpse of Hampton Court Palace and park, erst the stately abode of Cardinal and King, now a favourite rendezvous of the Cockney cheap-day-excursionist—from Harry the

Eighth to 'Arry the Tripper, so work Time's changes!

Then passing by some essentially utilitarian water-works with a tall chimney belching forth black smoke in the most approved factory fashion that would not have disgraced Manchester itself, we parted company with the river, and, striking a southerly course along the old Portsmouth road, we soon came to Sandown Park with its pretty race-course, and another half mile brought us to the little village of Esher, where the quaint and weather-stained bell-turret of its ancient church peeping above the lowly buildings around gave a certain feeling of picturesqueness to the otherwise featureless collection of houses that lined the roadway. At Esher the comfortable-looking old Bear Inn, standing well back from the village street, tempted us to call a halt, for the day was hot and mortals are sometimes thirsty, but we resisted its allurements in consideration of the short distance we had travelled, and mindful of the fact that did we linger at every attractive wayside hostelry we came to, our journey might be indefinitely prolonged—so we hardened our hearts and proceeded on our way.

Then began a gentle rise, and at the top of this, from a clump of Scotch firs that crowned a rugged knoll, we had a fine prospect reaching far away over a wild heathery common to a distance of dark woods, bounded on the horizon by low-lying faint-blue hills. Our eyes, so long accustomed to the confined prospects of town streets and squares, delighted to range unrestrained over this goodly expanse of spreading heath and shadowy wood away to the dim misty hills where the sky seemed to drop to meet the earth. It is well, as it is pleasant, to exercise the vision thus at times, for the eye wants training to understand the meaning that lies in the far-away, and to grasp the poetry of its mystery. The vision is apt to get cramped as well as the mind,—we should be able to see broadly as well as think broadly.

Our road now commenced to give us a taste of its scenic capabilities, and a finer or more varied drive of seventy odd miles than the old road from London to Portsmouth affords it would be difficult to discover in all fair England. From the time Kingston, and with it the last suggestion of outlying Cockneydom, is left behind till Portsmouth comes into sight the traveller on that once busy and famous naval highway has an endless succession of rural pictures and landscape panoramas presented to him, ranging from the quiet pastoral, to what may be honestly termed the grand, where the wild Hindhead Hill is crossed, with a long stiff pull of four miles or more. But as we shall drive along this old Portsmouth road as far as Petersfield (fifty-two miles and a quarter from London to be precise), we shall have a fair opportunity, as we proceed, of observing and enjoying a goodly portion of its changeful scenery and characteristic features at our leisure.

Continuing on our way, we passed Claremont Park to our left, shortly after which we crossed Fairmile Common with its excellent stretch of smooth straight road: surely it must be that this mile of good level highway has given its name to the common? Here, doubtless, of old the fast coaches made the most of the opportunity, and did the mile at their best speed : we also, for the mere delight of swift progress and the inspiriting feeling of the thing, indulged in a swinging trot that quickly brought us to the end of the common and to a sharp but short descent that took us to the very uninteresting, not to say downright ugly, hamlet of Cobham Street, which was primitive without, alas! being picturesque.

Just beyond Cobham Street we crossed the little river Mole, a river that earns its name by burrowing underground here and there; then followed a pretty stretch of road with grassy sides (an ideal spot for a quiet canter); after this we came upon another wide expanse of uncultivated ground, covered with gorse and heather, and encircled by dark gloomy pine woods. Wisley Common we made this out to be from our map. As we entered upon it no habitations were visible, nothing but the capital highroad we were on told of man. Here were we, within twenty-four miles of the mighty metropolis with its teeming millions, yet for all that a greater solitude you could hardly find anywhere, though different in kind.

The pine woods now grew close to the roadside, and the air became laden with the resinous odours of the trees, mingled with the peculiar perfume of the gorse. To simply inhale the sweet-scented air that was wafted to us on the warm summer breeze which, as it passed over them, gathered fragrance from tree and shrub and herb, made breathing for itself a delight,—we had discovered a new pleasure of life.

Suddenly, as we proceeded onward, we espied the shimmering silver of a sheet of still water surrounded by a forest of red-stemmed, pointed pines which were doubled in reverse on its glassy surface. This tranquil lakelet—it looked too large and, above all, too dignified to be called a pond—is marked as Bolder Mere on the Ordnance map; it certainly gave a sort of piquant picturesqueness to the landscape as well as an element of brightness, bringing down, as it did, into the heart of the sombre woods around a portion of the bright blue sky and glowing sunshine from above. It was one of nature's own mirrors reflecting and focussing together in sharp contrast the gloom of the dark woods and the sunny brilliancy of the sky.

A roadside inn, curiously called the Huts, stands close by the mere, possibly evolved from such primitive structures as the name implies. There was an ancient boat moored near to the shore, but as it appeared to be more or less leaky (rather more than less) we did not venture therein, a row in a leaky boat not being, according to a former Welsh experience, exactly an unalloyed pleasure; so in preference to a damp row we elected to take a dry ramble through the woods along the margin of the mere in search of a pretty peep just to make a beginning in our sketch-books. Somehow the beginning was never made; we could not find the exact point of view we wished, in fact we felt in a lazy mood, and allowed the camera to do the drawing for us. So we secured a photograph, but not a picture; sometimes we have, indeed, managed to obtain both, but disappointingly seldom.

We took a number of photographs of scenes and places during our outing, but with one notable exception, these were rather interesting than picturesque. A mechanical lens simply records facts, it never puts poetry into a scene, and it is just this glamour of poetry added to the truth of nature which gives the special charm to an artist's production; he has worked something of himself into his picture, he has given us more than a mere transcript of a scene. A mere matter-of-fact rendering of nature is not true art; a camera can reproduce what is before it in black and white—it can copy, but it cannot create. Somewhat in this fashion wandered our thoughts as we leisurely strolled along by the side of the quiet water. We found it easier to think than to work!

Pine woods, by the way, make delightful wandering, for the dead needles of their foliage form a dry and elastic natural carpet to walk upon; moreover, owing to their resinous nature, they dry up rather than decay, as do the leaves of ordinary forest trees, and they are inimical to any tangled undergrowth that so generally and unpleasantly impedes the pedestrian's progress in other kinds of woods.

What a delightful picture that little mere with its setting of pine woods presented to us! It is just these charming surprises that make driving about rural England so enjoyable. Truly England is a small country, but the diversified character of our home scenery, even that of a single county, is something to wonder at and to be grateful for. I do not believe that there exists an Englishman who knows thoroughly even the county in which he lives; if there be one, I have not come upon him yet. A gentleman once declared to me that he knew perfectly well the country all around his home within a circle of ten miles or so; he was a man who rode, and drove, and walked a good deal, and seldom slept out of his own house; yet I went out alone one day in search of the picturesque, and brought back with me a sketch that I had made within four miles of my friend's very own door. On seeing my sketch, he said I must have invented the scene, as there was nothing at all like it in the locality; yet afterwards, on going with me to the spot, he had to confess that, though he had often been near to it, he had never actually been there, and declared in manifest surprise that he had no idea that such a scenic gem existed within a walk of where he had lived for years!

There is no wearisome sameness in English scenery as so frequently obtains in foreign lands. Here have I been driving about England for many years now past, yet every time I find myself on the road, I am struck anew by the seemingly infinite variety and changefulness of all I see; the landscape always appears fresh, and therefore full of interest; at the same time it greets you with a familiar friendly face. Who could weary of travelling by road through a land like this? Such a journey is a continual feast of loveliness for those who have eyes to see and a heart to understand the mellow homelike beauties it reveals. Untravelled England is just as well worth exploring as any other land!

CHAPTER II

Ripley—The tyrants of the road—An old coaching inn—Old folk-lore—Guildford—Ancient buildings—A picturesque street—Past and present—A ruined fane—Godalming—A "thoroughfare" town—Gorse and heather—A lonely hostel—A gipsy encampment—At the sign of the Red Lion—Hindhead Hill—The highlands of Surrey.

So we drove on through this pleasant land of pine woods, of gorse-strewn commons, and wild heathery wastes, till we reached the sleepy little village of Ripley with its fine spacious green, on which some of its juvenile inhabitants were indulging in a game of rough cricket; happy youngsters, thought we, to have such a grand playground.

A famous halting and baiting place was Ripley in the old coaching days; then the village street was all alive with traffic, noisy with the clatter of many hoofs, and musical with the sound of the frequent horn; but times have changed, Ripley is quiet enough now, for it is left quite out in the cold by the iron road. To this day Ripley has never heard the sound of a railway whistle; though, as to this, let it be sorrowfully confessed that we had a good imitation of one from a huge ungainly traction engine that we met as we were driving in, a fine specimen it was, too, of one of those big bullies of the highway that, if the road be at all narrow, drive all lesser fry into the hedgerow or ditch. You cannot collide with a traction engine to your own satisfaction, so the weakest has to go to the wall, gracefully or grumblingly — we always do the latter.

I have often wished that two of these hideous iron vagabonds—surely the ugliest product of an ugly age—could only meet each other in a narrow lane and fight out the right of way between them, and "I be there to see" — but this is digressing and uncharitable besides. I cannot, however, be expected to see things exactly from the point of view of a traction engine driver.

At Ripley we drove up to the Talbot, an ancient inn so suggestive of a past age with its picturesque courtyard and weather-stained front. In days of yore, when mén made haste slowly, according to modern ideas of speed that is, forty or more coaches passed the old inn during the day, a number of which changed horses there; such, at least, the landlord informed us was the tradition handed to him with the historic house and was the only item that he had not to pay for on taking possession.

We determined to rest a while at Ripley and to proceed in the cool of the evening on to Guildford, where we proposed to spend the night. So having very satisfactorily "refreshed the inner man," as the country reporters delight to remark, and having seen that our horses were properly looked after, we set forth for a ramble across the wide-spreading green to the attractive-looking country beyond, and in search of the ruins of Newark Abbey, which we noticed marked on our map as lying in that direction about a mile and a half away by eye measurement. We somehow failed to find the ruins, or even to obtain a distant view of them, but what mattered it? We did not feel in any way duty bound to get there, and we had a most enjoyable afternoon's stroll which landed us at a pretty out-of-the-world spot by the side of the slothful river Wey, where we rested on the soft sward under the grateful shelter of some wide-branching trees, feeling much at peace with all the world and ourselves in particular. Newark Abbey ruins might remain unseen for all we cared. We were quite content to recline there on the grass and simply do nothing but dream dreams, for at times doing nothing is a virtue, especially in these days of push and brain pressure.

It was very peace-bestowing to while away an idle hour in that sweet seclusion listening to the liquid music of the flowing river and to the cawing and clamouring of some sleek-looking rooks who were holding an animated conversation on the topmost branches of the tall elms above us. I know nothing so soothing to the ear tired with town noises as the tranquil gurgling of a slowly-gliding stream singing its ceaseless song without words.

On our way back to our inn we came upon a man at a corner of the large common sorting a heap of rags out of a large hand-barrow: we felt no desire to go near him, so made a slight *détour* to avoid the locality whereon he had chosen to dump his unsavoury stock-in-trade. However, he saw and made straight for us, with the intention, we presumed, of requesting a copper, but for once we were mistaken; the man, after begging our pardon, simply civilly asked me if I could give him a light for his pipe. I gave him one and was quite prepared for the begging to follow as a matter of course, looking upon the match incident as a sort of preliminary for that purpose, but the unexpected does sometimes happen; having lighted his pipe, and not forgetting to thank me for my kindness, the man at once withdrew without another word. Somehow this individual interested me; he looked so poor and woebegone, he might so easily have concocted some dismal story, or still worse, might have told some real tale of sorrow, but he did neither.

Asking my wife to stroll slowly on I went to interview the man. It appeared from what I could gather from him that, after trying many ways of getting a living and failing in each in turn, as a last resource he had taken to rag-collecting. "It's not a pleasant job, and it's hard work too," said he; "so a lot of chaps shirk it, but a man must do something, and I've tried almost everything else and failed; now I can just get a living at this, and that's something to be thankful for these hard times." And he puffed away at his pipe, and still he did not beg. Certainly he was one of the most cheerful men under adverse circumstances that I ever met. I could moralise here but forbear, even children nowadays decline to read books with a moral!

Returning to the Talbot we ordered the horses to be put to, and whilst they were being harnessed we whiled away the short interval by opening up a chat with the landlord; for when on the road we never let slip an opportunity of gleaning any odd scraps of information, as by so doing we occasionally manage to add to our store of notes upon local histories and traditions, or perhaps to learn particulars of curious customs and quaint sayings, or, more welcome still, to pick up some of the old folk-lore that yet lingers on in a few remote corners of the country, and now and then we gathered anecdotes of the coaching days. Of course on the whole we collected a good deal more chaff than corn, but this was to be expected. Our present gossip resulted in unearthing nothing that interested us, besides learning the number of coaches that passed the place in the days gone by, as already mentioned. The landlord did, however, volunteer to give us a bit of information which *he* considered noteworthy. It appeared that his name was Monk, and that of the previous landlady was Nun. "So you see, sir," he exclaimed, "the Monks have turned the Nuns out." I merely give this as a fair sample of the chaff that has to be winnowed from the corn. To make amends let me here digress to record some of the old folk-lore about the weather as connected with the months of the year which we gathered at different points on the journey, but, for convenience' sake, I now chronicle together. These are all fresh to me, and some, if not all, may likewise be fresh to my readers. It is well worth while to glean all the folk-lore we can, while we may; to the lover of the never-returning past these old sayings are always welcome. Here then is my little list :—

> January cold and clear
> Makes a good grass year.

For the next month it would appear that fine weather is not desirable—

> All the months of the year
> Curse a February fair.

April, it appears, should be chill, as it often is, for

> An April chill
> The barn will fill,
> An April warm
> There's little corn.

The next concerns June and July—

> A wet June
> Sets all in tune.
> If warm July
> Need not be dry.

And with the following couplet my collection ends,

> Dry August and warm
> Crops come to no harm.

From Ripley on to Guildford we had a five miles' stretch of level winding road, and with it a complete change of scenery. Hedge-enclosed fields, in which the golden sheaves of the early harvest stood, and green broad meadows wherein cattle and sheep were contentedly grazing, took the place of the fragrant pine woods, spreading heaths, and open commons; and now and again beyond these we caught a peep of undulating wooded hills; green and gray and blue, as they were near or far away.

It is well in many respects to arrive at your day's destination late in the afternoon; and on a driving tour you generally do this of necessity. Then it is, when the light is warm and mellow and the shadows grow mysterious, that all places put on their most poetic aspect and therefore appear to the stranger at their best. The sunset hour wonderfully enhances any beauty there may be in town or country, and by its softened light and broad shadows helps to hide or gloss over the commonplace: mean trivialities do not then assert themselves, for they are more or less lost in the mass. I have seen even that dull and dreary row of highly-rented houses, known to Londoners as Harley Street, appear almost picturesque under the effect of the golden glow of a colourful sunset.

Under a similar glowing sunset, the west aflame with burning red and gold, it happily chanced that we entered the old town of Guildford and drove down its hilly and picturesque High Street—one of the most picturesque, I verily believe, in England—passing by on either side of us many a curious old building; amongst others we especially noted the ancient gray-stone Grammar School with its mullion, leaden-lattice windows and weather-worn doorway bearing the date of 1552: the Abbot's Hospital, also a charming bit of Jacobean architecture, with its tower gateway of red brick time-toned into a harmony of ruddy tints, delighted us. But, though less pretentious, what interested us more than all the rest was the quaint seventeenth-century town-hall with its picturesque bell-turret, projecting upper story, and recessed shadowy space below, together with its big, useful clock boldly stretching far over the roadway, supported by an elaborate bracket of wrought iron that would have done credit to a medieval craftsman. This eye-pleasing specimen of old-time building gives quite a special grace and character to the street in which it stands. Without it Guildford would be to me like "the play of *Hamlet* with Hamlet left out"; it seems a very part and parcel of the place, as much so indeed as St. Paul's is of London—and even more. It is curious to note how a well-designed building will oftentimes stamp a whole town with its own peculiar individuality, owing to the powerful impression it has on the observer over all else around; whilst the featureless commonplace is simply seen and speedily forgotten, or else passed wholly unregarded by,—we have that with us every day, enough and to spare.

At Guildford we drove up to the White Lion, where we found excellent quarters for the night. This inn, the landlady informed us, was rebuilt as far back as 1593. Its external appearance, however, suggests a much later date; in this respect it possibly resembles the old ship which had been so often repaired that at last there was hardly a bit of the original timber left in her, nevertheless to every one she was the old ship still. Anyhow the White Lion can boast historically of a considerable antiquity, a hostelry of that name having stood on the spot for over three eventful centuries, and still as of old the White Lion gives heraldic welcome to the tired wayfarer and offers "good accommodation for man and beast." This latter, by the way, is an important point for the driving tourist, as some modern hotels possess no stabling, naturally in an age when every one is conveyed from place to place by rail.

Having secured our rooms we set off whilst the daylight lasted in search of Guildford Castle; this we discovered—after threading our way along some mazy by-streets—to consist of a crumbling keep standing on a steep mound and surrounded by some well-kept public gardens. The gay flower-beds, neat gravel walks, and ornamental water hardly, it seemed to us, formed a happy or harmonious setting to the massive feudal keep with its four frowning storm-stained walls uprising dark and grim, as though the gathered gloom of unrecorded crimes hung over them. As a picturesque relic of the past Guildford Castle is distinctly disappointing; possibly this may be in some measure owing to its enclosed situation and unsuitable surroundings: we noticed some herring-bone masonry in its walls, and that was the only item of archæological interest that we could discover in the keep.

We were favoured by fine weather on the morning we left Guildford. A bright, warm, sunshiny day (the warmth being pleasantly tempered by a gentle breeze), and a rising barometer that gave promise of a continuance of such desirable conditions, caused us to set out upon our wanderings in the best of spirits. Indeed how could we feel otherwise than "jolly" (if I may be allowed that expressive term) with the whole of the day's untasted pleasure before us, the only thing really needful being to reach an inn for the night?

Leaving our hotel—the landlady coming to the door to bid us good-bye and a pleasant journey, in the frank and kindly old-fashioned manner—we soon "got away" once more into the quiet country. One of the great advantages of living in a small town is that you can so easily get out of it in any direction to enjoy a rural walk, and this without any undue exertion, or having to take to the railway, and to wait about wearily in draughty stations for unpunctual trains.

In about a mile we reached the ruins of St. Catherine's Chapel, which crown a sandstone cliff that rises directly from the roadside. This ruin forms a prominent and pleasing — not to say a romantic — feature in the landscape. Standing alone and boldly, as it does, on the top of an isolated knoll, it asserts itself out of all proportion to its size. The broken, bare, and weather-beaten walls of the desecrated fane have an indescribably pathetic look, all forsaken as they are except by wild birds, who as we drove along were holding a profane and noisy matins above the site where stood of old the high altar and bowing priests. The only purpose that the ruin now serves is to be picturesque, and this it does to perfection, though its pious founder (all such founders were, I take it, at least presumed to be pious) little dreamed that the sacred chapel he built would ever come to such a—to him—useless end. But to be picturesque, in this age of general utilitarian ugliness, is to fulfil a positive need.

Mindful of Emerson's injunction to the traveller—

> Set not thy foot on graves!
> Hear what wine and roses say—

we did not mount the hill for a nearer inspection of the ruin. The mind has many moods, and we elected that bright sunny morning, when all around was so full of gladsome life, to seek the "wine and roses" of the present, rather than to linger amongst the mouldering ruins of the past.

> Set not thy foot on graves!
> Hear what wine and roses say;
> The mountain chase, the summer waves,
> . . . thy feet may well delay.
>
> Set not thy foot on graves;
> Nor seek to unwind the shroud
> Which charitable Time
> And Nature have allowed
> To wrap the errors of an age sublime.

Now a level stretch of road that led us past rich meadow lands through which the little river Wey wound in and out like a ribbon of shining silver, brought us to the straggling town of Godalming, which appeared to us to consist mainly of one "long drawn out" High Street of old-fashioned two-storied and gabled houses—one of those places that earned for themselves the pertinent title of "thoroughfare town" in the olden days of road travel. Rattling along this extended and narrow street we came once more into the open country, and after passing through the neat and tree-embowered village of Milford we soon found ourselves on the wild and breezy expanse of Witley Common—a bit of unsophisticated nature, attractively picturesque in its unkempt, primitive beauty.

Climbing to the top of the common, on looking back, a glorious far-reaching prospect met our gaze. Here I may remark that when driving across country it is well worth while to take an occasional glance backwards; many a time has a wholly unexpected revelation of scenery been our reward for so doing. Looking back, then, from our elevated position in the direction from which we had come, our eyes wandered over a vast panorama of wooded slopes that dipped into valleys and rose again to fir-fringed hills, and to rounded downs over beyond where we judged the town of Guildford to lie hidden from sight in a deep hollow. But even more attractive than the view was the wild waste of common all around us: a miracle of colour this, glowing as it did with the harmless gold of the gorse, and painted purple with the sunlit heather; which rich intermingling tints were enhanced in glory by a background of dark-green pines and deep-blue hills. The gorse that grows so freely and flourishes on the poorest land, blossoming all the year round (even in the middle of December I have seen great patches of it on the South Downs in rich bloom), this little-considered plant excites my utmost admiration: were it only some rare exotic, difficult and costly to grow, and only to be secured in a heated greenhouse—like sundry over-estimated and delicately-nurtured plants—how charmed and enthusiastic we should be over it! Verily an English common seen under a sunny summer sky with the gorse thereon in bloom, looking like so much burnished gold, only far more beautiful, is a sight to behold, and sometimes I almost wish that it were not such an everyday one so that it might be more appreciated.

Who need cross the sea to distant Italy for colour? when we have at home the gorgeous gorse and purple heather, to say nothing of fields of crimson clover; the wayward wild poppy with its brilliant burning red, growing where it listeth; together with the spreading blue-bell and wild hyacinth making the ground below to rival the cerulean sky above; the hawthorn and apple trees with their pink and white blossoms, with many other plants and flowers and trees (such as the chestnut) that make gay this land of ours, which envious foreigners, who know it not, have called wanting in colour! Doubtless they have formed their judgment of the English country from the view thereof taken from a railway carriage window, for that is the way nowadays that travellers see the land. The railway is the best possible method of getting speedily from place to place, and the worst possible method of learning all that lies between!

Now the road dropped down to a desolate hollow where the landscape closed in around us, and took upon itself a gloomy air as darksome pines stood on either hand in place of the gay open waste with its acres of purples and golds. Here in this hollow we found a primitive and lonely hostel ycleped the Half Moon; how the landlord thereof could possibly make a living puzzled us, but the traveller by road has many such puzzles presented to him so that at last he ceases to ponder over them.

Even on that inspiring summer day the little forsaken-looking inn with its sombre surroundings appeared depressing enough, the only cheerful thing in the prospect being some stagnant ponds, which by reflecting some of the brightness from the sky above did lend a little much-needed cheerfulness to the scene. It was just one of those eerie out-of-the-world inns that a novelist of the old romantic school delighted to picture as the seat of some blood-stirring tragedy; the ponds would suggest a likely spot wherein to make away with the unfortunate traveller. The Half Moon looked as though one of G. P. R. James's ideal inns had come into actual existence, the mysterious belated traveller and the gathering twilight were only required to realise one of that author's descriptive opening chapters.

The Half Moon, though it led us into this train of thought, probably has had nothing but a dull and uneventful career, but somehow certain places suggest past histories, and look legendary as though they must have some weird story connected with them, if it could only be unearthed. A good deal depends of course on the momentary mood of the mind. Sometimes, too, traditions are innocently invented; I was told of a gentleman who, on going over an ancient manor-house, remarked in pure fun to one of the party who were being shown over the place, "That's the very window out of which the last Baron's daughter threw herself and was drowned in the moat below, all because of a love affair," and ever afterwards this legend, invented on the spur of the moment, was related as genuine history by successive servants who showed the house. So legends may sometimes arise and be handed down as facts from generation to generation!

Just beyond the Half Moon we had a charming wayside picture presented to us. In a wooded dell near to the road a rustic foot-bridge crossed a tiny stream, and leading from this hither and thither up and down the glen were wandering paths worn deep down below the general surface of the ground by the constant tread of generations of country folk on the soft sandy soil. Near to the stream was a gipsy's encampment consisting of an ancient caravan, a red-brown tent, and two tethered shaggy horses. Close to the tent was a tripod from which was suspended an iron pot over a wood or peat fire; from this a blue wreath of smoke ascended upwards to the bluer sky above. There is something very attractive and poetic about such a camp fire, it is so suggestive of holiday freedom from the ordinary restraints of society and gives a genuine flavour of out-door life; to me it also brings recollections of delightful evenings spent by similar fragrant wood fires on the lonely pine-clad mountain sides of remote California. A good deal of the pleasure of a scene lies not merely in itself but in what it suggests.

Then driving on in time we reached another humble but clean and bright little inn rejoicing in the familiar and favourite title of the Red Lion. Here we pulled up for a while and refreshed our thirsty souls with a mixture of ale and ginger beer which the cheery landlady recommended, and after sampling it we cordially approved of her recommendation. On that warm day the mixture seemed as very nectar, and we would not have exchanged it then for a bottle of the rarest wine nor most expensive brand of champagne. Hunger and thirst are excellent things—when you can satisfy them; and to show this, is there not a tale told of an American who exclaimed, "I guess I've such a thirst on me that I would not take five dollars for"?

Whilst resting in the grateful cool of the modest bar of the inn our eyes caught sight of a painted board hung on the wall and thus inscribed,

> This is the Red Lion Inn,
> When dreary without, 'tis cheery within.
> All who come here shall meet with good cheer
> and
> Those who are honest have nothing to fear.

Of this inscription the worthy landlady seemed somewhat proud, and asked me if it were not clever poetry. "You see, sir," she said, "a clergyman wrote that for me, and had it painted too." What could we do but appear to incline to her opinion? moreover, we were in a frame of mind to be easily pleased that day, as indeed we were on all the days we spent on the road. If you are a pessimist, a driving tour will soon turn you into an optimist; the health-giving out-of-door life induces an essentially cheerful disposition that makes all the world around you seem bright, your very soul is imbued with the cheerfulness of the sunshine, and the tonic air acts like a sort of natural champagne on your spirits. At any rate such is our experience of the benefits conferred on both body and mind by a prolonged driving tour, upon which you can walk as much as you choose. During the whole of our most enjoyable holiday we always had by us quite an over-abundance of spirits and health: we smiled on the world and it smiled back on us in return with interest added. We met with nothing but kindness everywhere, and every stranger seemed a friend. So long life to the road say I!

Then began the long and fine ascent of the Hindhead Hill, which for the pleasure of the thing we walked, pausing here and there, from time to time, to admire the wonderful views that opened out as we rose, views which culminated in one grand burst of a wide, far-reaching panorama, stretching over miles and miles of woodlands, meadows, and tilled fields; and beyond these we observed a faint silvery sheen which we imagined might be the distant sea. Now and again we caught a glimpse

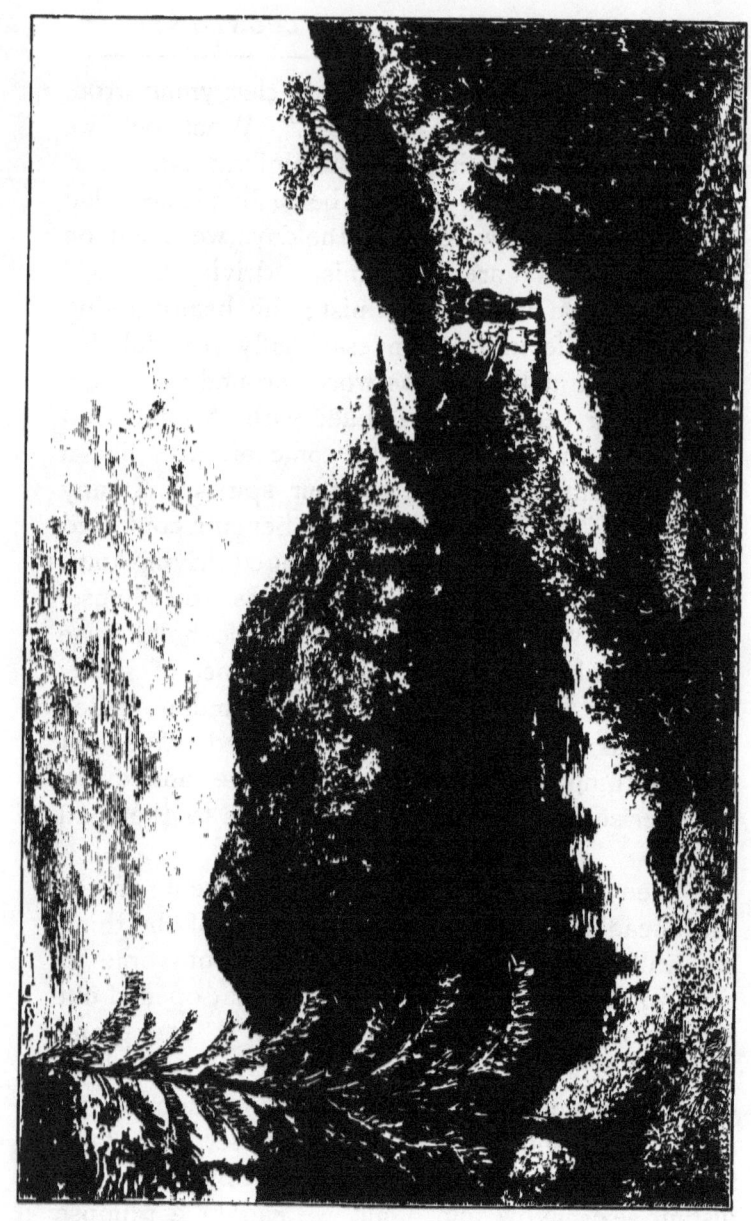

HINDHEAD HILL.

of a gray church tower, or the gables of a red-roofed farmhouse with cone-shaped ricks clustered around half drowned in foliage: and here and there the haze of lingering smoke showed the whereabouts of a hidden home or unseen hamlet; whilst white devious roads led our eyes away and away into the vast expanse of greenful country, roads diminishing by distance into mere traces of thread-like lines, which in turn vanished into nothingness, long before our visions reached the remote horizon.

It was a prospect to make glad and proud the heart of a home-loving Englishman, who seems, alas! nowadays to be so rare a being that it is a real treat to meet with one. When will English rural scenery, which of its kind and within its own limits is the most beautiful in the world, become fashionable, I wonder? Scotland, Wales, the Lake District, and portions of the sea-coast are overrun in the summer time, but who ever thinks of travelling in search of beauty or pleasure anywhere in Britain out of these tourist-haunted regions? To those in search of "fresh woods and pastures new" I say try rural England: you may cross the seas and travel far and wide (like hosts of perverse Britons do), and fare no better, if half as well.

From that breezy vantage height we looked down upon and over a world in miniature, it was a study of vast and vanishing perspectives. The landscape vigorous close at hand in the bold outline of rugged hill and wild common, softened down by degrees into a graceful pastoral peacefulness—a delightful blending of the grand and the sylvan; each enhancing the other by the charm of contrast.

How space-expressing was that glorious prospect of hill and dale, of wood and meadow; a prospect that as it receded grew more and more vague till in the distance all things became as shadowy and unsubstantial as the scenery of a dream. Our minds verily enlarged with the great expanse before us; the silence, the solitude, and restful peace of it made the ambitions and cares of the world below seem strangely trivial. It is good to be, and feel above the world at times, to see it from a changed point of view; it gives one a curiously combined sense of smallness and superiority not to be defined in words.

So full of radiant atmosphere was the scene that we could realise by the blueness of the bounding horizon the existence of a tangible something between us and it—an ocean of air (not a mere void) as real as the waters of the sea!

In this highland district of Surrey one might fancy oneself, without any undue strain on the imagination, in some remote corner of Scotland. But all this wild and lonely loveliness is reserved for the infrequent traveller by road, and is, therefore, known to but few of the present generation of Englishmen, for who ever goes by road nowadays when the rail avails? One can hardly realise that the Metropolitan county of Surrey possesses such truly fine scenery, for grandeur belongs to form and colour as well as to mere height, and Hindhead Hill can fairly claim these qualities.

CHAPTER III

A wayside monument—The Devil's Punch Bowl—A bit of primeval England—A legendary inn—A story of the road—The "Anchor" at Liphook—A misty day—Inn signs—Petersfield—Chats with country folk—A Hampshire "Hanger"—A railless land—Homes of the people—A pseudo Druids' Circle—A joke by the way.

STILL mounting and skirting the side of the wind-swept Hindhead Hill (that rose in a grand mass, purply dark, above us) we came to a desolate spot by the margin of the road, whereon we observed a solitary hewn stone set up—looking much like a grave-stone out of place; pulling up here we dismounted and found it inscribed as follows:—

> Erected
> In detestation of a barbarous murder
> Committed here on an unknown sailor
> On Sep. 24th 1786,
> By Edw. Lonegon, Mich. Casey, and Jas. Marshall
> Who were all taken the same day
> And hung in chains near this place.

Why the names of the murderers should be thus handed down to posterity, I do not quite comprehend. The stone stands on the very verge of a vast and gloomy hollow, known locally as the Devil's Punch Bowl,—and what more fitting liquor than the blood of a murdered man could the Devil's Punch Bowl hold? On the top of Hindhead Hill, which can be reached from this spot by a short stiff climb, is erected a tall granite cross which marks the site where the murderers were hung in chains. Truly a ghastly spectacle for travellers this way in the "good old days."

Reaching at last the summit of our elevated road we had, as a welcome change from so much collar-work, a glorious and continuous descent of three miles or more, that took us into the pretty village of Liphook. Just after commencing the descent we passed the Royal Huts Inn, not far from which a clump of storm-bent trees used to be pointed out as marking the highest part of the road. A little beyond the Royal Huts still another fine prospect opened out before us, a vast tract of shaggy woods, which on referring to our map we discovered to be Woolmer Forest. The view suggested a bit of primeval England, so wild and uninhabited it seemed save for a few solitary houses near at hand.

Then as we drove along, the brake hard on and the traces loose, we passed by, a little to our left, the lonely Seven Thorns Inn of legendary renown, a hostelry of importance at one time, which is said to stand exactly half-way between London and Portsmouth. Near here one stormy winter's night a century or so ago three coaches, one from London and two bound thither, were blocked in by deep snow-drifts. Fortunately for the passengers the Seven Thorns was within a walk, and let us hope that they all spent a sociable and merry evening therein, relating to each other over their wine and hot toddy the regulation stories of the perils and adventures of the road,—as such snow-bound travellers always used to do, at least in the good old Christmas numbers of the illustrated papers and magazines.

On this splendid stretch of favourable road the coaches were accustomed to make up for any lost time on the downward journey, and it frequently happened that they had lost time to make up. It was an ideal bit of road for the purpose; "pushing ground" it was termed in the slang of the period, though sometimes it was a case of "the more haste the less speed," for with a team of horses of all kinds and conditions, galloping down hill with a heavily-laden coach behind them, if anything went wrong, an upset was a possibility, and timid travellers were generally glad when this exciting stage was safely over.

On one occasion, so an old story has it, during the ascent of Hindhead the jovial Jehu who handled the ribbons had beside him on the box seat an over-zealous and manifestly nervous clergyman as a passenger. Now it chanced, like most of his kind and especially of that period, the Jehu indulged in numberless jokes and stories which he interspersed with a liberal supply of oaths. The clergyman, after many reproofs, at last managed to put a stop to the swearing—and the stories as a natural sequence: the "coachee" was silenced, but he waited his opportunity to be revenged. The Royal Huts passed, he whipped his horses into a full gallop, the coach rocked about, the clergyman held on fearful of a mishap, and remonstrated at the reckless driving. This is where the coachman scored; taking in the whole situation, he replied, "There's no good a talking any more, can't you see as how the whole —— lot are bolting? I can't hold 'em in, there's a bridge and a nasty bend at the bottom of the road, we shall be all smashed up there to a dead certainty. You'll be in heaven directly."—"The Lord forbid," exclaimed the clergyman! I beg to state that I am not responsible for the authenticity of this or any story picked up from strange fellow-travellers on the road, I simply relate them as they came to me.

On the last half mile into Liphook a complete and almost startling change came over the scene: the open heathery wastes, and fragrant fir forests, gave way to enclosed meadows and the leafy luxuriance of chestnut, oak, and elm. The trees, plants, and shrubs were of a different kind from those growing on the wild district about Hindhead: nature now took upon herself a more homelike aspect.

At Liphook we drove up to the Royal Anchor Hotel, on the roadway before which stands a great spreading chestnut that has doubtless afforded grateful shelter to many a thirsty traveller, driving or on horseback, whilst he quaffed a refreshing glass of cool, clear, nut-brown ale, home-brewed too I'll wager! Finding that we could be accommodated, we determined to spend the night here, though the horses were fit for another stage, and there was plenty of time on hand; but neither speed nor the "doing" of so many miles a day formed any part of our plans, and a sudden fancy took possession of us to see something of the pretty and inviting-looking country around, as far as a leisurely, desultory stroll might reveal it to us, that is.

The Anchor at Liphook is an ancient house, and one of wide renown in the old days; for its dinners and lunches were noted, and its wines were famed. From the *Diary* of Samuel Pepys we learn that during one of his official journeys to Portsmouth he visited Liphook on 5th August 1668; for he relates therein how coming from London he took "coach again" at Guildford (the worthy Samuel spells it "Gilford"), and so "got to Liphook, late over Hindhead, having an old man, a guide in the coach with us; but got thither with great fear of being out of our way, it being ten at night. Here good, honest people: and after supper to bed." And over two centuries later, we find likewise "here good, honest people, and after supper" we also "to bed."

Since Pepys' days the Anchor has outlived many changes, and has entertained many a royal and distinguished guest, including the allied Sovereigns, who in 1815 lunched here on their way from Portsmouth to London. In times past, naturally, this great naval highroad was often used by important persons, and the Anchor at Liphook was a convenient as well as a favourite stopping place—with good fare to boot as a matter of certainty. A complete list, if it could be obtainable, of all the royalties and notabilities who have rested here would be a long one. The names painted on the doors of some of the rooms of the old house in lieu of the usual numbers, such as "King," "Queen," "George," etc., suggest that they have been named after famous personages who have occupied them. On a newel of the staircase we noticed the date of 1629 deeply carved, which may be the date of the original building : one of the oak doors to a room upstairs we also observed was beautifully carved, telling of a past prosperity and a host who took a pride in his house,—not that the Anchor needs patrons now, for it was full of guests when we were there : fate has been kind to this historic hostelry that so pleasantly links the present with the past.

As I have already mentioned, of old this inn was famed for its wines, more especially for its port (indeed they were reported to be better than what his Majesty had), and this reputation was an important matter in an age of wine-drinking. After the coaches were taken off the road the Anchor's long and deservedly-earned prosperity departed for a while, though only to revive again : but, if what I have been told be true, the cellar of port remained and improved during all the outward changes. History has it, that a certain connoisseur and lover of good wine chanced, reluctantly driven by the force of circumstances, to have to spend a night at the then nearly-deserted inn, but finding that he could obtain a good dinner with a bottle of rare old port such as his heart desired, he frequently afterwards made it a special point to visit the ancient hostelry solely for the sake of enjoying the fine old wine. Many of the past-time coaching inns possessed cellars well stocked with the best of wines; most of these cellars were sold when declining custom caused the once prosperous landlords to abandon their houses. During a former journey we rested the night at an ancient hostel in the North, and found that the landlady still held a goodly supply of old port (she did not know how old it was) that had been in the cellars ever since the last coach had been taken off the road.

An evening stroll in the country round about Liphook revealed to us a wealth of beauty of the homelike, peaceful order, so rest-bestowing but so hard to convey in words. We wandered along deep hedge-bordered lanes whose green sides and leafiness would have done credit to even lovely Devonshire.

From all we saw we made a mental note to come again some day to leafy Liphook armed with sketch-book and camera, and to explore the locality more at our leisure. Sketching from nature and landscape photography are both delightful hobbies; the mere looking out for likely subjects to draw or take gives a greatly added interest to a country walk which otherwise might be without any special object. The exercise of the sketcher's art, too, affords him an insight into the loveliness of colour and the rare charm of form—an insight which no one who has not tried to paint carefully and honestly from nature, matching as far as he can tint for tint and form for form, can at all realise.

How many people perceive the charm of colour in a landscape till an artist has revealed it to them in a picture? Yet it exists all the same. Strange it is that so few people cultivate the art of seeing: nothing can be less costly or more rewarding. What a pleasant experience it is to take a walk with an artist who is trained to see and is willing to point out the beauties around where we, perchance, only see a succession of trees and green fields!

Leaving Liphook we still kept along the old Portsmouth road as far as Petersfield. It was a misty morning as we drove away from our comfortable inn, and the distant views were all blotted out by a gray veil of moisture. Now and then the mists dispersed in parts, revealing unexpected peeps of woods and hills, only to close in once more, and our horizon from one of miles again became limited to yards. But at last the sun asserted its mastery, and the mists rolled from off the land in mighty masses. It was a lovely sight, the open country being clear, to witness the lingering mists—of a delicate silver-gray in shade but touched with the palest gold in the light—wreathing in and out of the pine woods (which with heaths and commons still more or less lined our way); the mists gradually vanishing into space until we had visions of long vistas down the dim pillared recesses of the pine woods which our fancies tried to liken to the aisles of some vast cathedral. Then, as the sun shone down, the woods around, the gorse, the grass, the bracken and the heather were strewn with drops of suspended moisture that glistened like gems, and converted our little world into a veritable fairyland.

As we passed through the little village of Rake we noticed a public-house rejoicing in the sign of the "Winged Bull." This struck us as a novel sign, we had no recollection of having met it before. A flying bull would surely be a rather undesirable animal in reality, and it is not nearly so artistically effective for a sign as the griffin or the familiar lion. A real lion, though, is a very tame affair compared with the heraldic creation of last century's carver's brain, with his fierce glaring eyes, his twisted tail, his ragged mane, his pronounced half-opened jaws with his curled tongue projecting aggressively forth —a grim, grotesque, and very assertive creature, especially defiant-looking when rejoicing in a fresh coat of vermilion. A lion impossible in reality: the very embodiment of good-natured fierceness, a curious combination of most opposite qualities.

Petersfield, which we reached at noon, is a clean, sleepy, little town, unprogressive also, which is a fault that I have the bad taste to rather admire in these go-ahead days, neither is it picturesque, but it has the charm of naturalness which is not to be despised in an age when so many places ambitiously endeavour to copy London second hand. Here we drove up to the Dolphin, formerly a famous coaching house and still retaining its extensive and excellent stabling. In times past, we were told, over fifty horses were accommodated here, and for the mails one minute only was allowed in which to change the team, and pretty quick work too!

The country around Petersfield is as beautiful as the town is uninteresting. After our mid-day meal we took a tour of inspection round the place, which was soon seen, and eventually we found ourselves on an extensive common close to the outskirts of the town; this was enlivened by a large sheet of water, which with the old trees around and a background of undulating hills made a very effective picture; but just as we began to sketch it big drops of rain fell, and the sparkling, silvery sheet of water suddenly became leaden. The weather most unexpectedly had changed again in that charmingly inconstant way it does change in England; but I for one would not have it otherwise, variety has its attractions, and perpetual sunshine, however delightful for a time, becomes monotonous after a lengthened period, so at least I have found it on the Pacific Slope, where, by the way, a "perfect climate" is set off by earthquakes, and the dust on the roads, where roads exist, makes driving thereon anything but a delight. I have, after a few weeks of ceaseless, glaring sunshine, coming out of a changeless blue void above, actually sighed for our fickle English climate with its glorious cloudscapes and refreshing rains.

The wet drove us back to our inn, where, in the ample courtyard, I found sufficient entertainment for a time in chatting with the ostler, gleaning from him what I could of the coaching history of the old house; having exhausted the ostler, I ventured into the bar and opened up a conversation with sundry townsfolk and farmers I found there; thus I learnt their special views of the world, and gathered how it might be improved according to their ideas. The farmers grumbled, as is their wont; but I met with one exception, and thus he spoke, " Times is bad, they do say, for farming, but somehow I manage to get along. Well, corn won't pay for the growing, that's a fact, for you can buy it cheaper than what you can grow it for. Well, what of it, cattle pay, meat's a goodish bit dearer now than when I was a boy. I don't keep growing crops that don't pay just because my father grew them when they did pay. Not a bit of it. I raise stock and buy my corn to fatten 'em on—that pays! The cheaper the corn the better says I, I convert it into meat. It's all nonsense, with rents down, and good home markets close at hand, to say farming don't pay. It's the old-fashioned farming that don't pay any more than coaches would pay to-day." This was almost startlingly cheerful, so wholly unexpected was it coming from such a quarter.

But the day was now growing old, and the rain did not seem inclined to leave off; so as it was a long stage on to Winchester, our next halting-place, we decided to stop over the night at Petersfield, the more especially as we found our inn, though plain to ugliness outside, clean and comfortable within, our landlord most civil and obliging, and the chance company entertaining.

Amongst the number of men tramping through Petersfield that afternoon was a man who halted for a glass of ale, and who carried a long black cylindrical case, apparently rather heavy; this man puzzled me: I am accustomed to meeting all sorts and conditions of men on the road and can generally make out, or believe I can, their avocation in life; but this man with his curious case, what could he be doing? He looked contented enough, though evidently tramping on the road with his cumbersome burden. I managed to open up a conversation with him at the cost of a glass of ale and so solved the mystery. The case contained a telescope, his "profession" in life being to travel from one sea-side resort to another, where he set his telescope up on the parades, and by charging a penny a peep earned a decent living. He had been at Brighton early in the year, but that place was a failure, there being no ships on the sea there, and for his "profession" ships on the sea were a necessity; naturally "for people won't pay to see nothing," and because of this universal peculiarity of human nature he was off to Portsmouth as he understood that there were lots of ships there.

There is plenty of interest to be had on the road in watching and studying wandering humanity, from the useless begging tramp to the man who earns his living in a variety of unexpected ways,—the peripatetic photographer being perhaps the most common. One of these individuals, whom I came upon in a confidential mood, assured me that he did quite a profitable trade on the country side taking rural folk and their belongings; sometimes even he would manage to spend a whole day at a farmhouse (if he only found the right sort of people) photographing the farmer, his wife, and family;

sometimes as well his house, his horse, and his cattle. Thus sundry uncatalogued people (if I may be allowed the expression) move about in the world and get their living, and, as far as I have observed, they are, collectively considered, by no means a pessimistic race, as one might imagine. The most objectionable of this wandering class are perhaps the quack medicine vendors, who still seem to drive a flourishing trade in small towns and villages; the "only effectual cure for rheumatics" apparently paying the best—and this tells a tale of a prevailing malady, due possibly to badly built, draughty, and damp cottages.

Next morning on awakening we found that the rain clouds had cleared off, and as the rain would refresh the country and lay the dust we did not mind the half day's delay.

Just out of Petersfield we came to a level railway crossing, the gates of which happened to be closed against us whilst a long luggage train shunted backwards and forwards in a leisurely way; for a traveller in haste to get along to be stopped in this manner is most irritating. Fortunately our time was our own so the delay mattered not, still we could have spent five minutes more agreeably than in watching a slow shunting operation, and it seemed to us that railway directors might manage better than to do their shunting across a level crossing! Once I remember, when driving through Yorkshire, being delayed for some time in this provoking manner whilst a thunder-storm was in progress. As I was forced to stop in a bleak, exposed situation I did not at all enjoy the experience, and ever since I have looked upon level crossings as unmitigated nuisances, and have uttered many disagreeable things about them. But I have had my grumble out, let us get back to the dog-cart.

We had now a lovely stretch of country with a fairly level and pleasantly winding road that took us between wooded heights. We had all the beauty of a hilly country without the constant climbing and descending that traversing such a district generally entails. The country truly looked bright and fresh and green after the rain, and the clear air was laden with all sorts of sweet odours; for not only does moisture bring out the fragrance of flower, herb, and creeper (such as the delicate perfume of the honeysuckle), but it also brings out the colours of everything in a wonderful manner. Watch by a pebbly sea-shore, and note how rich is the colouring of the damp stones where left by the receding tide, and then observe how comparatively colourless they look above where dry in the sun, so in a modified degree the same obtains in a landscape.

So we journeyed on through this lovely country of green fields, of many-tinted woods, and gently-sloping hills : a country dotted here and there with humble cottage homes and an occasional farmstead all mellowed by age and so blended with the soft southern landscape as to seem more like a natural growth than something added to it. You had to look for these quiet homesteads, for they did not intrude their presence with the glare of white-wash or the assertiveness of a modern villa. It was essentially a bit of old England wherein all things were time-toned into a restful harmony!

At last we came to a very pretty little hamlet picturesquely placed under the shelter of a thickly-wooded height, or perhaps a steep wall of wood might better describe it. These wooded steeps, which abound about this part of Hampshire, are called locally "Hangers," from the way the trees overhang the hillside, I presume. Though we had heard of these "Hangers" before (White of Selborne and other writers make mention of them), we had never seen any, so abounding in variety is this small England. Here our road led right up to the wooded height, and we wondered what it would do next, but a narrow glen opened out before us, and up between its tree-clad sides we climbed. It was a deliciously cool and shady glen, and through the foliage above the softened sunshine shone, making moving patterns of green and gold around us, and sending here and there shafts of light across our road. The warm summer wind, too, as it passed through the trees made an indescribable "sur, sur, sur," a sound that reminded us of the surging of a distant sea. Inland thus as we were, it was a pleasant deception to shut our eyes and let our ears do the romancing for once.

At the top of the glen we reached, once more, the open country and basked in unclouded sunshine. We were now traversing a railless land, which, doubtless for this very reason, has retained much of its old-world primitiveness and picturesqueness. For if railways attract ugliness and modern eye-sores in building they keep such things much to themselves, for which small mercy the lover of the beautiful should be thankful.

Just after we got on to the high ground we noticed to our left a small stone-built mansion, a charming old home with the bloom of age upon it, standing well back and retired from the roadway, not isolated in a park. It seemed to us the very outward expression of a real English home of the people, picturesque rather than stately, and essentially homelike: anything but grand, yet a residence in which a prince might live and not be ashamed. We also noticed some old half-timbered farmhouses and thatched cottages whose doors opened rustic fashion with a latch. One of these farmhouses had a small outbuilding, the timber work of which was all open,—the intervening places not being filled in with plaster,—we could not imagine the reason of this unless the building were intended for a larder; but the deeply-recessed shadows were undoubtedly picturesque, and quaintly effective.

Now we found ourselves driving through a country that seemed almost like one vast park,—a country that looked as though it were above being merely agricultural. The trees had ceased to be mountaineers, and great elms and sturdy oaks contrasted forcibly with the light and graceful larches and the tall pointed pines of our past stages.

Then as we drove on our road opened out into a large and extensive common; at one corner of this were some pretty cottages that looked for all the world as though they had stepped out of one of

Birket Foster's pictures. On the common, not far from this spot, we saw a circle of rude stones that we took to be some Druidical remains. This circle consisted of a number of huge rocks or boulders set upright supporting several large stones horizontally on the top, Stonehenge fashion. We referred to our map but could not find any Druids' Circle marked at or anywhere near the spot. Pulling up here we proceeded to both sketch and photograph the stones. I think that this was the only time on the journey that we took a photograph without any one coming to watch the operation. Having finished our sketch and packed up our camera, we strolled back as far as the cottages in order to learn, if possible, the name of the Circle, and to gather any other information about it. We found a man at work in his little garden who seemed of a communicative mind, and thus he spoke in reply to our query: "Them stones over yonder, them ain't a real Druids' Circle, why they ain't as old as I be." This was rather severe upon us as we really thought we had come upon a "genuine article," otherwise we should not have taken the trouble to have sketched and photographed it. Then the man continued, "Lots of folk have been taken in with them stones. You see it happened like this; a goodish many years ago, I don't rightly recollect how many exactly, but when I were a boy, Colonel Greenwood as was, and who owned the land all about here, had 'em put up for a lark like. There were some great rocks lying about on the common, and one day the Colonel he says, 'We'll do something with these.' So he gets a big crane, and with a lot of men and horses and levers he got the stones put up as you see. It were a tremendous job, however." Certainly this precious pseudo antique deceived us, for the stones of themselves looked old enough for anything (as naturally they would lying on the common exposed to the storms of ages); and there was positively nothing to show how long they had been raised, for aught that the eye could tell it might have been countless centuries ago.

It really is too bad to manufacture Druidical Circles in this way to the deception of innocent travellers. Indeed, according to the old cottager, some "learned building people" (qy. an archæological party) driving past there one day were, like ourselves, attracted by the circle of stones, and stopped a while to examine them, and our informant overheard one of the company giving a short discourse to the rest about their high antiquity and prehistoric origin! "Lor, sir, how learned like he did talk to be sure, a wonderful clever man he thought himself; and when he had finished he turned round and seeing me there asked if I knew the name of the stones. Says I: 'They ain't got no name as far as I be aware, you see they ain't very old yet.' With that he gets mighty angry, and said I was a stupid fellow and knew naught about them. This were a little too much for me, so up I spoke a bit sharp too as well as he. Says I, 'Well I don't know about being such a stupid, but as I saw 'em put up when I were a boy, I do know positive sure as how they cannot be older nor me'; then I told him the whole history of how the Circle were made, and all the rest of 'em they did laugh just." And here the old man chuckled to himself, manifestly enjoying the joke: so did we. And he was still chuckling as we left him to rejoin the dog-cart and proceed on our way.

CHAPTER IV

A country inn—An ancient poster—Changed times—A new mode of spending a holiday—A barren upland—Winchester—A hostelry with a history — A fifteenth-century half-timbered house — Winchester cathedral—Izaak Walton's tomb—A bit of eleventh-century ironwork—Ancient builders and modern restorers—A quaint conceit in words—Where Jane Austen lived and died.

LEAVING this curious joke in stones to puzzle future travellers this way, in about a mile we reached the scattered village of Bramdean and pulled up at the Fox, a humble little inn whereat we obtained an excellent meal of bread and cheese and ale, followed by some fruit, freshly gathered from the garden for us,—and to a traveller hungry with a long drive in the open air, bread and cheese and ale, provided they are good, is a repast not to be despised.

We had a chat with the homely landlady whilst she laid our simple meal, a cheerful body in spite of seemingly adverse circumstances, for she acknowledged that "times were rather trying," as they had mainly to depend on the chance custom of the road, which was precarious. She said: "I'm so sorry we have nothing better to offer you," notwithstanding that we expressed our entire satisfaction with what she had provided. Anyway, we are not of those who grumble when people do their best, nor do we either expect or desire luxury on the road. We were quite prepared to rough it at any time if needful, and to enjoy roughing it, but we did not consider that we were doing so on this occasion; for the bread and cheese was very good, the ale cool and clear we deemed excellent. Moreover, we were made free of the garden to gather what fruit we liked for ourselves (besides the plentiful supply that the landlady brought in for us), and this without any extra charge, though we insisted on making a little addition to our modest bill; and even this trifle was almost reluctantly received with grateful thanks, on the condition that we would "take some of the fruit to eat on the way, perhaps it might refresh the good lady." So, indeed, wherever we wandered in old England out of the beaten track, we always found the same manifest desire to please and do the best for us. The landlords and landladies of the little country inns did not appear (like the managers of some big company hotels do) to look upon us merely as so much money-making material.

During our conversation with the landlady we learnt from her that the Fox was a very old inn, and before the coming of the railways did a large roadside business. The house, she further told us, was repaired in 1893, and when the plaster was taken down from off the front an ancient and well-preserved poster, dated 1674, was discovered beneath it; this related to a sale of property at Alton. Most unfortunately, in trying to get this off it came all to pieces, and no previous copy of the wording had been made, which was a great pity, as a poster of this nature and over two centuries old might have been of considerable interest.

Then we found our way to the stables to see how our horses were faring; here we discovered the worthy landlord, who was doing ostler duty. On arriving, we had noticed that the top of the sign-post of our inn was carved in the representation of the Prince of Wales' feathers, so we asked the landlord if he could give us the reason of this, and he said that there was a tradition that the Prince of Wales in former times had halted here, for it had been a frequented posting-house, and a goodly number of well-known people had "looked in when passing, but that was all over now; however, we still sometimes have racehorses and their owners stopping over night on their way from Goodwood to Stockbridge." Like the landlady the landlord was of a cheerful disposition, and happily given to look on the bright side of things, though he confessed that the brightness nowadays wanted a good deal of looking after, as it was hard work to get a living at a roadside inn when nearly everybody travelled by rail. Strolling around the small holding that belonged to the place we observed an unfortunate hen that was tied by her leg with a string, the other end of which was attached to a post set in the ground; we had seen a tethered cow and a tethered goat, but never a tethered hen before! In this little property of an acre or so we were told by the landlord that he had taken that year as many as 200 wasps' nests; a startling number it seemed to us, but all round about the district they had suffered from a plague of wasps.

We next extended our wanderings to the top of a wooded knoll that rose above our hill, in search of a view, and we were not disappointed. From a clump of trees there we had a charming prospect over the surrounding country, and looked down upon a picturesque old farmhouse with a rambling colony of irregular, red-roofed outbuildings gathered about it in a delightful planless manner. Certainly of all English homes such an old-fashioned farmhouse is the most picturesquely pleasing to look upon, and the most rewarding to sketch; it is, moreover, so suggestive of the poetry of country life.

There is always something of interest going on in and around a farmstead; the work of a farm too is carried on in a leisurely sort of way that seems the very poetry of labour. What can be less suggestive of toil than hay-making, or the shepherd watching idly over his flock, or the big waggons crawling slowly over the fields to gather in the sheaves of corn, or the meek-eyed cows tending sleepily homewards to be milked as the evening closes around? Now and then one may obtain comfortable apartments at a pleasant old-fashioned farmhouse, and if this be only situated in a pretty country (a district in which heaths and commons abound to be preferred) how delightful a holiday spent therein might prove; with the hay and harvest fields for the children to wander over, and the green lanes and country round to explore!

Nor should the advantages be forgotten of a plentiful supply of pure milk and cream, butter, new-laid eggs, chickens, and last but not least, fruit and fresh vegetables. Does the picture please you, kind reader? Of course there are farmhouses and farmhouses, and the right one needs searching for, but it is attainable. I have spent three most delightful holidays in farmhouse apartments, and the pleasure those holidays gave me, the "good times" I had, is still a delightful memory. Possibly I was peculiarly fortunate, but on two of these occasions the farmer's wife proved to be the cook, and, what is to the point, a most excellent one. We lived on the fat of the land, lived well and inexpensively. All the houses were scrupulously clean, or they would not have suited us. At one of the farms there was some very fair trout fishing in a little rocky river that flowed almost past the very garden; at least I presumed that the fishing was fair, as I managed to catch four presentable trout in about two hours, which is far beyond my average of piscatorial achievements. All the farmhouses were situated in a pretty, not to say romantic country; for this I made a *sine quâ non*, as beautiful scenery so greatly enhances the pleasure of walking, and gives, besides, a zest for sketching from nature,— that most innocent and interesting of hobbies.

For a paterfamilias with a large family in search of health-giving and reasonable holiday quarters, I strongly advise to try the experiment of taking farmhouse apartments. The only difficulty in the matter seems to me to be the rather serious one of

IN THE HEART OF HAMPSHIRE.

finding such quarters, and the necessary loss of time the search entails; for it would never do to take rooms without a personal inspection. I know from the experience of friends as well as my own that there are numbers of most desirable farmhouse apartments to be had and at a very moderate price; driving constantly about country as we do, the finding of these presents no special difficulties. Indeed, though it is rather a delicate task, we have never had any trouble in procuring them for friends, and sometimes very exacting friends too.

Leaving Bramdean our road took us through a thinly inhabited country, through which, at infrequent intervals, as we drove on we caught sight of the gables and chimneys of some solitary farmhouse, or the roof-trees of a lowly cottage nestling in foliage. It was, verily, a lonely road, without even the song of a single bird to cheer us on our way. And the gentle summer wind had dropped so that even the rustling of the leaves above did not break the prevailing quietude. By the roadside, we passed a deserted-looking public-house called the "Jolly Farmer"; but the jolly farmer himself, of the sturdy John Bull type, where has he vanished to? I regretfully confess that he is very hard to find—outside the pages of *Punch*. I have sought for him here in old England diligently, and despairingly, as I have sought in America for *Punch's* typical Yankee. An American gentleman, who once visited me, asked where he could find a living specimen of John Bull as he had seen him portrayed in the illustrated comic papers, and I was fain to confess that I did not know. "I guess," said he, "that your ideal John Bull is just as much a fraud as your ideal Yankee!"

As we proceeded, to the right and left of us low beech-crested hills came into view, and then our road began to climb in right earnest; up and up we went for two good miles or more, all hard, honest, collar work every yard of it! And as we rose we left behind and below us the softly-wooded valley, the air became perceptibly cooler, the trees grew fewer and fewer till at last they ceased altogether, save a few stunted thorns that seemed to have a severe struggle to exist at all, and so we presently found ourselves traversing the top of a bleak, barren upland. High up there, even on that calm summer noon, we found a steady breeze blowing from the south (not a cold quarter), yet it made wraps and a light overcoat actually acceptable. What it must be to experience a bleak Nor'-easter in the winter time, therefore, on these unsheltered heights we could imagine,—and felt that we would much rather imagine than experience!

The hills almost encircled us with their rounded ridges darkly outlined against the bright white sky, excepting in one direction where, between their great green slopes, we caught a peep of other distant hills dreamily indistinct. This upland waste was wild almost to weirdness in parts, as where a bent and broken sign-post, black with age, rose up grim and solitary from a dank pool of water, and was darkly silhouetted against the blue void beyond; its dilapidated, drooping arm—that should show the way—pointing aimlessly to the ground, and where near at hand a few straggling thorns, storm twisted into fantastic shapes as though they had been tortured, gave an added feeling of sternness to an already sufficiently dreary prospect. Yet in spite, or perhaps rather because, of its very uncouth wildness, this barren upland had a peculiar fascination for us. Such scenes powerfully impress one with the sense of solitude and space; they give a feeling of the vastness and strength of nature that has an indescribable charm to a vigorous mind, which can never be realised amidst the sylvan surroundings and the gentle graces of lowland meadows, fields, and woods; of a nature softened, subdued, and made homelike by the ceaseless toil and occupation of man through long centuries.

At last our elevated road came to an end and was followed by a long descent that still led us through a sombre, treeless tract of exposed downs. It must surely have been some such stretch of barren land that made the canny Scotchman, with an eye to the profitable rather than the romantic or sublime, exclaim, "Nature is unco' wasteful!" However, the bleakness of the nearer prospect was forgotten in the beauty of the panorama that was suddenly revealed to us as we began our descent, a far-reaching panorama that led our eyes over a richly-wooded valley of sunlit, unshadowed greenery that faded away into a horizon of hazy hills. Down far below us, so that we looked rather upon the roofs of its houses than their walls, was the city of Winchester diminished by space so that it seemed like a toy town. Unlike Canterbury, Salisbury, and most other cities, Winchester is not dominated by its cathedral; neither by tower nor spire nor the mass of its structure does it aggressively assert itself above the humbler homes of man around. The distant view of the city suffers for want of a prominent and central feature, as much as on the other hand Salisbury gains by its graceful soaring spire.

At the end of our long descent we found ourselves in the outskirts of "the city of memories," as some one has somewhere called Winchester, but who the some one is, or was, and where he made the remark I cannot call to mind; which is one of the disadvantages of reading many books and making few notes. Driving along devious and hilly streets, passing by many a quaint and picturesque old building—of which we made a mental note, for further more leisurely inspection and admiration a-foot—we found our way to the old George Inn, I beg pardon, I mean hotel, for the ancient coaching hostelry of that name, formerly beloved by artists and anglers, has taken upon itself the dignity and title of hotel.

The George Inn dates as far back as the fourteenth century, when it covered the same extent of ground as at present, so that if not quite as old as the cathedral, it can claim a very fair antiquity. Of late years it has been altered, internally at any rate, beyond recognition. The old courtyard, into which erst the coaches and post-chaises drove, has been enclosed with a glass roof, the ancient roadway is covered with encaustic tiles on which plants, rugs, and easy-chairs are placed, and here the modern tourist lounges in a lazy fashion. We remember the old inn as it used to be in years past, and rather resented the improvements. A homelike inn always appeals to us far more than the luxurious modern hotel where the tweed coat of the wayfarer seems strangely out of keeping, and the foreign *table d'hôte* takes the place of the plain old-fashioned English dinner with its honest joints. In a fashionable seaside resort one looks for a fashionable hotel, with possibly a lift, and other presumed advantages, but in an ancient city like Winchester, a flavour of the past in hostelries seems more desirable and more in harmony with the old-world surroundings.

However, of one alteration we did heartily approve. The ancient kitchen with its big, wide chimney—up which a man might climb, and looking up which we saw a great patch of blue sky—has been converted into an almost ideal smoke-room, panelled in oak from floor to ceiling, having also a most delightful ingle-nook that always gives a peculiarly cosy charm to a room. I know of a certain grand modern house wherein, according to my opinion, the only really comfortable room is the old kitchen (the only remaining portion of an earlier mansion) with its ample recessed fireplace and cross-beamed ceiling. I fancy also that the owner, in spite of his finely-decorated rooms, thinks likewise in his heart, for it is the custom of the house, after the servants have retired, to make up a blazing wood-fire in the great open range; and here the gentlemen of the house party are invited to smoke their midnight pipe of peace, with a simmering kettle on the hob suggestive of certain hot, comforting accompaniments, which the host terms "toddy."

Most visitors to Winchester, I imagine, arrive by rail, see the cathedral, and depart. But Winchester—with its gabled houses, its many quaint nooks and corners, its odd bits of stone and wood carving, its weather-worn, loop-holed walls scattered about here and there—apart from its cathedral, deserves more consideration. Unfortunately the railway enters a place, as it were, by the back door; so coming thereon one loses the charm of a gradual approach along a highway which houses and buildings have faced from time immemorial, and thus greet the arriving traveller with their best look,—a gradual approach by which the quiet country roads, according to a natural process of evolution, become by imperceptible degrees the city thoroughfare, and all that is of interest on the way is plainly to be seen.

Setting out from our hotel, sketch-book in hand, we went in search of some of the picturesque and interesting buildings that we had noted as we drove in. Winchester is built on the little river Itchen, and close to the stream stands a picturesque old water-mill that we sketched; this mill represented with trees around in place of houses, would make a charming picture. It is not often that you find an old mill, and a pretty one, by the side of a city street thus—a mill, whether driven by wind or water, seems so essentially of the country.

Retracing still farther back the road by which we had entered, we came to and sketched the picturesquely quaint old church of St. Peter's, Cheesehill, originally, judging by certain portions, of Norman construction; but it has manifestly been so altered from time to time in an apparently haphazard manner as now to be but a jumble of architecture. The interior is square, which for one thing is unusual in a church; it, moreover, possesses such curious details for an ecclesiastical edifice as Tudor windows, weather-tiled walls in the topmost part of the tower, which has also a roof above of red tiles. This tower, with its lower story of cool gray flint, crumbling stone windows of unique design, homelike weather-tiling, wood-framed bell chamber black with age, and lichen-laden russet roof, is a very picture in building; and the contrasting colours of its cool gray flint walls with the warm red of the tiles is most pleasing and effective. You might cross the sea to old-world Nuremberg and find nothing more quaint or more sketchable. When will artists learn the picturesque qualities of some of our ancient towns? Take Ludlow in Shropshire, for instance (which we shall visit later on), with its charming old half-timbered houses, ruined castle, ancient gateway, mills, bridges, and other buildings, all so effectively grouped; where else will you find such a wealth of picture-making material? to say nothing of its romantic surroundings of rock, river, wood, crag, and hill.

Near to this quaint old church of St. Peter's stands an interesting half-timbered gabled house, bent with age, and otherwise bearing the undoubted traces of antiquity; it has a projecting upper story and a carved oaken porch. This house now does duty as a shop, but was formerly, as is evident, a private residence. On its time-toned face we read the following inscription :—

Old Cheesehill Rectory
Known as
"The Oldest House"
1450.

It appeared to us a thoughtful act of somebody to thus make known, for the benefit of strangers, the history and age of this ancient building. I will not, however, weary you, kind reader, by a further account of our wanderings in and about old Winchester; suffice to say that for the artist, archæologist, or antiquary this ancient city has much of interest to show,—and it is a good and pleasant thing for each one to make his own discoveries.

Next morning we set forth to see the cathedral before proceeding on our way. For a regulation and detailed description of this venerable pile I must refer my readers to one of the numerous handbooks thereon. I merely propose, in due course, to note one or two matters that specially interested us, and that might possibly escape the notice of the general tourist, who is, as a rule, personally conducted, or guide-book led. On a previous visit we had ourselves in this manner duly "done" the cathedral, that is, under the guidance of an intelligent verger. We had inspected its many monuments in the prescribed order, its chantry chapels, mortuary chests (in which are presumed to be preserved the mingled bones of martyrs, saints, and—sinners I had nearly written, but I mean—Saxon kings), the rightfully famous William of Wykeham's tomb (an exquisite specimen of fourteenth-century work), the stone that marks the spot where William Rufus is said to be buried, and very much else besides that appeals to the lover of the historic past. But that morning we went in a different spirit; we desired not details, however interesting; we simply wished to rest a while in the sombre old fane and to let the spirit and the mystery of its grandeur and gloom impress itself upon us.

As we entered we found that the morning service was being held to a congregation of four besides the verger,—two of these four, however, as we afterwards discovered, were simply waiting till the service was over in order to view the cathedral,— and I sincerely trust that the tiny congregation of five, all told, appreciated the fact that the intoning of the officiating clergymen, perhaps I should say priests, and the superb chanting of the choristers was for their sole benefit. By the way, it struck us that the chanting was superior to the intoning. A cathedral service is a very fine thing, but is it not sometimes a waste of energy? We could not help wondering whether it ever chanced that the congregation consisted merely of the verger, or vergers!

As we walked to our seat we trod on tombs, for almost every stone here marks a grave, though the inscriptions on some are obliterated by the tread of generations of worshippers, and of others who come, not to worship, but to see. As the choir chanted in tones of wonderful purity, and the organ's note —mellowed by the vast arched and pillared space— rose and fell again like a dream of music, a sense of the grandeur and the glamour of the medieval faith came over us; but poetry is not faith, neither is romance religion; they are as far as the poles asunder. "God . . . dwelleth not in temples made with hands; neither is worshipped with men's hands, as though He needed anything."

We listened, charmed beyond the power of words to convey, to the trained voices of the choir, and whilst we listened questions would come to us unbidden and unsought: Was this majestic fane the outcome of a mighty faith or of superstition, or a mingling of both, combined with a deep and true love of art? Has priestcraft, with its dogmas, been the friend or foe of Christianity? Is Le Gallienne right in saying that "Organised Christianity has probably done more to retard the ideals that were its Founder's than any other agency in the world"; and again that "Not by the persecutor, but by the priest, has the world so far won the battle against Christ"? Says Russell Lowell also, "We have tried the Christian religion for eighteen centuries: is it not time that the religion of Christ were tried?" Poor doubting humanity asks for a sign in a faithless age, and no sign is given it. The days of miracles are over, and the modern scorner sneers at the medieval miracles, and states that the only miracle was that they ever were believed.

> Whence? Whither? Wherefore? How? Which? Why?
> All ask at once, all wait reply.
> Men feel old systems cracking under 'em;
> Life saddens to a mere conundrum,
> Which once Religion solved, but she
> Has lost—has Science found?—the key.

And as our thoughts wandered thus, and questions arose that we could not answer, and problems that we could not solve, our eyes wandered also to

> The great minster transept,
> Where the lights like glories fall,
> And the sweet choir sings,
> And the organ rings,
> Along the emblazoned wall.

Through the stained-glass windows, that glowed in the light like molten jewels, the glorified sunshine streamed and painted the hoary walls and pillars of the hallowed pile with glowing prismatic colours as though a gorgeous page of an illuminated missal had been transferred there. The mysterious gray gloom beyond acted as a foil to the miracle of colour of stained window and pictured wall; and whilst we were deep in thought and admiration, the service ended and we were left to meditate alone in peaceful solitude, which is more religious and impressive to some minds than the grandest ritual or most sumptuous ceremonial, that indeed disturbs rather than helps many a true worshipper.

After a time we shook off our reverie and wandered over the vast cathedral, whose very stones are histories, in search of the last resting-place, not of saint or martyr, proud prelate or crowned king, but of a simple fisherman—worthy Izaak Walton, to wit. However, we could not discover, even by the most careful search, where that honest-hearted old angler rested, so that after all we had to appeal to the verger for guidance, who conducted us to the South Transept, where, after removing some protecting matting, he pointed out to us a flat tombstone laid in the floor, on which we read :—

>Here resteth the body of
>Mr. IZAAK WALTON
>Who dyed the 15th of December
>1683
>
>Alas ! Hee's gone before,
>Gone to return no more,
>Our panting Breasts aspire
>After their aged Sire
>Whose well-spent life did last
>Full ninety years and past.
>But now he hath begun
>That which will nere be done
>Crown'd with eternall Blisse,
>We wish our Souls with his.

No wonder that we could not find his tomb if it is kept thus covered over, we thought ; perhaps the verger divined what was passing in our minds, for presently he exclaimed, "You see, sir, we take great care of it : we've plenty of bishops and kings, but only one Izaak Walton." Well and truly spoken, worthy verger !

Returning down the nave our attention was arrested by another slab laid on the floor of the north aisle; this marks the resting-place of Jane

Austen the novelist, who, we learnt from the inscription, was interred there in 1817.

Close to the vestibule of the cathedral, on the wall of the north aisle, we noticed the original elaborately worked iron grille that formerly protected the shrine of St. Swithin (or Swithun, according to ancient documents, but this is a detail for learned antiquaries), who, as the pluvial saint of Winchester, has made an undying fame for himself. This grille dates from 1093, and is the oldest one in existence. It is interesting as showing to what perfection such early iron-work attained, and the ornamental skill of its unknown designer.

Before leaving the cathedral we took a farewell glance down its grand old nave, the longest in England, stopping some time to admire the splendid effect of light and shade that was presented to us, together with the vanishing perspective of wall and window, vaulted roof and springing arch. We tried to imagine how the sacred fane must have appeared before the ambitious Bishop Wykeham converted, or rather completed, the conversion of the earlier grim and massive Norman masonry into veritable walls of light by his graceful perpendicular windows. It was a bold conception that of transforming the sombre walls of gray stone into walls of coloured glass and light; but it was done, and the building was brightened and beautified thereby.

Here perhaps one may pause to remark, anent the modern restorer, that the great architects of past times were neither over-careful nor considerate in preserving the work of their predecessors; as a matter of fact they were very much the contrary. Here at Winchester as well as elsewhere they frequently entirely altered or even pulled down great portions of the fabrics which their forefathers had raised, and left those fabrics very different from what they found them, to the actual complete changing of their styles as far as opportunities permitted. Were the modern architect to do likewise, what an outcry there would be! Yet these men of old thought no harm of what they did,—however, there were no art critics in those days to enlighten them, or to dispute their doings, though there was plenty of art,—they but added a chapter of history to a volume in stone, as plainly to be read by the initiated as any printed page. The question arises, Is this volume in stone ended?

What peculiar distinctive architectural features do we add to buildings now that reflect the art feeling of our age? Do we add a page of the present to the stone history of the past for our descendants to admire or wonder at? I am not now referring to the Churchwardens era, for this came not of art but of ignorance; and if modern additions to or alterations of old buildings be blameworthy, even though made to suit the spirit of the times and changed forms of worship, should we not, in common fairness, also blame William of Wykeham, who did the same thing on the grandest scale? What would be thought of the modern architect who would treat to-day, say, the Norman Abbey of Romsey as Wykeham treated the Norman Cathedral of Winchester of his day? What, I wonder?

There is such a thing as consistency, and were one logically to carry out a restoration of a fabric to its original intention, as manifestly revealed in its earliest parts, according to the line laid down by many learned and enthusiastic antiquaries and archæologists, what would be the result? Why, we should have to restore backwards many a now glorious Gothic fane to a grim and gloomy Norman structure stamped with the sternness of centuries past.

Outside the cathedral, on a projecting buttress of its fine west front, cut in the stone, is the following anagram; this we made out with difficulty, for the lettering is somewhat weather-worn and indistinct :—

☞ ILL⟍   ⟋PREC
    ⟍AC   ATOR⟋
   ⟋H   ⟍VI ☞
        AMBULA.

Which may be put into Latin thus: " Illac precator: Hac viator ambula"; and translated into terse English: "That way to pray: this way to walk." I may perhaps explain that one hand points towards the cathedral door, the other in the direction of the pathway that leads away from it. This is a happy specimen of one of those quaint conceits in words that the scholarly builders of old delighted in; and for the poor, unlettered people they provided jests in stone which the medieval carver knew so well how to tell.

Rambling about the byways of the city we

found ourselves in College Street, and upon the front of a pleasant-looking, unpretentious little house we observed a tablet fixed and thus inscribed :—

In this House
Jane Austen
lived her last days
and died July 18th, 1817.

CHAPTER V

An ancient dole—A wonderful jump of a horse—Hursley—The grave of John Keble—Romsey and its Norman abbey—A beautiful monument—A ghastly relic—An evening walk—A curious mistake—The wrong use of words—An amateur angler—" Merrie England"—A lighthouse for land travellers—The finest view in England—Salisbury.

WINCHESTER lies in a hollow, surrounded by sheltering chalk hills that slope gently down to the valley. Trust the monks of old to select a well-favoured spot to build in, and if they felt assured of the world to come they knew very certainly also how to make the best of this one. We arrived at Winchester by a long descent, and we left it by a long ascent, passing, just beyond our hotel, beneath a hoary, crumbling archway (the West Gate) of truly medieval aspect, which appears to divide the ancient original city from the less ancient suburbs that have grown up around its former boundaries.

At the end of our long ascent, to our left, we caught sight of the gray old hospital of St. Cross, an interesting relic of past times; at the gate of which is given to this day the "Wayfarer's Dole"—consisting, we were told, of a horn of ale and a piece of bread—to all who may demand it. Had the hospital not been so far out of our way, we latter-day nineteenth-century pilgrims would much like to have tested the St. Cross brew, if not its baking, just for the sake of old romance. This hospital was originally founded in 1136, and with its daily dole forms a strange and picturesque survival of a primitive past, and long may it remain unchanged to us in an age of change. We can ill afford to lose such graphic reminders of a vanished and never-returning epoch.

After the long rise our road began gradually to descend through hedgerowed pastures and brown tilled fields, and before us lay a lovely stretch of undulating country that gave our visions and our minds a charming sense of spaciousness. On the summit of a near isolated hill we observed a small stone obelisk, very conspicuous owing to its prominent position. We inquired of an intelligent native the meaning of this, and for once received a clear and fairly concise answer. "That," said he, "marks the spot where a horse lies buried which ran away with its rider in the hunting field and jumped down into a deep chalk pit; but neither rider nor horse was hurt, which was considered almost a miracle. Afterwards, when the horse died, his master had him buried there on the exact spot from which the horse jumped, and placed that monument above him in memory of the event."

Then we came to a level country, and our road led us past a beautifully-wooded park in which were a number of fine big beech trees, a tree so much more graceful than the elm that it seems a pity it is not more cultivated in parks. Some neat little cottages followed the park, and we found ourselves suddenly in a charming little tree-embowered village; this we discovered from our map to be Hursley. Here the ivy-covered church, with its gray flint tower and cared-for God's acre, attracted our attention; it was a spot to make one almost "in love with death." A peace, hardly of this world, seems to brood incumbent over that tranquil sleeping-place of the dead. I have to own, with shame if needs be, that until we had entered that peaceful and pretty church and seen the brass on the chancel floor placed there to the memory of John Keble, author of the *Christian Year*, I had no idea that he was vicar here for over thirty years. The simple inscription on this brass runs as follows:—

> JOHN KEBLE
> Vicar of Hursley
> 1835-1866
> Fell asleep in the Lord
> March 29, 1866.
> Aged 74 years.

The open timber roof of this gem of a country church is curiously lighted with top windows. The only other instance of this quaint arrangement we have come across during our wanderings over England is at the ancient Saxon wooden church of St. Edmund's at Greenstead in Essex (which I have described in a former work *A Tour in a Phaeton*), perhaps the oldest church in the world, and whose walls are upright halves of the trunks of trees perpendicularly placed.

Leaving Hursley, surely one of the sweetest villages in all England, we drove through an avenue of trees that lined the highway and would have been an ornament to any park; then it was up hill to the hamlet of Ampfield, which possesses an ugly church, charmingly situated in a wooded God's acre wherein we found a stone fountain. Here an old roadside inn, with a big bay window full of flowers and a great grass plot in front, looked clean and inviting, nevertheless we proceeded along without calling a halt, as Romsey was only a few miles farther on and we desired to see its famous abbey that day. Now came a prolonged descent, bounded by thick woods on either side, so that our view was limited to the long lines of the road and ruts thereon ahead vanishing far away into a narrow point; an object study in perspective.

Then the woods ceased and the old town of Romsey came into view clustering around its glorious Norman abbey, and encircled by bright emerald fields through which the silvery Test wound in and out, the distance being bounded by tree-clad hills of greeny blue. The prospect was a picture, and but for the intruding, assertive railway—that ugly necessity of the nineteenth century—we might easily have imagined ourselves medieval pilgrims looking down upon a medieval city! But a truce to romance. In due course we found ourselves in the sleepy cobble-paved market-place of Romsey, and, driving under an old-fashioned archway, we entered the courtyard of the old White Horse hostelry, whereupon a motherly landlady came forth to greet us with a ready, cheery smile that made us feel at home forthwith. How pleasant it is to be received thus, as we frequently were! There is a something about the road, I cannot precisely define what, that seems to make one a real traveller,—a somebody quite apart from the individual merely arriving by rail,—and that appears to engender a more natural and a more hearty welcome. Finding the town, as well as our inn, much to our liking, we secured rooms for the night so as to have ample time to not only see the abbey but to ramble round about the quaint old place and make some sketches should the mood incline, for we did nothing under compulsion.

Our first visit was, naturally, to the abbey, which we were fortunate enough to find open and the clerk within, so we were saved a tiresome hunt after that individual, who, according to our experience, is to be found anywhere but at home. The clerk was conducting a party over the building when we entered, so we began a quiet inspection of the interior on our own account; this, however, was not fated to last long. Having seen his party out at the door, the clerk approached us manifestly with a view of offering his services. Somehow this making a sort of a show place of a temple of worship—whether by gratuities or by charging so much a head as prevails at times—is not to our mind. One cannot contemplate in peace with a guide at your elbow like a walking handbook, telling you what to see, and giving you particulars of this and that in a mechanical, parrot-like manner begotten of long years of repetition of the same things. On the whole I prefer a handbook to a clerk, you can put it in your pocket safely out of the way! However, in this case, we managed to strike a bargain with our would-be guide,—on due presentation of a silver coin of the realm,—to be allowed to inspect the interior of the grand old abbey in our own way and at our leisure; promising faithfully on our part and on our word of honour as utter strangers that we would not run away with any of the monuments, cut our names anywhere, or do anything else that we ought not to do. The clerk looked at us somewhat doubtfully at first, as though considering whether he ought to trust us or not, but our "tip" was on a generous scale, so that we managed to overcome any latent scruples he might have had.

Romsey Abbey was one of the many pleasant surprises and discoveries of our journey; we knew of its existence certainly, but we were not at all prepared to find it a most perfect and little spoilt example of Norman architecture—solid, sombre, with a grandeur of mass and rounded form that is as different from the light and graceful Early English Gothic as a fortress from a palace, or a ponderous tome of prose from a dainty volume of poems. A Norman fane is impressive on account of its strength, powerful contrasts of light and shade, and rich, suggestive gloom, as well as from its right-down honesty of building and lasting-looking solidity. The Norman mason never scamped his work; he knew better, for they had a rough and ready way in those times of dealing with such dishonesty; in fine, scamping was a dangerous thing to do for the scamper, not, as in the reversed order of nowadays, for those who follow after him. "Buggins" the speculative builder, and the old firm of "Jerry Brothers" would have had a bad time of it in those days.

Amongst the monuments in the abbey one specially struck us as being exceedingly beautiful and chaste in design, as well as in feeling and conception. It was to a little child, who was represented as lying down on a couch asleep with some wild flowers crushed in her tiny hand as though she had just gathered them and had come home tired to rest. It was a pretty and touching idea, and the sculptured figure was tenderly rendered and true to nature. The inanimate marble seemed almost to breathe. The name of the artist of this poem in stone I know not, nor whether he be alive or dead; but I do know that no other monument, however beautiful, ever appealed to my feelings in the same degree. Before it we stood silently impressed. On it we read the following brief inscription:—

<blockquote>
To the Memory of
ALICE
Daughter of Mr. Francis Taylor
Surgeon of this Town.
</blockquote>

And that was all, but sufficient; for true sorrow is ever retiring, there is that which words cannot say because too deep for words.

On the floor of the chancel we noticed an ancient tomb-slab which is of interest from its high antiquity—if genuine. I make this reservation as the lettering thereon, as follows, appeared remarkably clear and clean cut considering its age; but I presume that the authorities ecclesiastical would not allow any inscription that was not above reproach within the sacred abbey walls. This then is it:—

Johanna
Abbatissa
de Rumeseye
1349.

Near to the doorway we found the clerk waiting for us; his office of guide was not to be ignored thus slightingly by two strangers. He had something, he said, to show us that we could not possibly discover for ourselves,—for the all-sufficient reason that it was kept carefully preserved out of sight under lock and key. We submitted to the inevitable, it is ever thus; it is man with his trivial details that worries the contemplative pilgrim in these glorious shrines of ancient devotion. And what, think you, this valued treasure was that needs be guarded with such jealous care,—gold or jewels from sacked tomb of Prior or Abbot, of Bishop or warrior knight? No such thing! The clerk brought forth a semi-circular box, and, lifting the lid, disclosed a woman's scalp, to which was attached a long tress of auburn hair carefully braided; this rested on a block of black oak. "That," exclaimed the clerk, "was discovered in a curious triangular coffin by some workmen over forty years ago. When the coffin was opened a beautiful woman was revealed with her face and features perfectly preserved, but everything fell to dust immediately on exposure to the air except what you now see. Who the woman was could not be discovered, but from the shape and make of the coffin, antiquaries" (he said antiquarians, to be literally correct) "have concluded that it dated from the early part of the tenth century," that is, of course, before the present abbey was built, and whose outer walls are now also crumbling to dust, to which all earthly things come in time, from the mighty mountain to the marble monument.

Before we parted from him the verger would conduct us to the beautiful Nuns' Door, beyond which, on the external wall of the south transept, he pointed out a curious stone sculpture of the Crucifixion: though why it was inserted thus is not very clear, for, architecturally, it seems strangely out of place; possibly thereby hangs some history we did not unearth.

Leaving the abbey, as we walked along we observed that our way was paved in parts with what appeared to be old grave-stones; at least we noticed one slab with the following lettering:—

Here lyeth
the body
. . . . .

and that was all, the remainder of the inscription having been worn away by the tread of worshippers —or passers-by. So hard is it to know how long our memorials will last after us when we are gone. But I am moralising again!

From the abbey we walked down to the river,

and wandered over some level luxuriant meadows to a quiet spot from whence we obtained a most poetical and impressive view of the gray old Norman fane which loomed lordly up above the surrounding town, a fit emblem of the ancient ecclesiastical supremacy. Then, strolling on, we passed by some picturesque water-mills, and reached a pleasant footpath that led us for a while alongside of the slow-gliding, troutful Test to a fine ivy-covered bridge that spans the river with one bold, graceful arch. From the top of this bridge we obtained a good view of Broadlands, formerly the seat of Lord Palmerston; and a charming home it looked, comfortable rather than stately, with its velvety, emerald lawns sloping gently down to the river and big branching trees around. After this we sought the restful ease of our inn; for the west was growing golden, our long and pleasant day was drawing to its end, and we felt agreeably tired.

Early in the morning, before starting on our day's pilgrimage, we took a stroll round the town and sketched two exceedingly fine specimens of iron-wrought sign supports; one that belonged to another inn, and that stretched daringly half-way across the narrow street, and one in the market-place that had evidently erst upheld a sign, but which was now signless and meaningless, as the old hostelry had been converted into a private house. There is a subtle charm in the graceful forms, twists, and changeful curves that the craftsman of old gave to his iron-work, always mindful of the limits of his material that to the artistic eye is most pleasing. The English workman in past times must have possessed an inherent taste for art that his modern descendants appear to have entirely lost, in spite of the multiplication of art schools. The real reason for this it would be interesting to discover.

Having finished our sketches we entered a draper's shop to make a small purchase, and the man who served asked us, as we imagined, if we had seen the habit-shirt. We presumed this to be some new-fashioned garment, so we asked him if he would kindly show it to us. Whereon he politely went outside and pointed out the way to the abbey, for which we thanked him, and realised that he meant the abbey church! But he spoke with such a puzzling local accent that I do not wonder at our amusing mistake. Another loquacious body we met elsewhere, also vastly amused us by her wrong use of words; she spoke of a disease as "debating," meaning doubtless abating; and of some one who had suffered from "an abbess on her head" instead of abscess! Country folk, too, I have noticed, in speaking to strangers are given to using long words, the exact meaning of which they do not clearly comprehend, instead of employing simple words they do. Is this the result of the school-boards, I wonder?

From Romsey we drove to Salisbury, and a lovelier drive of sixteen miles I know not in all fair England. The country we passed through appeared to be the very essence of quiet pastoral beauty with one most glorious panorama thrown in. The weather did not look promising as we started forth, gray louring clouds were driving above us before a freshening southerly wind, our aneroid had fallen over-night, the ostler cheerfully prophesied rain,— though we asked his opinion in the hopes that he would do the very reverse,—so we got our waterproof aprons out and made all "snug and taut" against stormy weather, prepared for any mood our fickle climate might take upon itself.

We had at first a level bit of road, then a long rise uphill followed; at the top of this rise we rested a while to enjoy the charming vision of Romsey that was presented to us on looking back,—a town that appears so happily picturesque from almost every point of view. In this case, however, the much-abused English weather greatly enhanced the ordinary natural beauties of the prospect, for over beyond Romsey the gathered rain-clouds of pearly-gray were dissipating themselves in descending moisture, and the sunshine on the misty rain caused a rainbow to span the sky and frame the picture with a semicircle of opal loveliness. Our changeful cloudscapes are full of interest, and abound in a wealth of beauty and colour, if we would only see it; but who ever troubles about the sky above except to learn whether it will be fine or not? The wet roofs of the houses of Romsey reflected the warm glow of the sunny gleam; only the ancient abbey remained sombre and gray, standing apart in solemn majesty from the brightness around, as though it could not shake off its century-gathered gloom.

There is such a thing as character in buildings, and Romsey Abbey takes upon itself a serious air.

Having reached high level ground above the greenful valley of the Test, we maintained our elevated position, more or less, for several miles. On either hand our road was bordered by grassy margins, with woods and fields alternating beyond. The variety of trees we passed on our way surprised us; from one spot on looking around we noticed, growing and flourishing, oaks, elms, pines, yews, chestnuts, ashes, thorns, and, I believe, beeches. Different kinds of trees that one would imagine, to flourish thus, would require varied soils and climates.

Some one somewhere has said—I think I read it in the leading article of a daily paper—that "there are too many people and too many things in the world," and regarding towns perhaps there is some truth in the remark; but it could hardly hold good of the country that we drove through that day, for it appeared to be very sparsely populated; and as for things that told of man, besides the cultivated fields, these were confined to a few scattered homes.

At the curiously-named hamlet of Whiteparish, we noticed a humble wayside hostelry called the Hatchet, another new sign to us. Beyond this hamlet we came to a fine open common, with a few picturesque cottages, possessing ample gardens, gathered about it. I would the house I live in looked upon such a glorious open prospect as these humble cotters' homes do! In parts the common was bounded by dark woods, through openings in which we here and there caught charming glimpses of the distant lowland country looking dimly blue. By the roadside was a reed-grown pool where a budding Izaak Walton was practising his 'prentice hand. "What are you catching?"—"Nothing," honestly replied the lad. "What kind of fish do you catch, when you catch any?" we ventured further to inquire. "I don't knows, I 'a never caught one yet, but I hopes to do some day; you see I'm merely a beginner, I only took up fishing this summer," whereon we left this enthusiastic and easily-pleased young sportsman. "Sir," said Izaak Walton, "when I go a-fishing, an' the fates decree that I get no fish, then I am still a gainer, for, God's body, I 'get flesh!'" Possibly so, but I have known a goodly number of amateur anglers who only catch colds.

Farther on by the common side was a quantity of fallen timber around which some sun-tanned children were playing at a rustic game, and as they romped about in boisterous jollity, the rippling music of their merry laughter gladdened our hearts by its very joyousness, a joyousness that infused itself into us. We had before us a vision of "Merrie England" that now in our cities seems so sad; a merry England that the poets love to sing about, and the painters of the simple countryside (like Birket Foster) so delight to portray. How different the lot of these happy youngsters from that of the poor man's children in overgrown London, who have only the confined narrow streets for a playground, scant sunshine, and no fresh country breezes to redden or bronze

AN ENGLISH COMMON.

their cheeks, and make strong their tiny frames! All the sadness and ugliness of England is crowded into its cities, and alas! the tendency of the times is for the rural population to gravitate more and more towards towns.

Proceeding onwards, in a few miles the aspect of the country underwent a complete change; the fruitful fields and shady trees ceased, and we found ourselves facing a long ascent leading over some barren downs. Before us our road climbed upwards till it was lost above in a mass of wandering gray mists. It was as though we were driving right into the clouds, and we had the feeling of being very high up in the world. As we rose, however, the mists blew over and revealed right ahead a ridge of dark downs, their dreary length of outline being broken in one spot by some desolate-looking, wind-blown trees.

On a commanding crest of these downs we noticed a curious six-sided tower built of brick, this was at some little distance from the road, so we pulled up and walked across the close, springy turf—that made the mere effort of walking a delight—to inspect it. The tower looked old, deserted, and decaying. We imagined, wrongly as it afterwards turned out, that it must have been erected for the sake of the view, which from this point is of great extent, stretching as it does right over the spacious Salisbury Plain, the vast panorama having no visible termination. From our reduced Ordnance map we made out that we stood here on the topmost point of Standlinch Down, and that we were 700 feet above the level of the sea, though it seemed much more.

At our inn on the following day we learnt from a gray-haired ostler, who had in turn learnt it from his grandfather, that this tower was raised to act as a beacon by day and a lighthouse by night, and so to serve as a guide to travellers of old over these then trackless downs. For in times past there was no regular road across this wild district, and men—and women too for that matter—had to traverse the downs on horseback carrying their limited amount of luggage with them on packs. Even to this day some of the ancient wayside inns possess outbuildings in which the packs of travellers were kept; and at one of these inns to my knowledge such a building is still known by the title of the Pack House. This old tower, from its prominent position on the topmost edge of the downs, plainly showed, to all who had need to take the journey, the point on the downs that it was necessary to make for in crossing them; so that, however rough the way—or want of way—the wanderer was at any rate aware of the direction in which he should go; unless rain or mist obscured his vision, or the highwayman had not put a veto altogether on his further proceeding.

Returning to the dog-cart we passed through a deep chalk cutting, and upon reaching the other side of this a most glorious and far-reaching prospect was revealed to us. Miles upon miles of wooded country lay spread out map-like beneath, interspersed with towns, villages, roads, railways, streams, and mansions surrounded by their parks; beyond all this was a vague distance of blue hills, excepting to the north, where the more level landscape faded away into a dreamy dimness. In the very centre of all this spreading loveliness the thin tapering spire of Salisbury's famous cathedral rose gracefully above the ancient city. "How beautiful!" we both involuntarily exclaimed, and truly if ever a prospect deserved that appellation, this did.

I have seen many a panorama of excelling loveliness during my numerous drives through the length and breadth of England, but when all were so beautiful, which was the most so I could not tell. That one revelation of scenery, however, settled the matter. Salisbury's soaring spire, with its graceful, arrowlike rise into the air, gives a special character to the view, that makes it, in my opinion, the finest in England.

Now we had a long and glorious run down hill almost all the way into Salisbury. As we drove on we passed a smart caravan, drawn by a pair of stout horses, which from our vantage height we had watched for some time slowly, very slowly, proceeding along ahead of us. This proved to belong to a gentleman who was travelling with his wife by road like ourselves, only he took his little home with him; however, as we shall meet the caravan again farther on we need say no more about it at present. Arriving at Salisbury we drove up to the White Hart Hotel, where we found very comfortable quarters for ourselves, and excellent accommodation for our horses, besides a welcome budget of letters from home.

In the evening we could not resist the temptation of strolling forth to get a glimpse of the cathedral. Leaving the busy street in which our hotel was situated, we passed under a quaint and shadowy old gateway, and thereupon found ourselves in the peaceful seclusion of the close, with its smooth sward, and fine old elms whose foliage was rustling in the soft summer breeze. There, looming up grandly right in front of us, was the venerable fane itself, showing in the low light of the gloaming a mighty mass of mysterious gray, excepting where its many windows reflected in parts the luminous sky above. It was a sight for a pilgrim! The sacred edifice stood a silent witness to the mighty genius of the master minds of the medieval age; solemnly impressive it appeared at that moment, vaguely undefined in sombre shade; the beauty of its architectural details being felt rather than defined, excepting where the roof and topmost pinnacles stood out darkly silhouetted against the clear soft sky, and where the wonderful spire soared heavenwards, etherealised by the last rays of the setting sun,—so light and unsubstantial it seemed in the tender evening glow, that it looked like the outcome of a dream, not an actual reality.

We had not seen Salisbury Cathedral before, and we certainly had a most poetical first view of it under the bewitching influence of that tender-toned and quiet evening hour. Would the garish light of day bring with it a disenchantment? that was the question we could not help asking ourselves. Whether or no, that one vision of beauty we could never forget! In truth, so entranced were we that for very dread of disappointment we almost made up our minds not to come there again, even though we had to leave the interior unseen. It is wise sometimes not to risk a disillusion by a second visit to a spot whose beauty, under the conditions of first beholding it, has sunk deep into your very soul! But it is easier to make resolutions than to keep them.

CHAPTER VI

Old Sarum—A windy spot—Gigantic earthworks—Salisbury Plain—Amesbury—Vespasian's Camp—Stonehenge—A chat with a caravanist—Over the downs—An ancient home—Old houses and new ones—Where Charles II. secreted himself for five days—"Hiding holes"—Woodford—A second Stratford-on-Avon—Old inscriptions.

THE next day we devoted to Stonehenge. We decided that we would drive there and back from Salisbury, going one way and returning another, as we discovered by our map that we could do this. So, early in the morning, we started forth to inspect that wonderful enigma in stones which has puzzled so many learned antiquaries. Who will solve this mystery of the ancient ages? What the Sphinx and the Pyramids are to Egypt, so is Stonehenge to England,—and more, for the Egyptian structures have revealed something of their purpose, Stonehenge nothing!

About a mile out of Salisbury we came to the deserted site of Old Sarum, where erst the cathedral and city stood. As we approached this, it appeared like a low hill cut into three mighty terraces. Pulling up here we entered the spot through a cutting in the outmost of the entrenchments; in these we observed portions of the ancient walls of the fortress in the shape of flint and rubble work as well as some small remains of hewn stone. Within this vast circle of high ramparts that protected the old city there is not now a single dwelling, nor even the visible remains of one left, all is given over to silence and desolation. Of this spot might well be written "*Sic transit gloria mundi.*"

Mounting to the top of the external ramparts, we walked right round them, and a breezy walk it was, of a mile or more by rough guess work; on one hand we had comprehensive views over Salisbury Plain, and on the other over the "City of New Sarum," as we discovered Salisbury to be called by a public notice posted in the cathedral close. According to tradition, one of the chief reasons for the removal of the cathedral to its present position in the valley was that the old site was so exposed. "For when the wind did blow, it made so much noise the people could not hear the Priest say mass." The people with a small "p" be it noted, and the priest with a capital "p." But facts tend to show that in the confined space the ecclesiastical and military authorities continually clashed, till at last the friction became intolerable to the former, and on 28th April 1220—the Pope Honorius having given permission for the see to be transferred— Bishop Poore laid the foundation-stone of the present cathedral at Salisbury, and eventually Old Sarum was deserted, even its very stones being carted away to help to build the new city,—all of which is a matter of history. "Until the passage of the Reform Bill in 1832 this deserted hill without a single resident elector returned two members to Parliament." Cobbett, indignant at this, called it "the accursed hill."

Mr. Samuel Pepys (whom I have already quoted, and shall do again as an old-time traveller in these parts) also visited this spot on his way to Salisbury from Hungerford on 10th June 1668; and it seems deeply to have impressed him, for thus he writes, "So all over the plain by the sight of the steeple, the Plain high and low, to Salisbury by night; but before I came to the town, I saw a great fortification, and there alight, and to it and in it, and find it prodigious so as to fright me to be in it all alone at that time of night, it being dark. I understand since, it to be that, that is called Old Sarum." Reaching Salisbury our seventeenth-century traveller went to "the George Inne, where lay in a silk bed, and very good diet." Luxurious days!

Leaving then these gigantic earthworks, to which William the Conqueror once came in regal state to receive the submission and the homage of the most notable Saxon landowners, we found ourselves on the lonely Salisbury Plain. Around us, far and wide, stretched a great expanse of undulating, uncultivated country, bounded on the circling horizon by blue distant downs, whose smooth outline was marked here and there by rugged prehistoric earthworks; for this vast plain and its surroundings seem, in the unrecorded past, to have been one great battle-ground. After proceeding for about a mile, on looking back we had a curious vision of the tapering spire of

Salisbury Cathedral peeping over the level top of the entrenchments of Old Sarum, and appearing as though it sprung from a religious edifice therein.

Salisbury Plain has been often described, but words have hardly the power—unless aided greatly by the imagination—to convey the peculiar impression that mighty open region gives to most beholders. The sense of limitless space it suggests enhanced by the almost painfully profound stillness that reigns around, and also by the great expanse of open sky above unbroken by tree or building. Salisbury Plain is by no means a level stretch of land, as one might expect from its title; indeed the hilliness of the Plain generally takes travellers by surprise. Salisbury Plain is a vast rolling prairie, a succession of rounded hills, like as though a gigantic sea with its vast billows had been, by some magic, suddenly arrested and turned into land! I have seen the mid-Atlantic a day or two after a prolonged gale, when the wind had dropped, and the mighty crestless waves rolled majestically along one after another in vast hills and valleys of green water,—and such a sea, suddenly stopped on its onward course and converted into solid earth, would in form and outline make a very passable representation of Salisbury Plain.

Before us stretched our bleak road in a lengthening line of whity-gray, now rising to the top of one bare hillock, only to dip down into a wide hollow, and so to rise and descend again in a wearisome monotony. Here and there over the plain were apparent tracks on the grass that did not deserve the name of road, indeed no defined way could be traced very far; yet for all this, at one point, about five miles from Salisbury, we noticed a solitary decrepit sign-post pointing aimlessly over the sweeping expanse of open country with "To Marlborough" thereon, and there could be traced for some short way faint marks on the rough sward of wheel-ruts and horses' hoofs as though the route were used at times. Indeed, on our return from Stonehenge, we crossed a portion of the plain for a mile or more on such a track, having first learnt from a driver there, who had brought a party over from Salisbury, that we could save a considerable distance by so doing; and delightfully easy and noiseless driving it was, though rather hard work for the horses.

Then as we proceeded we found that parts of the Plain here and there had been conquered by man and were cultivated; we saw at one time nine teams ploughing, and also an occasional shepherd watching stray flocks of sheep; after this we dropped down into the lonely little town of Amesbury. Here we pulled up to give our horses a bait at the ancient George Inn, an old coaching house that had evidently witnessed more prosperous times. In this sleepy town we noticed several picturesque old houses with red-tiled, lichen-laden roofs, and some even of homely thatch — houses that had never known the hand of the modern builder. Over one primitive shop we observed the uncommon name of "Soul"; and this reminds me that on our return, as we passed through the village of Stratford, we observed the noble name of "Beauchamp" above the shed of a carpenter and wheelwright. It may be remembered (I say this, though as a matter of fact we were not aware of it till we saw it so stated in a local guide-book we found in the evening at our hotel) that it was to Amesbury the repentant Queen Guinevere, wife of King Arthur, came and retired into a nunnery which existed till the reign of Henry II., when the nuns were expelled for dissolute living and scandalous conduct. Some slight remains of the nunnery are said to exist, but we did not see them.

Amesbury possesses a charming old Early English church pleasantly situated close to the Avon side; this is built of flint; and in its ancient tower we noticed and sketched a lovely little unglazed window, that shows the beauty which comes of simple design and careful proportion. This window is a gem, and proves the power of small things—if only good—to arrest attention and delight the eye; when much grander work, less skilfully designed, may wholly fail to impress.

Crossing the quiet-flowing Avon (how many different Avons there are in England!) on an ancient bridge, we climbed a hill and reached a great earthwork now-overgrown with wood, marked on our Ordnance map as "Vespasian's Camp." Shortly after this the Plain became treeless and bare again, and presently, right in front of us, a mile or so away on a brow of the rounded downs, darkly outlined against the bright sky, stood the mighty monoliths and trilithons of Stonehenge! Some travellers have expressed their disappointment at this first distant view of the prehistoric structure. In fact, on reaching this spot, I heard from a driver at our hotel who took them there, that a party of Americans exclaimed "That Stonehenge!" in disgust, and forthwith ordered the coachman to turn back, and would not be persuaded to proceed, as they explained they had only a fortnight in which to see England and they could not afford to waste their time on such a fraud! The fact is that seen thus from afar the actual size of the great stones is not realised, they being so dwarfed by distance and the vastness of their natural surroundings.

Unlike Salisbury Cathedral, which is so enclosed by buildings that you do not see the grand edifice coming by the general approach (excepting always the soaring spire) till you are close upon it, Stonehenge (standing as it does alone on the top of the desolate downs) *must* first be beheld from afar; there is not even a solitary tree near by to afford a scale as to its real size, therefore to one who cannot allow for the diminishing effect of distance the first view of Stonehenge may prove disappointing. It is not till you have really reached the circle and stood at the foot of one of the great upright stones that you can realise how huge they are, and the strength and skill that must have been required and employed to bring and raise them thus there, especially the trilithons. Then it is that their majesty is apparent, and the glamour of the mystery in which they are enshrined takes possession of you.

Having decided before leaving home that whatever else on our journey we might or might not see, we would see Stonehenge, I took the trouble to hunt up as many authorities as I could about the mysterious structure. Sundry learned archæologists and antiquaries I found had a great deal to say on the matter, but very little of real information to impart, and nothing whatever approaching to anything like a certainty as to its uses. The majority inclined to the old-fashioned belief in the Druids as being the builders, though this is manifestly a pure hypothesis, as there is absolutely nothing to show that the Druids ever performed their rites otherwise than in woods or groves of oaks.

I discovered that the various authorities I consulted, both old and modern, varied very widely in their estimate of the probable age of Stonehenge. Some endeavoured to prove that it was erected centuries before the Christian era, others as confidently (?) held that it was post-Roman; and when the learned in such matters so disagree, what is the ignorant layman to conclude? Some maintained that the rude edifice was a temple; others that it was a place of assembly for the chief of the tribes, a sort of primitive Parliament; others again that it was raised for astronomical purposes,—conjectures all, wholly unsupported by any evidence that would stand investigation. Verily, as Horace Walpole once pertinently remarked, "it appears that those who write upon Stonehenge ascribe it to that class of antiquity they are themselves most inclined."

I made for myself a précis of the only solid facts I could gather out of the mass of conjectures; but perhaps before giving this it may be useful to consider, as far as can be judged from the present position and condition of the remains, what Stonehenge was like in its perfect state. In trying to arrive at this, my own plans and observations made on the spot have been aided and confirmed by an excellent model of a conjectural restoration of Stonehenge that I saw in the museum at Salisbury. Externally, the circle appears to have been surrounded by a bank of earth, at the north-east end of which was an avenue approach, also banked with earth on either side. In the centre of this approach stood (and still stands though leaning) a solitary monolith, known as "the Friar's Heel." The structure itself consisted of two outer and complete circles, and two inner ovals of stones somewhat resembling horse-shoes in form. The outmost circle was composed of thirty stones set up on end, and at equal distances apart; these were joined together on the top by a series of imposts that formed a continuous horizontal ring of stones above. These stones were all more or less square hewn; and the horizontal slabs had mortice holes cut in their undersides and were secured to the upright posts by tenons made thereon to receive them; plainly showing a certain skill in construction. The outer circle is of local silicious sandstone popularly known as "sarens." Next came an inner circle of small unhewn stones of no great size; these stones consist of primary igneous rocks, of which none exist in the country around, nor indeed nearer than Wales or Cornwall. Then came the oval of five great independent trilithons, with their imposts secured by mortices and tenons. Inside these huge trilithons was another horse-shoe of small unhewn igneous stones; and in front of the largest and central trilithon was a large flat "saren," supposed to be an altar stone, which to this day shows signs of fire.

Now, having conjecturally restored Stonehenge, let us as briefly as possible (apart from purely speculative theories) consider the few facts thereon, which I gathered from the many and various authorities I consulted. On Midsummer morning in the year 1858, Dr. Thurnam, standing on the site of the supposed altar, observed that the sun rose exactly over the top of the solitary monolith known as the Friar's Heel. This fact has also been testified to by several other observers, and a photograph showing the sun rising thus has actually been taken. The plain around Stonehenge is literally strewn with sepulchral tumuli, making of it one vast unenclosed cemetery. These tumuli have been opened and examined by Sir R. C. Hoare and other barrow explorers, and were found to contain skeletons of men, burnt bones, and tools or weapons, ranging from the uncertain neolithic time to the age of bronze; besides, in one instance, fragments of the primary igneous rocks and silicious sandstone of which the small unhewn monoliths, and the hewn outer circle with its imposts and the mighty trilithons are respectively composed. In forming the earth bank around Stonehenge some of these barrows were cut through and partially destroyed. Several authorities agree that the nearest spot from which the igneous rocks could come would be either North Wales or Cornwall. The outer circle and the trilithons still show tool-marks. And after consulting many books and magazine articles this was really all of positive information that I could gather respecting this mysterious relic of the past.

Now what-conclusion can we arrive at from such scanty data? Like the rest of the writers on Stonehenge one can only make guesses, probably more or less wide of the truth. Still certain *facts* strike me as worthy of consideration. In the first place no other so-called Druids' Circle has the connecting imposts; in this Stonehenge is absolutely unique. The upright stones supporting the imposts and the imposts themselves have been certainly hewn, though roughly, and are skilfully and firmly connected by means of tenons and mortice-holes. Now may we not conclude from all this that Stonehenge, though primitive in construction, shows a most marked advance over any other structure of the kind, and is, therefore, of later, possibly much later, date? This fact might suggest that it was post-Roman, and that the builders had learnt something from the civilised Romans, if indeed they had not endeavoured to copy some of their temples that they had seen? Even Inigo Jones, the famous architect, who made a careful study of Stonehenge by order of James I., was so struck by its rough resemblance to a Roman temple as eventually to conclude that it was one!

From the difference in construction and in the kind of stones employed, does it not seem probable that we have here two actually distinct structures raised at different times, and not one structure raised at one time? It appears to me that the two circles (let me call the ovals, circles for convenience) of small unhewn stones possibly formed the original and ancient temple,—presuming Stonehenge to have been a temple,—and at a vastly later period these were surrounded by the much larger hewn stones with their imposts; a period when the builders thereof had learnt something of the use of tools and construction.

Now as to the purpose of Stonehenge. We find that the small unhewn stones must have been brought from afar, and at an enormous expenditure of time and labour. Now what other inducement but that of a sacred nature could have caused its builders to have brought these stones from such a distance, when the local "sarens" could be had at hand? Then may not the fact of the sun rising precisely over the solitary monolith known as the "Friar's Heel," as seen from the altar stone, point to some form of solar worship, as prevailed in so many heathen systems of religion? This could hardly have been accidental, and would account for the curiously isolated position of the monolith outside, and apart from the circle.

As to the age of Stonehenge, may not something be gathered by the weathering of the chisel-marks on the hewn stones, taking into due consideration, of course, the exposed position of the structure, open as it is to all the fierce storms and winter blasts that sweep unrestrained over the unsheltered

Plain, to say nothing of destructive frosts? There are houses built of this same kind of silicious sandstone, and the approximate, if not exact, date of their erection is known; and by judging of the amount of weathering of the tooling on these stones to make them square for building purposes, some rough estimate might surely be formed as to the date of Stonehenge. I merely throw this out as an idea.

The encircling bank of earth cutting right through and destroying at least two of the ancient barrows proves, at any rate, that this bank was formed subsequently to those barrows. It certainly proves no more, but it does suggest that if the surrounding earthworks were (as appears most probable) coeval with the hewn stone circles, Stonehenge itself is of later date than the barrows.

We have now to consider the fact that a few fragments, both of the primary igneous rocks and of the "sarens," have been found in one or two of the tumuli. But it appears that in ages past these barrows have been opened, possibly in the search of buried treasure; and if so, there is no telling when, or how, these bits of stone may have got there: so such finds are of very doubtful significance.

Stonehenge fascinated us, as it has fascinated countless other travellers. The structure grows upon you as you come to realise its true proportions, and ponder over the profound mystery that surrounds it. The grandest cathedral ever raised by man (as far as I have seen) never impressed me half as much as this rude structure open to all weathers, and whose stones are sculptured by the storms of ages. Standing within its encircling stones we seemed, somehow, suddenly to have stepped back long centuries; the railway, the telegraph, and all the other modern miracles of science for the moment appeared unreal and strangely out of place. This feeling was a very actual one at the time, though I cannot analyse it nor define it in words, for there are certain impressions beyond the power of language to convey. Like ourselves, Mr. Samuel Pepys appears also to have been greatly impressed with Stonehenge; for, to quote once more from his entertaining *Diary*, he writes : " To Stonehenge, over the Plain and some great hills, even to fright us. Come thither, and find them as prodigious as any tales I ever heard of them, and worth going the journey to see. God knows what their uses was! they are hard to tell." It will be noted that even this old-time traveller, accustomed to road travel as he was, found the Plain hilly!

We remained for a long time at Stonehenge, sketching and photographing the storm-stained structure; after which we engaged in a chat with an intelligent photographer we found installed there, and who seemed to take quite a paternal interest in the place, as though his remote ancestors had erected it; this quite apart from the selling of his productions, which he did not unduly press upon us. Later on, we culled the following from a local paper which, we presumed, related to this individual : " The old photographer at Stonehenge told us of an incident which is not without interest. Many years ago, whilst following his profession at the stones, a party drove up in the manner in which scores of tourists come from Salisbury. He took no more notice of them than of others. After they had inspected his views, at the suggestion of a lady of the party they were photographed against one of the stones, a gentleman giving an address in London to which the photographs were to be sent. It subsequently transpired, to the astonishment of the old man, that the lady was none other than the Queen, whom he had not recognised. The photographer kept the negative, until by accident it was broken, and it brought him in an annual revenue of fifty pounds."

As we sat sketching, chancing to cast our eyes for a moment around, we noticed the caravan we had overtaken the day before coming slowly up the hill towards us. On reaching the nearest point of the road to Stonehenge, it stopped, and curiosity led us to go and inspect it. The genial owner, seeing the interest we took in his novel conveyance, most kindly invited us inside, introduced us to his wife, who was travelling with him in this refined gipsy-like fashion, and showed us over the interior, which was fitted up like a state-room of a fine mail steamer, only more sumptuously. And besides the state-room there was a compact little kitchen for the cooking of meals. The caravan was a veritable yacht on wheels; called, if I remember aright, the "Vagabond." We had a long and most interesting chat with the owner, whose name has unfortunately escaped my memory, nor would he let us away till we had drunk a glass of wine with him. Who would have expected to be thus entertained on the lonely and inhospitable Salisbury Plain? Our unknown friend was most enthusiastic about his special mode of travelling, and expatiated upon its advantages and delights. Notwithstanding all of which, we felt no inclination to exchange our old-fashioned and comfortable dog-cart for the more luxurious and, it seemed to us, somewhat lumbersome caravan. Moreover, wherever it goes a caravan, by its uncommon appearance, unavoidably attracts attention; and speaking of ourselves, when we drive about country we seek to avoid publicity as far as possible; we set out to see what we can and care not to be seen. Our more humble dog-cart is, to a greater or lesser extent, an everyday sort of conveyance, and is, therefore, not specially conspicuous. But *Chacun à son goût.*

During our pleasant chat in the cosy interior of the caravan, a change had come over the weather, and when we parted company with our entertaining caravanist we observed that great gray clouds, rounded and bulging with aqueous vapour, were sweeping across the wide expanse of blue above; and broad masses of shade mingled with golden patches of sunshine were pursuing each other over the far-reaching landscape. We made haste to rejoin our dog-cart, as big drops of rain and a gusty wind foreboded a coming storm, and we were mindful of the warning given in the *Ingoldsby Legends*—

> It's a very bad thing to be caught in the rain
> When night's coming on upon Salisbury Plain.

Just after starting we gave a farewell glance back, and by doing so secured a most impressive view of Stonehenge which we shall never forget. The gloomy, brooding clouds above suited well the wild scene, better far than the soft summer sunshine of the morning; the great stones stood out gaunt and weirdly black against a transient glow of light in the sky. It was a fitting last view of the mysterious structure, and we were glad to have had it. In spite of the weather we could not resist making a hasty sketch of the effect, which sketch is given in the illustration with this chapter.

Then we proceeded back to Salisbury across the Plain in a direction that was pointed out to us, for there was no regular marked way. Driving down over the gently-sloping sward we found, after a time, a fairly-defined track which led us through a rambling farmyard, and eventually brought us to a very decent country road. We had not proceeded far along this before we came upon a most charming and picturesque old home of the Elizabethan period, with mullioned windows of leaden panes, carved stone doorway with a coat of arms above, great roof and clustering chimneys—a home eloquent of the past, and raised in the days before the art of building beautifully had been lost.

The ancient walls of this delightful abode were time-tinted and mellowed into a delightful harmony of soft colours. There is no painter like Time, though he may take two centuries or more to perfect his work. This thoroughly old-world English home was a picture in stone, a romance in building;

STONEHENGE.

more like an artist's dream than a bit of reality. Yet there it stood, not too good to be true. We would have liked very much to paint it, but alas! just then the rain came down in such earnest that to make even a pencil sketch was an impossibility, and it caused us to take shelter for a while under some spreading trees. There we found a native taking shelter likewise, and he informed us that the place was called Lake House, and that it was over three hundred years old.

How is it that an ancient English home like this so charms us with its picturesqueness, whilst most modern ones, when they do not actually offend our eyes, are so uninteresting? It is surely because the men of the past built their homes to live in. We have learnt otherwise; the speculative builder has arisen in the land, who merely produces houses to sell. The old homes are naturally eye-pleasing because they are the outward expression of their original owner's requirements, or even "fads"; wherever a window was wanted there it was put, wherever a chimney, there it was raised, so there was no undue formality nor mechanical feeling apparent, the thoughtful architect was everywhere in evidence, the engineer nowhere. So these buildings had the charm of variety and irregularity of outline, causing a pleasing effect of light and shade; they looked like homes to be lived in and enjoyed; and it is this quality that unconsciously charms the eye. Each old home has its special distinctive character, and when they have been added to, or altered, by succeeding generations, these changes have been purposeful, have rather enhanced their picturesqueness than otherwise, and have given them a further interest by adding, as it were, a chapter of history to the building. The modern "eligible mansion" and "desirable villa" are so often manifestly intended to be picturesque that they utterly fail to achieve that quality; indeed they brim all over with it with their meaningless, *cheap* decorations, that fail to decorate; ornamentations (save the mark!) stuck on, not sound construction ornamented. And what can be more out of keeping than a showy mansion meanly built with a sort of veneer of decorations added—an architecture *appliqué?* Yet, after all this saying, is the speculative builder wholly to blame? he merely produces what the public demand. The fact is that the means of cheap communication and rapid transit have made us a restless race, we do not, as a rule, live long in one place. A modern house is but too often only a place of temporary abode; we merely come and go. The old home where father and son succeeded one another for generations is gradually becoming a thing of the past. Our homes are, consequently, less homelike, less beautiful, they lack past associations; we live in them, they are not a part and parcel of us: strangers had them before we took possession, and strangers will have them when we leave; they lack the flavour that comes of long indwelling and personal ownership. I know people who think that if they reside in one house for seven years they have made a lengthened sojourn. We live in an age of change. It is the nineteenth century that invented the flat with one owner and several separate families housed under one roof.

Some distance farther on we came to a fine avenue of trees that led to another interesting home of the past called Heale House, with its own little old-time romance; for Charles II. came thither after the battle of Worcester, and there he was secreted by the then owner, "one Mrs. Hyde, a widow," in the hiding-hole which, according to the account he afterwards gave to Mr. Pepys, "was very convenient and safe, and staid there all alone for four or five days." Not very desirable quarters, one must imagine, but perhaps the hiding-hole at Heale House was convenient and comfortable in comparison with others; for the Prince must, during his wanderings, have had some considerable experience of such places. It seems that hardly any house of importance in those days was unprovided with a regular hiding-hole; the architects of the time would as soon have thought of omitting a kitchen in their plans as such secret chambers, or "holes" for concealment. Truly, as Oliver Wendell Holmes says, "England is one vast museum." You cannot well take a day's drive anywhere therein without coming upon some spot instinct with memories—some ancient home fraught with old-time associations that link the historic and picturesque past with the prosaic present; and so it proved that day.

Then we came to the side of the gently-gliding river Avon, which we followed most of the way back into Salisbury, through a pretty, green, and treeful country most refreshing to look upon after the bleak Plain.

The banks of the river were beautifully wooded; and, passing through the scattered hamlet of Woodford, we reached an old mill built right over the stream on a series of stone arches, the mill-wheel being between two of them. In front of us was a stretch of smooth water that reflected the mill and dark woods beyond, above which woods some rooks were circling around, not without a considerable amount of cawing, and farther away were the bare uplands that we had so recently left. We could not pass by such a ready-made picture without attempting to make a sketch of it, for though it was growing late the rain had ceased. This valley of the southern Avon is full of a quiet, soft beauty that is most soothing and restful to the eye, and should delight the painter of sylvan scenery.

Driving on we came to Stratford,—an unfamed Stratford-on-Avon,—a picturesque though unnoted village. Over the doorway of an ancient and rather quaint old house there we noticed the following inscription:—

Parva sed Apta Domino
1673

which may be done into plain English: "Small, but adapted to its master"; notwithstanding the fact that the place did not seem particularly small to us. Many of the old houses of the time had legends like this inscribed on their walls or over their porches, though more generally they were adorned with coats of arms carved in stone. Some of these inscriptions are interesting; here is one that I copied which bears its own moral :—

> Heir I forbeare my name or arms to fix
> Lest I or myne should sell these stones and sticks.

I have it also on good authority that a certain Manchester cotton lord who bought a fine estate in the North and built a magnificent mansion thereon had, in place of an invented coat of arms, the following pithy inscription placed over his doorway :—

> Who'd have thought it
> Cotton bought it.

And I would there were more such witty and anti-snobbish men as he!

In the church at Stratford here is a curious relic of the past in the shape of an ancient wrought-iron hour-glass stand; not many of these now remain, though once they were quite common in the land. A sermon was a serious thing in those days! Let us hope that there was no truth in the old saying, "The longer the sermon the worse the parson." Little wonder that they had high-backed pews then, they were a necessity! Soon after Stratford we found ourselves once again in Salisbury, well pleased with our day's wanderings, and so back to our comfortable inn.

CHAPTER VII

Salisbury Cathedral—Wilton—Good roads—A church and a museum—The flag of the ill-fated *Captain*—The valley of the Wylye—Wishford—A curious incised slab—Codford—A chat with an old villager—How the poor live—Legendary inns —Warminster, past and present.

EARLY next morning we set out to see the cathedral, though not without considerable misgivings that a daylight view might rob us of our first pleasing, poetic vision. On this occasion, however, the sunlight brought no disillusion with it; for once the real came up to the ideal! The prospect of the gray old cathedral as you approach it from the northeast is, I think, the finest revelation of architectural beauty in the world; not possibly the grandest, though it is grand; but there is a something about this one comprehensive view of what is surely the crowning glory of Gothic art that charms and fascinates the beholder beyond the reach of words. There are certain things in the world of which any description is as a shadow to the substance, and of such is the first sight of Stonehenge and of Salisbury Cathedral; two structures the very antithesis of each other; the one rude, mysterious, strange; the other a dream of beauty, a poem in stone!

Salisbury is unique amongst English cathedrals from the fact of its unity of design, being built as it was from one plan and of one period, in the graceful Early English style when at its prime, pure and undefiled. One cannot but feel that none but a medieval architect, aided by the medieval craftsman, could have conceived and successfully carried out such a miracle in building. The stately beauty of the old fane is wonderfully enhanced by its happy surroundings of wide velvety lawn—the product of centuries; of old trees with their soft green foliage, and of clustering, time-mellowed, irregular-grouped buildings,—a delightful blending of nature and art amalgamated into a perfect harmony.

Both at the Reformation and at the hands of the Parliamentary troops Salisbury suffered less hurt than any other English cathedral; but the despoiler came at last. In 1791, Wyatt the architect was employed to restore the building, which he commenced doing in a most curious way, by destroying all the priceless stained windows which had marvellously escaped till then; these he ruthlessly removed, and actually threw the rare painted glass " by cartloads into the city ditch." The next thing he did was to level with the ground the ancient belltower or campanile that stood at the north-west corner of the close. Then he set to work in this thorough manner to improve (!) the interior of the cathedral by sweeping away "screens, porches, chapels, tombs, etc." Yet, at the time, these changes —I believe they were termed restorations—were considered by the authorities " to be tasteful, effective, and judicious." What untold destruction has been wrought in the name of restoration! Old buildings must of course be maintained, but why in the name of common sense cannot they be simply repaired?

There is one thing, however, that Wyatt did, which, though archæologically indefensible, has still, to my mind, given a unique grandeur to the interior of Salisbury Cathedral. By the removal of the altar-tombs of ancient bishops, mailed warriors, and other noble and notable men from different parts of the building, and by the placing of them in two rows between the arches of the aisles, a certain stately and imposing effect is given. There is an unquestionable impressiveness in this succession of noble monuments, with the sculptured effigies recumbent thereon. Marshalled thus in a long and orderly array they at once arrest attention.

Owing, doubtless, to Wyatt's "restorations" the interior of Salisbury Cathedral seems a little chill and bare; it suffers from the absence of the rich old stained-glass windows through which the softened sunshine streamed, laden with countless hues, on to arch, pillar, chapel, tomb, wall, and floor, taking warmth and beauty everywhere. There are so many excellent guide-books to the cathedral that I will refrain from entering into a needless competition with them; rather would I describe the unfamiliar and the little known. Suffice to say, then, that we wandered all over the beautiful old building, nave, aisles, choir, chancel, Lady chapel. We duly admired the noble chapter-house, the groined ceiling of which is supported by one light central pillar. Around the walls are a series of quaint medieval carvings in high relief representing the history of the world from the Creation to the giving of the law by Moses. And lastly we walked round the superb cloisters, through whose pillared arcades we caught picturesque peeps of the hoary old cathedral, and watched the shadows come and go across the emerald green sward of the cloister-garth or Paradise, whilst above we caught patches of the brilliant blue sky which the soaring pointed spire seemed verily to pierce.

There is an old rhyme respecting the cathedral that I give here, though I cannot vouch for its correctness. I wonder if it has ever been verified :—

> As many days as in one year there be,
> So many windows in this church we see;
> As many marble pillars here appear
> As there are hours throughout the fleeting year;
> As many gates as moons one year does view—
> Strange to tell: yet not more strange than true.

Leaving Salisbury we drove westward to Wilton and Warminster, at which latter place we proposed to spend the night. We found some difficulty in getting out of Salisbury, the many streets leading in all directions were as confusing as a maze; but at last, by dint of persevering in asking our way, we managed to strike the right road. It is astonishing how hard it is to find any one in a large town who can direct you as to the way out to a neighbouring place, though almost anybody is able to direct you to the railway station. Nowadays most people who travel patronise the iron horse, and so know little of the roads—cyclists excepted.

I note in my diary a memorandum underlined as to our day's stage; it runs thus: "Excellent roads, frequent signposts, and legible milestones all the way." It is not often that the driving tourist is so blessed! On the other hand, we hardly met a soul on the road to make use of these conveniences.

Passing through a level country with a near distance of wooded hills, in about three miles we came to the clean little town of Wilton, where the first carpet in England was woven, and where excellent carpets, known by the name of the place, are still made. Here in the centre of the town, surrounded by its old God's acre, stand the ivy-grown ruins of the ancient parish church; and in the roadway, close by the churchyard wall, is still in position the deeply-carved but much weather-worn shaft of an old market cross. The old church, with its ruined arches draped with ivy, is a most picturesque object, and we wondered why it was allowed to go so to decay. It is not often one comes upon a ruined church in the midst of a small country town.

A little farther on we came to the grand new parish church (which has taken the place of the old one), erected in 1844, in the Italian style, or, to be precise, in the Lombardic of the sixth century; therefore, as may be imagined, it looks strangely unfamiliar, set as it is in an essentially English country town; about as much in keeping therewith, indeed, as would have been an ironclad at Trafalgar.

This church is truly an astonishing and gorgeous edifice, besides being a perfect treasure-house of works of art; so much this latter, in fact, that it made it seem to us more like a museum than a place of worship. We fortunately found the clerk within, and after payment of a prescribed "fee" of sixpence a head *à la* South Kensington, we were provided with a card with printed particulars thereon of the building and its art stores, and to this card I am in part indebted for the following particulars.

The entrance pillars to the main doorway resting on lions are typical of the strength of the church. The tower for the bells—which stands apart from the main building, but is connected therewith by a light-pillared cloister—is a copy of an Italian campanile. We entered through the cloisters and by a side door, above which is an old Jacobean tomb to a William Sharpe and his wife dated 1626, which was removed from the old church and is now cleverly utilised as a sort of ornamental entablature to the doorway, though it hardly harmonises with its intensely classical surroundings. One window in the church is of rare old fifteenth-century Flemish glass, and very lovely and gem-like it is. The marble pillars of the nave have alabaster capitals, and are alternately carved with representations of good and evil angels. The chancel floor is covered with an elaborate mosaic in coloured marbles; and above the altar (which is adorned with rich and ancient needlework) are stained-glass windows of the twelfth or thirteenth century. The pillars that support the arch of the chancel are two massive monoliths of Italian marble brought from Portus Veneris in the Gulf of Spezzia. Over the vestry door is a painted copy of the earliest emblematical representation of our Lord, from the Catacombs at Rome. The pulpit is a grand though composite work of art, being partially formed of a thirteenth-century shrine removed from S. Maria Maggiore in Rome. The font also came from Italy. In the vestry we noticed a massive and very ancient wrought-iron alms-chest having four padlocks; this came from Venice. The rest of the stained-glass windows are of the thirteenth, fourteenth, and fifteenth centuries.

It would, however, take a small volume to describe, at all worthily, the rare treasures contained in this truly unique church, which may fairly be termed magnificent, but thoroughly un-English. It is a building to admire but not to love; it does not appeal to one's tenderest feelings as does an ancient village church, simple and unpretentious, hallowed by the prayers of bygone generations of humble worshippers.

On the chancel wall we observed suspended a large flag with St. George's red cross thereon, looking strangely out of place in the midst of its anti-English surroundings. What did it do there, we wondered? And as we could not answer the question we sought out the clerk and asked of him. "That," said he, "is the flag that belonged to the ill-fated man-of-war the *Captain*, which, as you may remember, was capsized at sea and went to the bottom. But there is a curious bit of history about it; when the *Captain* left Portsmouth on her last voyage, by some strange blunder her flag was left behind—and there it is." We thanked the clerk for his information and took our departure; if the story he told us be correct, it was certainly a curious coincidence.

This wonderful church, with its priceless art treasures, came upon us as a revelation; it was one of the "finds" of our journey. And after this who shall say that the man who takes his holiday exploring the byways of his own country sees nothing noteworthy? As a matter of fact not a day of our journey passed without some scenic surprise being presented to us, or our discovering some spot of antiquarian interest, as will be gathered from this unvarnished account of our most enjoyable outing.

On coming out of this foreign-looking church directly into the homelike English town, it was as though we had in a moment travelled hundreds of miles from fair sunny Italy to beautiful mellow Old England; the sudden apparent transition from one to the other was almost startling in effect.

On a wall of a building in the town we noticed, as we passed along, an old fountain, at which we were bidden by an inscription above to "Drink and thank God." But the fountain was dry; and a tramp who happened to pass by just then saw his opportunity, and with an aggrieved tone asked us if we knew what it was "to be thirsty and never even a drop of water to drink." We replied that we did, we too had been thirsty, and had even been driven to quench it with a glass of ale; whereupon the tramp sympathised with us, and said it was a hard thing to be compelled to take intoxicating things, but if we would give him the price of a glass of ale he would buy with it a glass of milk. He certainly did not look like a milk-drinking tramp, and as we handed him the inevitable twopence and received his blessing in return, we thought that we caught the faint mingled odours of beer and tobacco, but this must have been fancy on our part!

Leaving Wilton our road took us through a lovely country, and along a well-wooded and hill-enclosed valley watered by the winding Wylye, a river of whose existence we were unaware until that day; truly a driving tour teaches one a good deal about the geography of one's own country besides many other things. We followed this pretty little river up as far as Warminster, near to which town is its birthplace, as far as we could make out from our map.

This little-travelled valley of the Wylye is one of great beauty, and reminded us very much of Devonshire. As we journeyed on, the little river kept us pleasant company, winding in and out of the green meadows to our left, and was crossed every here and there by picturesque foot-bridges. The landscape all around had a thoroughly rural look; gently-sloping hill and wooded vale, gleaming stream and verdant meadow, cottage home and time-toned farmstead, all went to compose a perfect picture of rural contentment. Scenes like these made us wonder when Englishmen will learn to travel in their own land, and not merely to rush through it by rail to some more or less fashionable watering-place. We want a guide-book to untravelled England! If we could only post across country as our forefathers did in the days of old, what a changeful and pleasant holiday might be spent thus! It is a great pity there was not room for both coaches and railways. Fancy being able, in the fine summer weather, to take a seat on a coach and drive all the way down to fair Devonshire, what a treat that would be, and what a revelation of lovely scenery to the modern generation of railway travellers!

The first village we came to was Wishford, a snug little hamlet situated by the side of a beautiful bend of the river, which is here crossed by an ancient stone bridge. Close to the bridge stands an old inn, and when we passed an angler was trying his luck in the stream. We made a hurried sketch of the scene; the figure of the fisherman gave just that touch of life and interest to the prospect that was alone wanting to make a perfect picture.

Then a long pull uphill with wide views opening out as we ascended, followed by an equally long descent, brought us to Stapleford, another charmingly situated little hamlet by the river-side—primitive and picturesque. Some of the garden walls here appeared to be built of mud, and very unsubstantial they look; but a native said they were cheap, and assured us that with a little patching up now and then they would last a lifetime; still I would rather have one of stone or brick, that does not require such frequent attention and looks much better. It is astonishing, though, what can be done with mud; I have an excellent teapot, serviceable and ornamental, which is made simply out of Nile mud.

On now, with great barren downs to our right, to the clean and scattered village of Steeple Langford, its hoary old church standing in its well-kept graveyard close to the roadside. We took a sudden fancy to inspect this church, and so pulled up and went in search of the clerk, who as usual happened not to be at home, but his wife was and offered to show us over. Upon entering the rural fane our attention was at once arrested by a very curious marble slab, built into the south wall of the nave; on this was a boldly-incised figure of a man in a loose robe, with his hands holding, apparently, a heart over his breast; on his right side was a horn slung from a strap. The head of the figure had a strangely Egyptian appearance, but the slab was in a bad light for inspection. This quaint figure had no inscription, and our guide knew nothing about it excepting that it had been found buried in the chancel when the church was repaired some years ago. We wondered what the horn signified; could the man possibly have been a hunter? Those who erect monuments might really inscribe them with some particulars for the benefit of future generations!

In a deep recess of the chancel wall is a carved and painted wooden effigy of the Rev. John Collier, who, the clerk's wife told us, dropped down dead when preaching from the pulpit "some two hundred years ago." This effigy is painted in natural colours, and evidently intended to be lifelike, and consequently has a somewhat grim effect. Finding nothing else to interest us, we remounted the dog-cart and proceeded on our way.

The valley now became wider and less well wooded; the scenery was, for a time, bold rather than pretty. To our right stretched forth a long continuous range of treeless downs, whose dark-green outline rose and fell in grand curved sweeps that gradually faded away in the far distance to a pale purple-gray. The foot of one of the outlying spurs of the downs that descended to our road was simply covered with a mass of poppies; and never saw I such a blaze of burning colour before, half blinding in its brilliancy. All the rest of the landscape seemed, by comparison, of washed-out tints. The rich purple of heather, and even the glowing gold of the gorse, have no chance against the powerful scarlet of the gorgeous poppy when massed thus.

After this feast of colour, descending into the valley we had, by way of contrast, a little quiet-toned Birket-Foster-like bit presented to us. A small gurgling stream close to the roadway was crossed by an old wooden foot-bridge; below this was a shallow ford, and behind were great tall leafy elms. To complete the picture, a girl was on the bridge with a faded red shawl thrown across her shoulders, standing just where an artist would have placed her, and she was talking to a sunburnt lad who was driving a donkey down to the stream to drink. There's an idea for a picture, we thought, with "Wayside Gossip" for a title!

Soon afterwards, we found ourselves in the

curiously-named village of Codford (why a fish should want a ford, we could not understand), where, at the homely George Inn, we made our midday halt. Our refreshment here consisted of a simple meal of bread and cheese and ale; and hungry as we were we pronounced it to be fare fit for a king. Just then, with our healthy appetites, dainty dishes, I verily believe, we would have scorned, though certainly we should not have objected to a cut from a sirloin of cold roast beef in place of the cheese; but we did not sigh for the unattainable.

Whilst our horses indulged in an extra rest after our long morning's stage, we took a stroll round the place. The first thing that we observed was a flag flying from the old church tower, and we asked of a pleasant-faced woman who was standing knitting outside her cottage door the reason of this. "Oh," she replied, "I expects it be a saint's day; the parson is a bit High Church you see, and we've lots of saint's days here, and whenever there's one they puts the flag up."—"Indeed," we exclaimed, "and do many people go to church on those days?"—"Sometimes I believe that there's three or four who goes," said she; "but I don't think as how the people as goes to church so often is much better than the rest of us. No, I never go to church"; this looked rather bad, but she qualified her statement by adding, "*when I go to church I go to chapel!*"

Then, as we chatted on, we learnt that she was "seventy-eight next February"; her father died at ninety-three, and she felt good for some years to come. Certainly the old body looked hale and hearty enough, and all the time she talked she never once stopped her knitting. Her husband, she said, was seventy and worked on the road; he used formerly to be a gardener and earned good wages, now he got about 10s. a week; they took in a lodger, who paid them 1s. 6d. a week, and out of these sums they managed to feed and clothe themselves, paid a subscription to a club, and 2s. 6d. a week rent for their cottage. This cottage, though poorly furnished, looked neat and cleanly kept, so I think they contrived well. All these particulars I discovered during the course of our conversation, and it showed us how some of the poor live. The woman appeared quite contented, and seemed to think that they had much to be grateful for, in the fact that they were able to keep out of the "union"! These patient English poor folk, after a life of toil, do they not deserve a better fate than the workhouse in their old age? I am speaking of the worthy, not the worthless ones. I wonder, could not some little cottage homes be built (they need not be costly) wherein the deserving poor, when too old or weak to work any longer, could live and die in peace, being of course provided with what small weekly allowance might be needful? Surely unavoidable poverty is no sin; and a worthy workman in a Christian land, who has spent the best of his life in constant toil, has earned some quiet resting-place other than the dreaded workhouse, as a right of his humble but useful citizenship,—not as a charitable concession! But I will say no more: it was that uncomplaining woman, so manifestly thankful for her small mercies, that started my pen awandering thus.

From Codford on to Heytesbury we had a good stretch of level road; at the latter place we noticed the name of the village painted on the side of a house (railway-station fashion) as was the custom in the old coaching times. Here also we noticed the Angel Inn bearing the date of 1692. Farther on our way we passed another roadside inn ycleped the Royal Oak; but the painter of the sign thereof had, by some extraordinary mistake, copied a cedar tree —and not at all badly by the way—instead of an English oak, which was presumably intended.

On to Warminster we had fine views of the open downs to our right, plainly marked here and there by rugged earthworks, some of great size, and doubtless of British origin. There is no monument in the world so lasting as earth mounds, when grass-grown like these. Old Sarum has disappeared without hardly a trace, but the ramparts around are still almost entire.

At Warminster we drove up to the Bath Arms, formerly a famous coaching house, and its weather-worn and time-stained stone front proclaims it to be an ancient hostelry that doubtless possesses its own unwritten history. Most of these old-world inns have some legend or tradition attached to them waiting to be unearthed, and when there is a communicative ostler on the premises a good listener may reap a rich reward in the shape of strange stories of the past, more or less true: at least such has been our experience. Here, however, though the inn looked legendary, the ostler failed us.

There is not much of beauty or of interest in Warminster, or at least if there be we failed to discover it. What pleased us most in the place was some rather quaint gargoyles on the church of St. Laurence. These represented some griffins, and though modern had a good deal of the medieval spirit about them; but after all they were merely superfluous ornaments, serving no real need, rainwater pipes being used. How strange it is that what the builders of old employed as a necessity and then afterwards ornamented, now that they have outlived their functions, we to-day add to our buildings solely as decorative features. This shows a sad want of originality. I greatly doubt if the architect of the past deemed a gargoyle of itself a desirable thing, but being required for a particular purpose, he forthwith embellished it and converted an article of utility into a thing of art,—beautiful or quaint as the fancy took him.

Going into a shop to make some small purchases we entered into a conversation with the proprietor; country shopkeepers, we have found, are not averse to a chat with a stranger, it is doubtless a relief to the usual monotony of their existence. He was an old man, and said that he had lived in Warminster ever since he was a little boy. He remembered the days when the Bath Arms was "all alive," to use his expression, "and not the quiet place it is now. The coaches used to change horses there, and as they came in sight of the hotel the guard would blow his horn, whereon a postboy, who was always stationed at the gateway of the stable-yard on the outlook, would shout, 'Bring 'em down!' meaning of course the fresh team. What a big man we thought the coachman in those days; he brought us all the news. So punctual, too, were the mail-coaches that we used to set our clocks by them. Yes, sir, it was a lively town then, plenty of traffic on the road day and night. Them was good times for us small shopkeepers; now, thanks to the Parcel Post, we can hardly get a living."—"Why, how's that?" we exclaimed. "Well, you see, sir, folks now writes up to London for what they wants and gets most everything down by the Parcel Post next day. We used to have a great corn market here, the biggest, I believe, in the west of England, a ready-money market it was, but now we've hardly any corn market at all, as so much of the land around is laid down grass. No, sir, Warminster is not what it used to be when I was a lad; it was a busy place then, now it seems gone to sleep and never wakes up, we don't even get one busy day a month. Men rust out rather than wear out here." Poor old man, he took a somewhat pessimist view of things; and, possibly, in his case, with a certain amount of reason. He had evidently not moved with the times, and in these competitive days fate is hard upon those who lag behind.

CHAPTER VIII

A breezy day—A chartless cruise—Westbury White Horse—Turner's Tower—Beckington—Old English gardens—A quaint village—A fifteenth-century inn with a history—A great "hiding-hole"—Ancient chambers—Vanished curiosities—"The twin maidens of Foscote"—A horrible tradition—A haunted room—Cider-making—Farleigh Castle—A picturesque spot—Storm-overtaken.

It was a wild windy morning the one on which we left Warminster, great white rolling clouds, shaded with pearly-gray, were moving apace across the deep blue sky above, softened here and there into silvery mists where they dispersed themselves in transient summer showers. There was a delightful sense of freshness in the air; it had rained heavily over-night, and the storm had cleared the atmosphere; all nature looked bright and gay under the cheerful gleams of sunshine that came and went between the soft gray cloud shadows. The trees were bending and rustling in the wind, the scattered cornfields were waving like little golden seas, the long lank grasses everywhere were swaying in rhythmic lines of changeful curves; all was breezy and full of movement.

It was just the weather for travelling by road,

and we set out early on our day's stage so as to
have plenty of time before us, for we did not even
know where we should spend the night ; for once we
determined that we would drive on and trust to fate,
therefore on leaving the town we simply took the first
road out that led in a westerly direction. We were
bound for the Welsh Border, that was enough for
us; but we were not bound to get there by the nearest
or by any prescribed route. It was pleasant to start
in all the freshness of that summer morning with the
knowledge that it mattered not if we lost our way,
or where we should eventually arrive, so long as we
did arrive somewhere before nightfall. So we steered
a more or less westerly course, and where two roads
met we selected that which promised the best scenery
so long as it did not diverge too much to the north
or south, and waited upon events. " Fortune favours
the "—reckless; sometimes! In England, if you
follow a road long enough, you are sure to reach an
inn, or a town at last. A desultory drive has its
charms, and thus may you (as did we) make discoveries that you might not otherwise do.

After a few miles of pleasant and greenful
country we came to a steep descent that led us
down through a damp and deeply-wooded glen,
which presently widened out into a rough common.
It was in truth a lonely road, gloomy in parts,
where the dank, dark woods overhung the narrow
way; but when we reached the open common with
glimpses of distant hills all around, raked by golden
gleams of sunshine, the gloom vanished. Then
some cottage homes, with flowerful gardens, came

into sight, and our road once more assumed a cheerful aspect. On the slope of the downs to our right we suddenly espied the form of a great white horse, well figured and proportioned. Noticing a cottager at work in his garden we pulled up and asked of him its name and what he knew about it. "That 'ere," said he, "is called the Westbury White Horse, it were made long afore my time; they do say as how some great battle were fought there by King Alfred, who, after he had won it, had the horse cut there. But I don't rightly know whether it be true, but that's what they do say. It were long afore my time, you see. It shows very plain to-day, and when it shows like that it's sure to rain." We thanked the old man for his reply, and drove on apace mindful of his last remark.

We were now getting into a hilly country, as a proof of which our road began to mount in right earnest and eventually landed us very high up in the world. In all directions we had magnificent views over a vast extent of rolling country. On the top of a distant hill we observed a tall tower somewhat like a lighthouse. A shepherd chanced to be sitting on a wall just then (for we had reached a bleak stone district), and he told us that it was called "Turner's Tower," and that he had heard "as how it was built by a gentleman who had more money than what he knew how to do with." Then he added, "I wish as how I had more money than what I knew how to do with, even a sixpence more." We took the hint, for he was a civil-spoken man, picturesque withal in his sun-faded gray coat and old-fashioned crook; so much so that we ventured to make a sketch of him. By the way he called our drawing "a draft."

In the rural country, human beings are, to me, more interesting and vastly more picturesque than the monotony of multitudes of men and women of towns who slavishly, and all too successfully, strive to resemble one another in dress and who dare not be original. What artist could make anything out of a crowd of fashionable people, or a unit thereof? but the weather-beaten fisherman, sun-burnt shepherd, haymaker, ploughman, or even the unsophisticated tiller of the soil, how delightfully picturesque they generally are. So also is it with country buildings, an old cottage, with its lichen-laden roof, and ivy-covered walls, is vastly more pleasing to look upon than the finest palace that was ever raised. Beauty, it seems, ever delights to associate itself with simplicity.

Then we dropped down into the picturesque little village of Beckington, which possesses some interesting old stone-built houses, roofed also with thin stone slabs. These slabs are of a pleasant warm gray tone, and infinitely more delightful to the eye than the cold, cheerless hue of slates; but they are expensive, and require heavy and strong rooftrees for their support, whilst slates are cheap and light, and so ugliness as usual triumphs. Some of these houses were surrounded by high old-fashioned walls, over which we tried in vain to peer. In imagination, however, we pictured to ourselves behind them genuine old English gardens, abounding in homely, sweet-scented flowers such as our grandparents loved, with on the lawn, perchance, a moss-grown sun-dial, and beyond a trim-clipped yew hedge. Perhaps it was as well we could not see over, our dreams might not have been realised. And it is well to dream at times; a little innocent romancing in a prosaic age does no one any harm, even though one's poetic fancies are far from the actual truth!

Driving on, in time we came to a long uphill stretch; at the top of this a sudden dip landed us all unexpectedly in one of the quaintest old-world villages imaginable, built centuries long ago, and apparently little changed since. Then our eyes were gladdened by a vision that for the moment made us almost think that we were dreaming. There before us stood, not a poetic imagining, but a delightful reality in the shape of an ancient hostelry,—a veritable picture in stone and timber that we never expected to find out of a painting or a Harrison Ainsworth's novel. But there it stood an enchanting reality, with the bloom of ages upon it. A thrill of delighted surprise went through us as we gazed upon that charming old inn, built in the fifteenth century (as we afterwards learnt), and fortunately little altered since, at least externally, and not very much internally. In itself it was worth the whole journey to see, or a dozen such journeys for that matter. And how shall I describe it? Here I feel that pen and pencil both, alas! must fail me.

As we drove up to its ancient doorway, the

landlord came forth to greet us; and, stabling our horses, we could not resist the temptation to at once make a sketch of the grand old building, hungry as we were with our long drive. An engraving of our sketch is given with this chapter, and though a poor attempt to realise in black and white the indescribable charms of this rare old hostelry, it is perhaps better than nothing. Our camera, too, was called into requisition, and created such surprise amongst the junior portion of the population that we could not help wondering whether they had ever seen a photographer before. Then the claims of hunger got the better of us, and we sought the interior of our inn, where we found a modest repast ready prepared for us in a genuine antique fifteenth-century chamber lighted by a picturesque mullioned window, which verily seemed to enclose an atmosphere of the past. How far away the busy, money-making present appeared at that moment!

The architecture of this ancient inn is certainly unique; the ground story is of stone and somewhat ecclesiastical in the detail of the mullioned windows; the great Gothic doorway, too, suggests, rather the entrance to a church than to an inn. There is a tradition that the building was originally erected by the Prior of Hinton Abbey, which, if true, may account for the style of this lower part; but the curious thing is that above this are two stories of half-timber projecting one above the other. It would be interesting to know how it was that this peculiar transition from a stone building to that of half-timber came about.

GEORGE INN, NORTON ST. PHILIPS.

It seems to me most probable that the original builder failed to complete his design and left it unfinished at the first story, whereon the superstructure of half-timber was added by some one else. They are two such wholly different styles that one can hardly imagine them to be the work of the same hand, though I gathered from what the landlord told me, who appeared to take an intelligent interest in the old place, that it was built as it is from the first, and that the upper stories were not an after addition. Be this as it may, it is certainly one of the quaintest—I will not say the most harmonious in architecture—of old inns that we have ever set our eyes upon; and we have seen, at different times, during our many drives about England from one end to the other, a goodly number of quaint and picturesque past-time hostelries. It has sheltered, moreover, several important historical personages, if I may rely on the authority of our landlord, who kindly took us all over the rambling interior and gave us a most interesting account thereof.

Taking us up an octagonal stairway at the back of the building, our guide led us up to the first story and showed us the ancient chamber "in which Oliver Cromwell slept a night when in pursuit of Charles II." The old oak door of this creaked on its rusty hinges as we entered, and had, we noticed, on the inside its original wooden latch and bolt. In another room, where the ill-fated Duke of Monmouth slept on 26th June 1685, previous to his retreat on Bridgwater, was pointed out to us the window in which the Duke was standing on the morning following, and who was shot at and wounded for his pains, presumably in view of obtaining the reward offered for his life. The top story of all was one great long, hall-like apartment; this we learnt, "four hundred years ago, was used as a market for cloth and wool." At the end of this great upper hall was a false wall, between which and the real outer wall of the building was a space of some ten feet or so; this reached all the way down to the ground floor, and was used as a hiding-place. In this the fugitive Prince Charles secreted himself for a time. Then we were shown the recess in which a wooden wheel was formerly fixed, and by a rope therefrom food was lowered to the unfortunate person in hiding below: though it struck us forcibly that such a wheel would inevitably disclose the hiding-place. This top story projects fully two yards over the roadway, and through a crack in the oak floor we looked down and saw the ground beneath.

Our landlord further informed us that "the inn had been a licensed house for over 300 years, as long as houses have been licensed, and is supposed to be the oldest licensed house in England." Then we were taken downstairs and shown the stone-groined cellars, which, tradition says, were at one time used as dungeons, though why an inn should be provided with dungeons we could not imagine; however, they certainly looked prison-like and dismal enough. The curious little rounded chimneys at either end of the roof, we were told, never smoked; if this be so, they are effectual as well as picturesque, two things one cannot always combine in this imperfect world, and may be worth the study of modern architects.

On the return home from our journey an artist friend told me the following story. Being in a neighbouring town and hearing of this ancient hostelry he drove over with his son to see it in a hired fly. On arriving there, his son at once exclaimed, "Oh, father, you must paint the old inn!" Now it so chanced that the owner of the property was expected that very day to inspect it, and the remark being overheard by the driver,—who imagined that my friend was the owner,—he ventured to remark, "I don't think that I would paint the old place, sir, it would quite spoil its antique look, it will do very well as it is outside for a many years yet"; which shows that even a hired fly driver may have artistic tastes, and an idea of the fitness of things.

Strolling down the village street, we found ourselves close to the church, and whilst we were making a sketch thereof an old body came to us and asked if we would like to see over it, "it is very curious." So we replied that we would, whereupon she told us to walk inside as the door was open, and she would come after us, as she had a book at home with all about the history of the building, and she would fetch it; we begged her not to go, but she would; therefore we entered the church alone. This, though ancient, did not seem to us specially curious or noteworthy. Just as we were coming out, the worthy body reappeared with an old and much-thumbed book in her hand. "Have you seen the heads of the two ladies?" she exclaimed, somewhat out of breath with her hurried journey home and back. This sounded somewhat mysterious, and we replied, "The heads of two ladies? No, we've seen nothing of the kind. Where are they, and what are they like?"—"Not seen them; why, they's the great curiosity here, they stands on the top of the cupboard under the tower." Then we were led to that spot. However, "when she got there the cupboard was bare," or at least the top of it was, and our guide looked around bewildered. "Well I never," said she in manifest astonishment, "wherever can they be got to; they've been there as long as ever I can mind, and now they's clean gone. Some one must have run away with them." Then she looked at us, we thought, suspiciously for a moment as though we might have pocketed or perhaps made away with them whilst she was absent. But we managed to reassure her that we had not as much as even seen them. We had no idea how large they were, what they were like, or anything about them. Indeed, we felt a good deal mystified about the matter, and asked for particulars.

Then the old woman brought forth her treasured book and wanted us to read through some twenty pages or so of small print, giving, we noticed by the heading, "A true account of the twin maidens of Foscote"; but we felt disinclined to wade through this, and therefore said that we would rather hear all about them from her. "Well," she exclaimed, "it is all down in print, and I thought you would rather read it, that you might know it was all true" (Oh, dear! if everything that's in print be true, thought we! but we held our tongues). "The two heads is carved in stone quite natural like with hair down their sides; they are about this size," making a circle in the air with her finger, by very rough guess of about a foot in diameter. "They used to be on a tombstone that stood a long while ago in the floor of the chancel beneath which the ladies were buried; they had two heads and only one body. All of which is down in this book, and if you will only read their history in it, you will find it's all true, and a lot else about them." We thanked and rewarded the old body for her information, and glanced over the account of these "twin maidens of Foscote," as given therein, and found that she had given us the correct particulars as there recorded, concerning these personages, or one person with two heads is it?

On our return to London we sought for further, and, if possible, authentic particulars on this matter. In Pepys' *Diary*, edited by Lord Braybrooke, we came upon the following quotation taken from Collinson's *History of Somersetshire*, and this is all we could discover: "In the floor of the nave of the church of Norton St. Philips are the mutilated portraitures, in stone, of two females, close to each other, and called by the inhabitants 'The Fair Maidens of Fosscot,' a neighbouring hamlet, now depopulated. There is a tradition that the persons they represent were twins, whose bodies were at their birth conjoined together; that they arrived at a state of maturity; and that one of them dying, the survivor was compelled to drag about her lifeless companion till death released her of the horrid burden."

Norton St. Philips is a thoroughly old-world place, looking much the same now as it did generations long ago. It abounds in those effective and picturesque "bits" that so delight the eye of an artist, the antiquary, and the lover of old England. Some people might, perhaps, consider it a rather bleak and dreary village; for beautiful as they are in their varied tints of gray, the old stone houses have not the rich warm colouring of brick; by this I do not mean the dirty sort of yellowish brown of some modern bricks, which are cheap—and hideous.

Returning to our inn we consulted our map as to where we should drive next, for though we should much have liked to have spent the night at Norton St. Philips we were not by any means enamoured by the ancient and ghost-like chamber that was offered to us. Lover of the old and the picturesque as I am, I still have the bad taste to prefer a modern bedroom with modern appointments to an ill-furnished fifteenth-century one. I have slept in both panelled and tapestried chambers, with ancestral portraits in dismal black frames hung around, provided with stuffy four-posters and many big cupboards—haunted-looking chambers—but I cannot honestly recommend them. I consider that spending a night therein is carrying romance a little too far! They are well enough in the daytime and in pictures, but not so well to sleep in, especially for a nervous individual. By the way, a certain nervous gentleman I know, who I rather more than fancy secretly believes in ghosts, though of course he will not confess it, was paying a first visit to an old country house wherein was a large party gathered. On his arriving there late at night his host quietly took him aside and confidentially whispered into his ear, "I say, old fellow, I'm awfully sorry, but we shall have to put you up in the haunted room, it is the only spare one we've got; but I know *you* won't mind, you're such a brave fellow. A soldier never cares for anything!" My friend had been in the militia! I only know that he went to the place to spend a fortnight, but was obliged to return to town the very next morning "on urgent business." I once slept in a "haunted" room, and slept well, but then I did not know that it had that reputation till the next morning, which makes all the difference.

A glance at our map showed us that Bradford-on-Avon was the nearest town to where we were, and learning from our landlord that it boasted of a good inn, we decided to drive on there.

Going into the stable-yard to order the horses to be "put to," we found some men at work cider-making. The apples were placed in horse-hair bags, which were put under a press and the juice squeezed out into great vats beneath. We had never witnessed cider-making before, and the process interested us. One fact connected therewith we discovered that determined us never to drink cider again,—not a great deprivation, however, as it is not a favourite beverage of ours,—namely, that a quantity of half-ripe and some blemished apples were being used that were fit only for pigs, we thought. On inquiry we were told that they only selected the worthless fruit for cider, just that which is not good to eat; for "somehow you see, sir, that the bad 'uns makes the best cider, they give it a flavour!" But we did not see! If apples are not fit to eat, why should they be fit to drink? That's the question.

As we left Norton St. Philips dark, thundery clouds were spreading across the sky in front of us, which looked so threatening that we had almost a mind not to venture forth but to return to the despised fifteenth-century chamber; the choice lay between a probable drenching or an uncomfortable night. Madame preferred the drenching, and that settled the matter; besides, said she, "the room is a certainty, the drenching an uncertainty." So we whipped our horses up and put on our best speed, helped at first by an excellent road; but our course was across country and that a wild one. We only hoped that there would be finger-posts at the cross-ways, for it is not pleasant to be caught in a heavy thunderstorm in a bleak district when uncertain about your road. Nor is it improving to one's temper to have to consult a map in the midst of wind and rain. However, the clouds passed over harmlessly for a time, and we even began to hope that we might escape a wetting altogether. "Fortune favours the brave," exclaimed my wife. "Wait till we arrive at Bradford," I replied; for a strange stillness reigned around, which, under such circumstances, is generally the precursor of mischief. Not a leaf of the trees stirred, not a bird was to be seen.

Presently our road made a steep descent, which had to be negotiated with the brake hard on; down and down we went through a wooded gorge that only wanted a little sunshine to be exceedingly beautiful. Gloom is not suitable to purely pretty scenery. Some way down this long descent we came upon the very picturesque ruins of Farleigh Castle, with its crumbling arched gateway, ivy-clad walls, and ruined towers. The castle is romantically placed, standing, as it does, boldly on a rocky height, above a well-wooded dell, round the foot of which winds and tumbles the little river Frome.

Coming thus wholly unexpectedly upon this old ruin was another of the delightful surprises of our journey, the second one that day; and we were to have still one more on entering Bradford by its chapel-crowned bridge.

Not being in a tourist-haunted district, Farleigh Castle has no attractions for the ordinary guide-book compiler; neither, for the same reason, has it been painted, photographed, and engraved times without number from every possible point of view as have most famous old ruins on the beaten track. Therefore not having read about it, nor seen it portrayed in pictures, this ruined relic of the feudal past came upon us with all the freshness of the unfamiliar. We had the pleasure of discovering it for ourselves, and a more picturesque spot there could hardly be.

For over three centuries, Farleigh Castle belonged to the proud and powerful Hungerford family, and their coat of arms still exists over the entrance of the gatehouse. Their erst stately stronghold, in which they lived and entertained right royally for many generations, is now a mere shell :—

> Yet Time
> Has seen this broken pile complete
> Big with the vanity of state;
> But transient is the smile of Fate;
> A little rule, a little sway,
> A sunbeam in a winter's day,
> Is all the proud and mighty have
> Between the cradle and the grave.

Then we descended to the river, which we crossed upon a moss-grown, gray stone bridge of three arches. The stream, with its wooded banks, the ruined and weatherworn castle above, the old bridge below, together with some lowly cottages on the hillside, formed a perfect picture, and we took out our sketch-book to realise it on paper, when a roll of thunder, loud and long, followed by a sudden downpour, as though a second deluge were about to commence, put an effectual stop to our proceeding. We looked around for shelter, and hastily made for some overhanging trees by the roadside, but even their thick foliage failed to protect us from the heavy rain; moreover, trees do not always afford a safe retreat during a thunderstorm. Across the way, we noticed a tiny cottage which, though small and poor, was probably water-tight, and to this I hurried my wife to seek shelter for a time. The storm was sharp and short, and soon the sky grew lighter above, then it simply rained in an ordinary steady manner, not with the first tropical fierceness; with this improvement in the outlook we determined to proceed lest worse things should happen. The poor old cotter woman, who had been most kind and attentive, proved to be the wife of a farm labourer, and her eyes positively glistened with delight when we presented her with a whole shilling in return for her hospitality. What hard lives rich England's poor must lead to be so genuinely grateful for so small a trifle! I do not know how many comforts she made out that one shilling would bring her; it was hard work to live and pay rent out of a farm labourer's wage, she said, and work was not always to be had; moreover, there was illness to be taken into account, so that what with one thing and another at the end of a year they could never manage to put by a penny even. But the poor old woman spoke in no complaining tone, only, as it were, to excuse herself from receiving any payment at all for affording us shelter. "Deed, sir, I were only pleased to do it; I only wishes as how I had a more comfortable chair to offer the good lady. I never expected anything, deed I did not, sir, but I'm extreemely grateful all the same." And so we parted without the inevitable "God bless you" that the sturdy loafing tramp generally bestows upon a foolish donor; which is, in my experience, the unmistakable "hall mark" of the professional beggar.

Then we drove on in the rain through damp, dripping woods, when a sudden bend in the road brought us to a more open country; and there, a mile or so ahead of us, we saw the town of Bradford clustered on the hillside, the wet roofs of its scattered houses reflecting a transient gleam of watery sunshine through the momentarily parted clouds overhead; and we did not feel sorry to be in sight of our night's destination. For, in spite of that one sunny gleam, fitful flashes of light on the dark-gray horizon foreboded another storm, and the clouds were rapidly approaching. We raced the storm into Bradford, and won by five minutes! That second edition of bad weather lasted all night, so that we considered ourselves lucky to have escaped so well as we did on the road.

Passing over a quaint old stone bridge with an ancient and curious "mass chapel" thereon (of which presently), we found the town rising before us in a most romantic fashion on the steep sides of a hill, houses over houses happily grouped in picturesque irregularity and confusion, as though they had all been tumbled down there anyhow regardless of any formal plan.

Bradford in Wiltshire, or Bradford-on-Avon, however it may be distinguished from its ugly namesake in Yorkshire, is as romantic-looking a town as the other is ugly and commercially commonplace. Bradford-on-Avon takes its name, so antiquaries say, from the broad ford over the river, which was used till about the middle of the seventeenth century, the bridge originally being only serviceable for foot or horse passengers. Here we drove up to the Swan Inn, where we found comfortable if homely quarters, good fare, and a hearty welcome; and what more could the weary and storm-overtaken traveller desire? So ended our long, most interesting, and eventful day's wanderings.

CHAPTER IX

Two old manor houses—An ancient Saxon church—Unexplored England!—An old monastic tithe barn—A stately Jacobean home—A mass chapel on a bridge—Great Chaldfield manor—A curious inscription on a window pane—A quaint church tower—A fifteenth-century mansion—Sir Walter Raleigh's smoke room—An interesting interior—Places and pictures—The legend of the lady with the white hand—A well in a living room.

THE next morning proved showery, but in spite of the weather we were up early in order to take a short stroll of inspection round about the quaint old town before breakfast, and before proceeding on our journey. The result of our stroll revealed to us the fact that Bradford-on-Avon, with its outskirts, was so full of interesting ancient buildings, picturesque odd nooks and corners, and charming architectural tit-bits, that we thereupon decided that we would not proceed farther that day, but would stay where we were, exploring and sketching the place, and, if the weather permitted, photographing as well whatever specially took our fancy. By so doing we should also give our hard-worked horses a well-earned rest.

Bradford is one of those places that improve on

acquaintance; it has a decidedly old-world flavour about it; it is a spot to gladden the heart of an archæologist or an antiquary, as well as the eye of an artist.

At the end of our stroll, chancing to glance in the window of a shop nearly opposite to our hotel, we were struck by the many photographs displayed therein of quaint old houses, and other buildings situated either in the town itself or in close proximity thereto. We always make it a point when passing through a town to seek out a shop that sells local photographs,—not for the sake of purchasing photographs, as we greatly prefer to take our own, and still more prefer to make careful sketches, when time avails; but we have found that by inspecting a collection of local views we have frequently discovered places of much interest in the place or neighbourhood. Moreover, if the photographer be a man of the right sort, as he often is, you may glean from him much valuable information, and how best to reach and see certain spots. So it was that in looking over the store of photographic views in this shop our eyes were opened to how much of uncommon interest there existed in Bradford and the country around. Amongst other things we discovered that there was an ancient Saxon stone-built church in the very heart of the town, built about A.D. 700, and in an almost perfect condition,— here was a rare find, and one enough to make any archæologist's mouth water! Then there was the ancient time-worn bridge we drove over as we came in with its quaint "mass chapel" thereon, and in the meadows near by a grand old tithe-barn (one of the few that are left in the land), and almost in sight of this bridge (in another direction, as we were informed) a magnificent old seventeenth-century mansion of a most ornate and unique character known as Kingston House, with much else besides. We also saw photographs of the interiors and exteriors of two most beautiful examples of old English homes, one of which was a veritable picture, a poem in architecture. Both these delightful and stately manor-houses of the long ago were situated well within a walk of Bradford; their names were Great Chaldfield and South Wraxall respectively. Little wonder that we determined to rest over at least one day at romantic Bradford!

Breakfast over, we started forth on our rambles, sketch-book in hand. We first sought out the ancient Saxon church and found it to be a most remarkable structure and apparently unaltered since it was first built all those long centuries ago. The church, as might be expected, is a somewhat rude edifice; it consists of a chancel, nave, and porch. The height of the building relative to its size appears out of all proportion, according to modern ideas; the nave being twenty-four feet long and twenty-five feet in height, or one foot higher than long! Let in the wall, one on either side of the chancel arch, are two stone sculptured figures of angels; these angels, who face one another, are represented as flying, with a glory round their heads, and each one holds a napkin. We imagined that, most probably, there was originally a sculpture of the Crucifixion between the two angels, and that the napkins were upheld to catch the blood of our Lord; this, however, is pure conjecture on our part, but we have seen the same poetic idea carried out in an ancient fresco. These early sculptures are most interesting and noteworthy, being, doubtless, coeval with the church itself. Externally, the building is decorated with an incised arcade that runs round it, which is simple and effective. But the peculiar charm of this very ancient church (I believe the only perfect and unaltered Saxon church in England; and possibly in the world, but of this I am not absolutely sure) lies in the glamour of the never-returning and half-forgotten past that surrounds its rugged walls, gray with years but strong still. After it, even the hoary old parish church, which stands near to, seems almost modern; and yet again both these time-hallowed fanes are as of to-day compared with the ruined temples of early Egypt, that wonderful cradle of human civilisation. Who shall dare to say, after this find, that he who explores untravelled England goes unrewarded? Well may American Emerson remark upon the strange neglect of England by Englishmen, " whose British sense and perseverance is so whimsical in its choice of objects, which leaves its own Stonehenge or Choir Gaur to the rabbits, whilst it opens pyramids and uncovers Nineveh."

Next we made our way by a devious path to the river, which we crossed by a picturesque and very ancient foot-bridge; from this bridge we had a fine and comprehensive view of the town, and just beyond it we reached old Barton farm, the road curiously going under a projecting wing of the house. Everything about Bradford seemed quaint and unexpected. In this farmyard stands an old monastic tithe barn, a fine stone building, of grand proportions, built in the fourteenth century, and still in excellent condition, strong enough apparently, in spite of its years, to outlive many a speculative builder's modern mansion. This old barn possesses a magnificent open timbered roof, its thick walls are supported by massive buttresses,—how substantially and enduringly these men of the past built,—and it has two great arched gateways big enough for a corn-laden waggon to go under. These tithe barns belong to a past epoch, and but few in a perfect or imperfect condition now remain to us. There is, however, a very fine one that I have seen standing about a mile from the little town of Faringdon in Berkshire, and there is also another, I believe, in the parish of Lymington, and one at Glastonbury.

Following along the side of the quiet-flowing Avon and crossing the railway, we obtained a good view of Kingston House, the former residence of the Dukes of Kingston. It is a truly noble Jacobean building, with its high-pitched gables, clustering chimneys, great mullioned windows, and fine old-fashioned garden terrace in front. This mansion is most elaborately decorated with carved ornamentations that show no ordinary designer. It is a remarkable building. The last Duchess of Kingston, who frequently resided here, was a notorious character, and in the year 1776 was tried in the House of Lords for bigamy and convicted.

Then we retraced our steps to the ancient bridge with the "mass chapel" that stands in the centre on one of its piers. This chapel is a curious building; the roof is of stone, and it gives a very quaint look to the bridge. The illustration I have given of it will, however, afford a better idea of this odd bit of ancient architecture than pages of description possibly could. Here the pencil has the advantage of the pen.

Whilst we were sketching this a man came up to us and exclaimed, "Do you know what you're a sketching of?" We replied that we believed it was an old chapel. "Yes," said he, "it were once certainly, but it were used as a prison after that. You see the fish on the top," alluding to the weather vane which represented a fish, "well, when folk were locked up there, people used to say of them that they'd been under the fish and over the water. It was a polite way of saying they had been in gaol. You will excuse me a speaking to you, but I thought as how you'd like to know the old story, as I saw you was a stranger." Which was very kind of him; moreover, he was pleased to admire our sketch, which he considered "main correct, all but the fish; it be a gudgeon you see, sir, and you've gone and made it a perch." However, as we had done our best to draw what we actually saw before us we did not feel inclined to alter our sketch, the more especially as our informant could not exactly say where our drawing departed from the original.

MASS HOUSE ON BRIDGE, BRADFORD-ON-AVON.

Thereupon he departed, repeating, "more in sorrow than in anger," I trust, "It's a gudgeon, and you've gone and made it a perch." This sketch completed our very interesting and profitable morning's work.

In the afternoon, learning that Great Chaldfield manor-house was only about three miles from Bradford, we determined to walk thither; though we did not quite like the "about," as former experience has taught us that sometimes the "about" nearly equals the whole distance. Before starting we consulted the ostler as to the road, and he carefully directed us so that "you could not possibly lose your way." That ostler did not know our capabilities! We duly set forth with our waterproof and sketch-book, but foolishly without our map, and did the impossible very successfully; in fact we managed to get a good mile or more out of our way, which was not so bad considering we had only a margin of about three miles to do it in. Our directions from the ostler appeared very clear—till we came to put them in practice. We got out of Bradford by the correct road, which was something; then in a mile we reached the Plough Inn, where we were to turn to the right and go straight on for two miles, neither turning to the right nor the left, and that would bring us to Great Chaldfield House: well, it didn't. At least we went as straight on as a winding road would allow us, at a fair walking pace for a good hour or more, and as Great Chaldfield did not put in an appearance we felt puzzled, as there was nobody about of whom to ask the way, and our map was safely stored in the driving-box of the dog-cart. Then, to improve matters, it began to rain, and we sought shelter under a tree, wondering doubtfully whether we should reach our destination or not; for we had no idea what direction to take, nor, as far as our eyes could range, could we see any old house at all likely to be the one of which we were in search. So we waited where we were impatiently. At last the rain ceased, and a lad came on to the scene over a stile hard by; fortunately he was an intelligent youngster, and for sixpence offered to show us the way; we closed with him, and he led us over some fields along some footpaths, and across a road or two till we came in sight of the ancient manor-house hidden in a valley. I am sure that we should never have found it without our guide; he certainly earned his sixpence. It seems, as we afterwards discovered on returning, that we should have taken a rough, muddy, narrow by-way to the left that appeared simply to lead to fields. However, "All's well that ends well"; we enjoyed the tramp across the fields, though the grass was rather damp, and we learnt the names of one or two wild flowers and plants from the boy that either we had never known, or had quite forgotten.

Great Chaldfield manor-house proved even more picturesque than we imagined it to be from the photographs, and it was as interesting as it was picturesque. It is a place to thoroughly please alike an artist and an antiquary. Passing by a gray old water-mill, and skirting a weed-grown moat, which we crossed on an ancient stone bridge, we found ourselves before a many-gabled, ivy-grown, old-time abode of the fifteenth century—a picture rather than a building. This is one of the most beautiful examples of domestic Gothic architecture I have so far seen in all England. The house and garden with a small church areen closed by a moat; around the inside of the moat ran defending walls, strengthened here and there by towers, of which the remains of two may still be seen. Just over the bridge, standing in the old-fashioned garden, is to be had by far the best view of this most charming and interesting home of the olden days, which, however undesirable to live in, were undeniably picturesque. It now does duty as a farmhouse; fortunate farmer, thought we, to have such a beautiful old family mansion to live in!

We made a sketch of the place from the garden, and whilst so doing discovered that the gables were surmounted by quaint figures carved in stone; one appeared to be that of a man in armour holding a dagger; another, as well as we could make out, for the sculptures were much weather-worn, represented a man sitting cross-legged; and on the top of the two nearest gables were griffins upholding shields. The roof over the porch was stone-vaulted, the doorway was of oak, possibly the original one, and on either side of this were seats. At each end of the building is an elaborate oriel window, the one at the east end being specially noteworthy for its carving; over the other is a coat of arms. But a place like this requires pages of description and many illustrations to do it justice, and my space will not permit. The interior of the house has, unfortunately, been modernised; we must, however, be thankful for small mercies, in the fact that the exterior has suffered hardly at all in this respect, and is in an excellent state of preservation.

Having finished our sketch, we went to inspect the curious little church which stands close to the house; this is, manifestly, an ancient structure restored; it possesses a bell-turret crowned, in a strange fashion, with a tiny stone spire. The door of the church was carefully locked, but we managed to obtain a glimpse at the interior through a window, and observed a very fine carved screen with a series of coats of arms on the top, all "coloured proper," to use a familiar heraldic term.

We should like to have lingered much longer at Great Chaldfield, but the sun was getting low in the west, and as we had to find our way back to Bradford afoot, we deemed it wise to bend our steps homeward, or rather, to be precise, innward. We made a mental note, however, if ever we could manage it, to return some day and sketch, at our leisure, that picturesque old manor-house, with its ancient mill, sleepy moat, and rambling colony of outbuildings. An artist might come thither, and find ample material in and around the spot to keep him delightfully employed for a whole summer, only it is the getting to the place that is the difficulty; but perhaps, as painting means sitting still most of the day, a three miles' walk (when the way has been discovered) out of, and in to, Bradford, would only prove a sufficiently health-giving exercise; or possibly primitive but sufficiently comfortable quarters might be found at the Plough Inn on the road, and a portion of the distance be saved. I merely throw out the hint to any chance artist reader in search of "fresh woods and pastures new."

We reached Bradford late, agreeably tired, and well satisfied with our day's explorations. The window of our inn overlooked a spare space of ground where three roads met, and on this bit of ground a Cheap Jack took his stand during the evening, and we were both interested and amused, watching and studying his ways and the doings of the crowd that he gathered round him. He appeared to do a good business at the expenditure of a vast amount of talk. Umbrellas were offered for the small sum of five-and-sixpence that cost over ten shillings, he would take five for them. "No one give five shillings for an umbrella; don't it ever rain at Bradford? Well, now, I'll give 'em you for four-and-six; don't buy too many, for I shall lose by every one." Nevertheless, he appeared pleased to "give" some half a dozen away at the last-mentioned price. "I loses by every single one," said that truthful man; "it's only by selling a number that I can make it pay," which deep reasoning was altogether beyond us. So on in this fashion, he offered article after article, and when he had reached an irreducible minimum as to price, he would make a fresh start with something else. For two whole hours that man shouted at the top of his voice, and when he had finished we went to bed, it would have been no use going before!

The next morning, looking around our inn, we discovered the following curious inscription scratched on a window-pane, by a diamond, we presumed :—

> One stone now keeps Kitty down,
> Who when alive moved all the stones in town.

We pointed this out to our landlady and asked her the import thereof, but though she lived in the house she had never noticed the inscription before, and could in no way enlighten us as to its meaning. So we conjectured to ourselves that it might relate to some lively party of past times known as " Kitty," the fact of whom being dead and buried would account for one (tomb) stone keeping her down: the moving of "all the stones in town" might possibly be a figure of speech for her excessive liveliness. It may, however, bear a different interpretation; this was simply our guess.

We made an early start that morning bound for Malmesbury *viâ* Chippenham, a stage of twenty-two miles. We planned to see South Wraxall manor-house on our way, which we learnt from our map (not the ostler!) was only a short distance off our road. We had a steep pull up out of Bradford, then a long level stretch on high ground; our elevated position gave us vast views to the right over a well-wooded country, made doubly beautiful by a constant play of light and shade. This portion of the west of England abounds in such wide-reaching panoramas; and though the country is hilly the roads are excellent.

A short distance on our way, to the left, we

noticed the church of South Wraxall, which has a tower with an uncommon "packsaddle" roof of red tiles; this gives the church a charming quaintness as well as a pleasing individuality, and struck us as a relief from the usual monotony of ordinary church towers and spires; these, naturally, are prominent features in the landscape, and a little more variety in their outline would materially add to the interest of such structures—and the view. As a rule a church tower stands out boldly against the sky, and therefore is a specially notable object; and were they not, each of their class, so similar in design, it would be a relief to the eye, for you may even repeat a good thing till it becomes monotonously wearisome.

Shortly afterwards, we observed the gray gables, towers, and chimneys of an ancient mansion peeping above some thick-foliaged and rook-haunted elms; this we guessed to be South Wraxall manor-house, and so we made our way to it. Arriving there, the time-toned mansion stood before us

> Four-square, and double-courted, and gray-stoned,
> Two quaint quadrangles of deep-latticed walls
> Grass-grown, and mourned about by troops of doves—
> The ancient house!

A great gable of the building, with a wide entrance-way beneath, projected from the main edifice to the roadside; and looking over a low stone wall we could see one of its deserted, moss-encrusted courtyards. Just above the doorway is a remarkably fine oriel window of chaste design. Whilst we were admiring this, an old body came forth from a cottage adjoining the old mansion and asked us if we wished to see over it. This was just what we did wish, and told her so, whereupon she said that she would get the key and go round and open the great door.

South Wraxall, unlike Great Chaldfield, is built on the top of a hill from which there are wide views all around; it is presumed to have been originally erected by Robert Long in 1426, who was a Justice of the Peace, a member of Parliament, and who died in 1447. The mansion has evidently been altered since in parts, though fortunately not to any great or destructive extent, and it still remains to us a grand and most interesting example of medieval English domestic architecture.

Presently the great oak doors opened before us with a considerable amount of creaking, and the old body bade us enter. She told us (as we could see for ourselves) that the house was uninhabited, and that she lived in the cottage adjacent, "which was formerly part of the stables. It were a grand place once, the old house, that it were; and I think as how you will consider it so when you have seen all over it." Entering, we learnt that this projecting portion of the building was called the porter's lodge; from it a flight of stone steps led to a chamber above, where a servant was always stationed, ready to attend upon the door. In this chamber was the beautiful oriel window that we had noticed, which was used by the porter as an outlook to observe any one approaching. Opposite the doorway, on the other side of the way, stand two fine stone gate-posts; and we were told that, of old, there was a straight road of over a mile in length that led to the house, the road we came by being a comparatively modern innovation. From the porter's lodge we were conducted across a courtyard to the great hall, a truly grand apartment possessing a fine open timber roof of high pitch, the timbers springing from a series of stone corbels engraved with various coats of arms. At one end of the hall is a spacious minstrel's gallery with a richly-carved oak screen in front, and in the centre is a fine stone fireplace bearing the date of "Anno Domini 1598." This fireplace has manifestly been an after addition, and our opinion that it was such was confirmed by our guide, who said that she had shown a number of archæologists and antiquaries over the building and had taken careful notes of their remarks. She was, I verily believe, on the whole, the best guide it has been our fate to come across. She told us concisely all we wished to know, even to the translation of various Latin inscriptions; and when the opinions of archæologists varied on sundry points, she gave us, impartially, both sides of the question. Moreover, she appeared to understand what she talked about, which the average guide seldom does, according to our experience.

We were next taken to a delightful old oak-panelled room, the panels being decorated with what is known as the "linen" pattern; that is, the wood is carved like squares of linen folded in creases flatly, but very artistically folded be it minded. This charming chamber, disused and destitute of furniture as it was, had still a snug look. "This," exclaimed the old body, "is known as Sir Walter Raleigh's room; he was a particular friend of Sir Henry Long's. Local tradition had it that it was really in this very room that Sir Walter smoked his first pipe; anyhow he used to smoke with his host here, and a great deal was talked in the neighbourhood at the time as to his queer doings. You see, sir, smoking was considered a mysterious thing then, and the people around, when they heard of it, could not make it out at all. They do say that some of the servants of the house got hold of some tobacco and tried to smoke it out of pipes made of half a walnut shell and a straw!" This antique chamber has a deeply-recessed window, in which doubtless Sir Walter often sat, and looked out upon much the same landscape as we see now. The window shows the thickness and solid substance of the walls; built strongly thus it is no wonder that the mansion has withstood the hand of Time so successfully all those long years. The fireplace in this room is a very fine one (as are all in the house); on either side of it in the spandrels are cut respectively the initials S. H. L. and H. E., which are supposed to be those of Sir Henry Long and Helen Eleanor his wife.

Next we went to the kitchen, *temp*. Elizabeth, where the ample arched space for the fire suggested past-time preparations for sumptuous feasts. From the kitchen we proceeded to the dining-room, where we noted another fine carved mantelpiece, but nothing else of special interest. Then we were shown up some stairs to the " withdrawing-room," a truly stately apartment, and in its prime, we judged, must have been worthy to grace any palace. This room has an exceedingly beautiful arched ceiling of enriched plaster work in high relief, varied by pointed pendants. We are so used to flat ceilings (and these often merely a void of unbroken whitewash) that the charm of a groined ceiling in our homes is almost unknown, the curves of which contrast so pleasantly with the square of wall and window, besides affording a feeling of lightness and airiness.

In the centre of this great room is a curious projection on one side, which it is supposed was made to give a further support to the heavy roof. This is ornamented very cleverly with carvings and pillars, thus happily forming a pleasing decorative feature of a necessity of construction, that in less skilful hands might easily have proved an ugly eyesore. It was always so with these old-time builders, they first planned everything for use, then they proceeded to ornament their construction, not as we do, construct ornament. Their houses were the outcomes of the requirements of the time—beautified. But as to this quaint pillared projection, it struck us as quite a novelty, and yet it seemed strangely familiar. How could this be? Suddenly our memory enlightened us; we had seen it shown in a painting at the Academy, wherein this olden room had done duty as a picturesque background for a telling composition. I have, unfortunately, forgotten the title of the picture or the name of the artist for certain, but I fancy the former was called "Men were deceivers ever"; it portrayed a gallant (?) lover of times gone by paying court to a fresh beauty in ignorance of the fact that his old love was in hearing, if not in sight, behind the ornamental projection. By the way, I do not think that we have made a single lengthened driving tour in England without, at one time or another thereon, coming upon some place or spot that seemed to bear a familiar look, though we had never been in that part of the world before. And in each case, as our memory afterwards revealed to us, this apparently familiar look has arisen from our previously having seen the place or spot represented in a painting in some exhibition. Trust an artist for finding out the picturesque old homes and nooks and corners of the land. I have discovered many a quaint manor-house and beauty spot by the drawings on the walls of certain London galleries (mostly water-colour ones, I may mention), aided, of course, by the catalogue. Why, Stokesay Castle, which we made a special point of visiting this journey, and shall come to in due course, was thus brought to my notice by seeing a delightful sketch of it—or rather the unique Priest's Tower thereof—in the Water-Colour Institute.

But I am wandering; let us return to the stately "withdrawing-room" of South Wraxall manor. As this is the most ambitious room in the house, so it has by far away the most ambitious mantelpiece, where all are grand. This magnificent mantelpiece reaches from the floor to the ceiling, and is richly carved all over. In four recesses above the fireplace are four figures inscribed Prvdentia, Arithmetica, Geometria, and Justitia. Prudence is represented simply by a woman standing straight up; Arithmetic by a woman apparently doing a sum in a book that lies on a table; Geometry by a woman measuring a globe by a compass; and Justice holds a pair of scales, one end of which is, however, lower than the other, which does not seem quite the thing, and her eyes are open. Possibly Justice in those days was not blind, at any rate, alas! she often sided with the strong against the weak, with the rich against the poor. Nothing is inscribed under the figures of Prudence and Justice, but below the figure of Arithmetic the following Latin lines find place :—

> Par impar numeris vestigo rite subactis :
> Me pete concinne si numerare cupis.

Which, our guide told us, had been rendered into rhyming English as follows,—as our Latin has grown rather rusty, we frankly accepted her unknown authority in this and the rest of the translations into passable verse—

> Odd or even, my figures form results :
> He'll calculate well who me consults.

Under the figure of Geometry is inscribed :—

> Mensuras rerum spatiis dimetior æquis :
> Quid cælo distet terra locusque loco.

Which has been Anglicised thus :—

> By right measurements I mark off space :
> How far is heaven from earth, and place from place.

This great room has two large mullioned windows with double transoms and leaded lights; there being in all fifty-seven separate windows enclosed in the mullions and transoms, and I forget how many panes (I think over five hundred), according to the old body, who said that we could count them if we liked, but we preferred to take her word for them; one window or pane, more or less, what did it matter? The walls, we observed, were panelled up to the ceiling; and the oak floor, we were informed, was "the original one of three-and-a-half inch boards dove-tailed one into the other."

Close to the "withdrawing-room" is a bedroom or "guest's chamber," also panelled; but in the bad taste of a later period this has been painted all over a pale blue. Here is a quaint chimney-piece with a carved monkey in the centre supported on a bracket, and below is painted :—

>Mors
>Rapit
>Omnia.

"Death takes all." On the over-mantel, on either side of the monkey, are the following Latin inscriptions. To the left :—

>Faber est
>Quisque for-
>tunæ suæ.

Which we were kindly informed meant "Every man is the maker of his own fortune." To the right :—

>Æqua laus
>Est a laudatis
>Laudari et
>Ab improbis
>Improbari.

"To be praised by the good, and blamed by the bad, is equal laudation." This chamber, we were told, was haunted; though our guide, who had lived a long while on the spot as caretaker and showwoman, was obliged to confess as a truthful party (somewhat reluctantly by the way, we thought, as though unwilling to injure the haunted reputation of the place) that she had never herself seen or heard the ghost. "You know, sir," she continued, "it was the wife of Sir Walter Long that is the heroine of the legend of the White Hand." Manifestly she imagined that we knew all about the legend, and we were compelled to confess our deplorable ignorance thereof. "Well now, I am surprised that you never heard of it. You see, it's like this, Sir Walter Long was married twice and had two sons, one by each wife, and tradition has it that his second wife planned to get the estate for her son; so she induced her husband to make a will in his favour, but when he was about to sign it his first wife appeared and prevented him by stretching forth a white hand between him and the lamp, so that he could not see to write, and he and all around were terrified at the apparition and took warning thereby." It is also said—according to tradition—that the evening before Sir Walter Long died he went into his library and found a Bible lying open on a table there, and on going up to it the White Hand suddenly appeared and pointed to the words " This night shall thy soul be required of thee." What a lot tradition has to answer for!

We had now gone all over this interesting old

mansion (to use an antiquarian term, one of the many "finds" of our pleasure-giving outing), so we took a stroll around its weed-grown garden in order to see the ancient building from the outside, a building whose time-toned, lichen-stained walls speak eloquently of the days departed. An old home like this is suggestive of romance, and appeals alike to artist and novelist. We observed evidence, in the shape of a painting on canvas, half-finished, and placed away for a time in one of the ancient chambers, that the artist had found it out : whether the novelist has or not, I cannot say.

From the garden the old body led the way to her cottage, where, in the stone floor, she pointed out and lifted up a wooden trap-door and revealed to us a well. "It is only ten feet deep, yet it is always full of the purest water, which is curious, the place being right on the top of the hill." It also struck us as curious the having a well thus in a living-room. Supposing that the trap-door were left open one day, and some one chanced to cross the spot in the dark, they might undergo an unpleasant surprise! And then we departed, rewarding our guide according to her merits. On retracing our steps through the first courtyard we noticed some extraordinarily large and hideously quaint gargoyles. One represents a huge face swallowing a man head foremost, and another apparently reversing the operation. These gargoyles are more interesting to the antiquary than to the lover of the beautiful.

CHAPTER X

A land of stone—Corsham—Chippenham—A story of the road—Chance company at one's inn—Corston—Malmesbury—An ancient market cross—An ideal landlord—Trespassing—A "watching chamber"—Stories in stone—The Thames head—Cirencester—A misadventure.

LEAVING South Wraxall manor-house we traversed a lonely open country; our road for a time took us over high ground, and we had almost a superabundance of bracing breezes as we drove along, owing to our exposed position. That we were in a land of stone was made manifest to us, for, as far as our eyes could reach, long gray lines of rugged walls took the place of the familiar green, bird-haunted hedges; and here and there by the wayside stood great piles of stones ready for road-mending, all carefully built up in huge squares, or perhaps, to be exact, I should say oblongs. Such order and tidiness in this respect was a novelty to us. This part of England is but sparsely populated; now and then a solitary, bleak-looking farmstead came into view, but even these were few and far between.

At one spot at the top of a hill, and therefore conspicuous all around, we came to a few cottages, close to which was a curious little building with a bell-turret at one end; this, we presumed, was formerly a chapel of some kind, as it had an indefinable place-of-worship look. When we passed by, it was in a half-ruinous condition, and appeared to have been in that state for a considerable time. However, it was in the hands of the restorer, and brand new mullion windows were being inserted in the empty voids of its gray old walls. The result of the restoration produced a peculiar effect, for the new white stone of to-day and the old time-mellowed stone did not harmonise at all. "You cannot put new wine into old bottles" very successfully in an architectural sense. At the time there chanced to be not a soul about, so that we were unable to learn why this structure had come to ruin thus, or why it was being restored, or what its purpose was or had been.

Then, as we drove on, ahead of us appeared a long stretch of great earth banks ramparted like ancient fortifications; these were not marked on our map, nor were the banks much overgrown with greenery, so that their purpose and age rather puzzled us. However, some time afterwards, we noticed, near our road, an extensive stone quarry with mounds of refuse around, not unlike in form to the banks we had previously seen; so that we guessed that the latter might possibly owe their origin to the same cause; the quarries being worked out and deserted. But in ages to come, when the great earth slopes are all grass-grown, and the quarries are forgotten, perchance these embankments may perplex the antiquaries of the day.

Driving on we gradually descended into a more gentle-featured country; the air became perceptibly softer; hedges and trees, and even wooded parks made their appearance. Passing through the neat and clean village of Corsham, we noted its well-built stone houses, some with very good carving thereon, that was a pleasure to see in these days of cheap decoration. Possibly it is the material that gives the skilful workman a chance to express that which is within him; bricks, from their soft nature, are not so suited to the carver's tool. One thing I have noticed, that as a rule, the buildings in a stone country—on an average—are far superior to those in a land where bricks prevail. The chief exceptions to this rule are the *old* half-timber buildings, where solid oak was employed without stint in their structure.

At Corsham we struck the grand and broad old mail-coach highway from London to Bath, and we bowled along its well-kept and delightfully smooth surface at a pace that quickly brought us to the pretty and prosperous town of Chippenham; where, after a brief look round, we selected the ancient Angel Inn as our mid-day halting place, and such comfortable quarters we found there for ourselves, and such capital stabling for our horses, that we felt half inclined "to rest and be thankful" and not to tempt fate further that day. On the other hand, the weather was so beautifully fine, and our horses were so fresh and "full of go" after their day's holiday at Bradford, that we finally decided to proceed. We were now in a hunting country, which, doubtless, accounted for such excellent stabling at our inn. My very best wishes to all hunting men, artists, and anglers, for they support many a good old-fashioned hostelry in country places that without their patronage would hardly exist, if indeed they could at all. And these old comfortable inns, wherein he can really take his ease and feel at home away from home, are the delight of the traveller by road.

Chippenham is an interesting old town, with a lovely country around that affords many romantic and some hilly drives. We had rested there for a few days on a previous journey, and on that occasion had explored some of the scenery in the near neighbourhood which greatly pleased us. Chippenham, having a comfortable inn (which, let us trust, it may always possess), would not make at all a bad centre for a short holiday for those in search of something fresher and more novel than the familiar and crowded watering-place, who, by making excursions round about the district, might see and enjoy something of rural England, unspoilt by modern improvements, and severely let alone by the genus tourist, though none the less beautiful or attractive on that account. And besides the lovely landscapes and wild open uplands, there are many interesting old houses not far afield.

In the sunny coffee-room of our inn we found a gentleman seated at one end of a long table taking his solitary meal, whilst ours was placed as far as possible away at the other end, and neither of us spoke a word to the other, in truly insular British fashion. To the average American, foreigner, or even travelled Englishman, this awkward reserve seems much like rudeness. How could it possibly harm any one to make some civil remark when he sat down to the same table as a stranger, provided the stranger were well behaved? Being old travellers we could not stand the silence, and we took the very first opportunity to break it, and as usual our advances were courteously met. John Bull is not a bad fellow at heart, and when his inbred reserve is overcome, he can be even jovially sociable. Having broken the ice we soon found ourselves in the midst of an interesting conversation with our neighbour at table, who proved to be a most entertaining individual. Writing of our insular reserve, reminds me of a letter that I received some short time ago from an American friend; he had been on a visit to me in London, and upon his arrival in Liverpool on his way back to the States, wrote thus: "I had a pleasant run up to Liverpool in the railroad car; there were four other people in it besides myself, all very superior-looking, and no one spoke a word all of the way, so that I had (according to English notions) a most delightful journey." By the way, such a silent party would have been almost an impossibility on an old coach, the Jehu alone would never have stood it; the road is very democratic and a great begetter of sociability.

But to return to the coffee-room of our inn; our unknown friend was full of good stories, and what is more, he could tell them well. He gave us a very laughable account of an evening's experience of his at the very inn we had just left at Bradford-on-Avon; a good deal of the humour, however, lay in the droll manner in which he related the incident. I shall not attempt to re-tell it in full and so spoil it; but, briefly, it appeared that a commercial traveller who had dined well, and drunk not wisely, had taken possession of his bedroom, had unpacked his portmanteau, bolted the door, and nothing would induce that commercial "gent" to listen to reason, or to move. So our friend had to take an adjacent room without any of his things, and had the felicity of being kept awake all night by the snoring of the man who had his room. Another story, which does not lose so much in cold print, ran as follows: It appears that in the pre-railway days a certain nobleman happened to be benighted on the road, with a horse lame to boot and no fresh one to be had, under which untoward circumstances he preferred to put up at a small country-town inn called "The Bear" to proceeding farther. It chanced that the proprietor of the inn was so proud of having entertained a nobleman that he begged permission to change the title of his sign-board, and call his inn after his lordship, The Lord Dash. Permission was granted, the old sign-board was duly painted out and re-christened. Whereupon the other inn of the town at once appropriated the old-established name of "The Bear"; and the landlord of the original Bear, finding that a good deal of custom was lost to him by travellers "following the name," had painted immediately under the portrait of Lord Dash the notice—"This is the Old Bear"! When next my lord—who was of a fiery temperament—passed that way and saw those words beneath the representation of himself,—well, there was a commotion in the quiet little town.

Respecting those one meets at country inns: during our wanderings on wheels in England I may mention that every now and again at these quiet resting-places, we have come upon, and even made friends with, men whose names are known the wide world over, and others of lesser fame. In one special case, indeed, during a three weeks' sojourn at a lonely North Country hostelry, we made friends with a very famous man, without knowing who he was for some days; for, strangely enough, though we met frequently and talked much, and walked out on the hills around, and drove about together, I had not the curiosity to ask his name: those three weeks' sojourn gained for me one of the best friends I ever had! But it is, I think, only at the homely, old-fashioned inn that such pleasant experiences are possible, the grand, modern, company-managed hotel with its showy comfortlessness effectually freezes such budding friendships, or rather they never have a chance of budding at all in such uncongenial environments.

It was late in the afternoon when we left our comfortable quarters at Chippenham. Driving out of the town we skirted an extensive park, with great sweeps of green sward and many a fine oak thereon, between whose rugged trunks the sunshine glinted and formed long broad lines of green-gold light across the smooth grass; causing also, by way of contrast, blue-gray shadows from the trees themselves. After a few miles, the scenery became rather monotonous, but it was a monotony of beauty; green hedgerowed fields, with spreading elms, formed the staple of our prospect on either hand, and reminded us of Dr. Johnson's definition of the country: "It's only a succession of green fields. Let us take a walk down Fleet Street." But we preferred even "a succession of green fields" to the noisy city street. At length we arrived at the rambling village of Corston, the name of which was painted on a board attached to the first house on entering, and also on a similar board attached to the last one on leaving. The name of Corston was barely legible when we were there, but we could just make it out. These boards have, doubtless, existed thus uncared for ever since the coaching days, and in a few years will probably be things of the past.

From Corston we had a grand run down hill all the way into Malmesbury, which most picturesque old town we reached just as the sun was setting behind fire-fringed clouds in the golden west. It was a perfect ending to a perfect summer day, as though to show how supremely lovely the much-abused English climate can be when it likes; and it likes oftener than possibly many people imagine who judge of it from a town residence. During the whole of our enjoyable expedition, I do not think that we had really an hour too hot, nor an hour too cold; and though we did have more than an hour too much rain, still we were little troubled by bad weather.

We had a short stiff rise into Malmesbury, and

at a sudden bend of the narrow winding road, what a poetic vision was presented to us, a vision of beauty that impressed us the more because it came upon us wholly unexpectedly. There, some distance ahead of us, the ancient half-ruined abbey loomed up a solemn mass of mysterious gray, a memory in stone; in front of this, at the end of the street, stood a most beautiful old market cross, with its arched recesses below deep in shade, and its curved flying buttresses above uprising to a central shaft with a canopied pinnacle, elaborately decorated. But the indescribable beauty of the scene lay in the fact that the graceful market cross, with its pinnacles and buttresses, was lighted up with the last warm rays of the setting sun, and showed with a wonderful effect against the cool gray gloom of the massive abbey walls. It was an impressive scene! I think that this old market cross, abbey, and street of Malmesbury, as viewed from this point, form the finest bit of architectural grouping in England: an artist could not have designed it better had he the placing and planning of the buildings. It may be all a happy accident, or the builders of the past may have purposely placed their structures so for the sake of picturesque effect, which they sometimes considered.

Entering beneath the archway of the King's Arms, we soon found that "our lines had fallen in pleasant places." The landlord was standing at the doorway,—a portly and polite individual (at last we had met John Bull in the flesh), who received us with a smile of welcome; then his wife, a motherly body and also an ideal landlady, came forth with another smile, and showed us to our bedroom, the very pink of neatness, with a broad bow-shaped window full of sweet-scented flowers. Landlord, landlady, and old-fashioned inn were all exactly after our own heart. There was none of the indifference that prevails at the large modern hotel, where your coming or your going seems a matter of no concern to the stony-eyed officials. At this homely, provincial little hostel everybody seemed pleased to see us, from the jovial-looking landlord to the obliging boots. It was a pleasant evening we spent in the low-roofed sitting-room of our inn, and very cheerful it looked under the soft lamp-light, the table spread with a snow-white cloth and a friendly meal of tea and toast and eggs thereon: a good old-fashioned meal that "kettledrums" and late dinners have but too effectually killed. We were attended to by a be-ribboned, civil maid, who brought us a vase of freshly-plucked flowers to grace the table. Had we been millionaires, I know not what else we could have desired just then; one cannot be more than perfectly satisfied and contented.

Indeed, an out-of-door life like ours is so health-giving and invigorating that it begets that state of mind which thoroughly enjoys life, and consequently also a happy condition to be easily pleased. With health one sees the world through rosy-tinted glasses; be we well or ill it is just the same world, it simply differs from our point of view: I prefer the rosy prospect.

In the following morning early we set forth with

camera and sketch-book on a tour of inspection round about the picturesque old town, leaving the grand abbey as a sort of *bonne bouche* to the last. On an ancient cottage, at the bottom of the main street, we noticed a curious inscription, which we copied literally as follows:—

> Memerand that where as King Athelstan
> Did giue unto the Free School within this
> Burrough of Malmesbury Ten Pounds & to
> the poor peoplem y Alms house at St Iohns
> Ten pounds to be paid yearly by ye Alderman
> and Burgesses of ye same Burrough for Euer.

This was somewhat puzzling to make out; we presumed the first word to be intended for memorandum, but we had no idea that Free Schools, not to say Alms-houses, existed in the reign of King Athelstan, yet if they did not how could he have made a gift to them? We gave the puzzle up.

Then we drifted towards the abbey, which had a sort of magnetic attraction for us; from an elevated terrace on the north side of the old pile is a fine view over a pretty country, through which the fishful little Avon winds, and, alas! an ugly branch railway, too! At the east end of the abbey stands a charming old Elizabethan house, a most delightful abode— externally. For I must fain confess, in all honesty, it is not always that a picturesque exterior means a desirable home to live in. It may, or it may not. Descending by a footpath to the river, which we crossed on a small two-arched bridge, we discovered a very comprehensive view of the gray old abbey on the hill above, which we at once set to work to sketch, and this sketch engraved is given herewith. Then we went to work with the camera, and secured several pleasing photographs; one of the best of these was taken from the railway just by a notice-board warning all trespassers that they would be prosecuted! This reminds me that once, when trespassing on a railway elsewhere (in search of a picture that I could not get so well from any other point), and sketching harmlessly, as I imagined, right on the top of an embankment, where of course I could not get in the way and throw a train off the line! I was accosted by a somewhat too officious official, who demanded my name and address with a view to a prosecution for trespass. In this dilemma a happy inspiration came to me; I remembered that I was a shareholder in the company,—a very small one by the way,—and so I ventured boldly to ask how I could be a trespasser on my own property, as I was a part-owner of the railway. The query was too much for my interrogator, and I was left with "I'm sure I didn't know, sir, as how you was" to finish my sketch in peace. After the abbey we sketched and photographed the market cross, during which latter process we secured, I should imagine, unwilling on our part but with much willingness on theirs, about half of the juvenile population of the place, who did not improve the picture by standing straight in front of the camera, "the forty staring like one!"

Next we went to the old abbey, but found the ponderous door locked; so we had to set out in search of the clerk, who, as usual, was not at home,

MALMESBURY ABBEY.

but his wife said we could have the keys if we did not mind going over the "church" by ourselves. So we thanked her, and on being handed them offered a small but what we deemed a sufficient tip. This was actually refused. "You'd better see the church first," she said, "then when you brings the keys back will do for the rest. The south door isn't locked, you put the skewer in the slit and lift up the latch." This sounded a rather primitive way of entering a stately old abbey; what would the monks have thought of it, I wonder? Looking at the big bunch of keys, we found there something like a blunt skewer, which we made use of as directed, and obtained an entrance to the building; had we known of this arrangement the blade of our penknife might have gained us admittance. The abbey interior is certainly impressive; it has not been over restored, so that it still looks ancient; the architecture is of the later Norman time, when the lighter grace of the coming Gothic had just begun to show itself. What interested us most in the building was a curious small square stone chamber with window-like open spaces therein that projected from the triforium above; we had never seen anything like this in any cathedral or abbey before. At first we imagined that perhaps it might have been employed to exhibit certain relics; but afterwards, on mentioning the matter to a catholic priest whom we met at Worcester (and who appeared to be an enthusiastic antiquary as well as a priest), he suggested that the uncommon structure might possibly have been a watching-chamber from which the sacristan observed the rood-loft and altar lights. This peculiar departure from the usual scheme of abbey architecture deserves attention. We next inspected the reputed tomb of King Athelstan, which consists of an altar tomb with a much-mutilated and crowned effigy thereon. It is, doubtless, a monument to some king, and it may as well be that of Athelstan as of any other ancient sovereign. Tradition positively says that it is that of Athelstan—and who can now prove otherwise!

Leaving the abbey by the south door, the one we had entered it by, we stopped a while to admire and puzzle over the elaborate and quaint carvings of figures that decorate its deeply-recessed arches. These sculptures, though sadly worn by time, still give a crude epitome of the religious history of the world, from the Creation down to the Crucifixion and Resurrection, forming a sort of poor man's Bible, suited to an age when only the learned few could read. These primitive sculptures were the ignorant people's only literature; they told the sacred story in stone easily to be understood by the common crowd. But sometimes we have found that these old carvings have told of meaningless miracles unknown to Scripture. The Puritans, however, took care not to leave many of these "superstitious imaginings" intact; the few we have seen were in out-of-the-way places.

We were loth to leave quaint, quiet Malmesbury. The old town, with its gray abbey, age-worn butter-cross, and ancient houses, has quite a medieval look—a look that gave us a delightful feeling of remoteness from the rush and striving of the busy outer world. Malmesbury seems to belong to another century, and we rejoiced to give ourselves up to the illusion of the seeming. We resented the little branch railway line as an intrusion on its ancient peace. Here the iron horse seemed almost an anomaly, the one thing in and around the place that told of the nineteenth century, excepting, possibly, a telegraph wire to the primitive post-office, which, if it did exist, did not intrude its presence; the fussy locomotive makes itself heard even when not seen, it is noisy as well as ugly.

We had a steep descent out of the town followed by a sharp ascent that took us into a pleasant open country of wide green fields reaching to a deep-blue distance of wooded hills. There was a soft south wind blowing, laden with the sweet mingled essence of country perfumes, that made us enjoy the very act of breathing. The air had a refined quality about it. Overhead was a gray lowering sky that suggested rain and caused a gentle gloom to lie over the landscape; now and then the sun tried to filter through the clouds, but it gave the attempt up at last, and we settled down to a regular gray day. If we had no sunshine to cheer us on our way, at any rate there was no glare of light, which was a relief to the eyes, and the country had a tender, mellow look that was not without its charms. Whatever else it may do, the English climate seldom wearies you with a monotony, its worst enemies cannot put that to its charge, and I like variety in weather, even at the cost of an occasional wetting. A cloudless sky may suit the poets to sing about, but it does not suit artists to paint. Clouds are picturesque; their changeful forms give an interest to the sky, which without them would be a mere blue void. The sky scenery of Great Britain is the finest in the world! Why should I not make a virtue out of the presumed faults of our much-abused climate? It has its faults of course, but so has every other climate I wot of in the world. Why, I was in the south of France last year in the spring-time sitting sunning myself in a beautiful old garden on the hills above Nice; there were orange trees golden with their fruit around me, palms as well, and far below through these trees I caught a peep of the blue Mediterranean. Had I found an earthly paradise at last? Well, hardly! I had not sat out in the sunshine long when a gentleman came up to me and excused himself for speaking to a stranger, but, said he, " It's really not safe to sit in the sun without an umbrella over you, several people have taken sunstroke here by so doing." So I went and sat in the shade, when some one else came up and told me that it was really not safe to sit out there in the shade without a wrap, so many people had got chills by so doing and had been made seriously ill. So I found in the town of Nice, one side of the street in the sun would be baking hot, the other sunless side would be quite uncomfortably chilly, and the sudden change from one to the other was very trying, and you could not walk about the town without encountering these sudden changes. I was informed, moreover, that it was not safe to venture out of doors about the time of sunset. Thus, everywhere abroad have I found some drawback to the climate. Strange it seems that our own, which we so despise, should be so praised by many Americans, including Nathaniel Hawthorne, who declared that, "take it for all in all, *it is the best climate in the world.*" The italics are mine; I really could not resist putting them. But I am digressing; it was that gray, dull day that set my pen a wandering thus. I desired to defend it; some might call it cheerless, and talk of foreign skies,—I wanted to be beforehand in the matter.

We were still in a stone country, but the quality of the material seemed to be sadly deteriorated; for we noticed that the walls were built of thin friable slabs, and not of the solid hard blocks that prevailed on our recent stages. Passing through the pretty village of Crudwell we came to one of the sharp dips and equally sharp rises in which our road abounded. Climbing up the rise through a small fir forest we came to a post at the junction of two roads with "Wiltshire" inscribed on one side and "Glo'shire" on the other.

Then another long descent and ascent brought us to a bridge that took us over a winding canal; some little way down the towing-path of this we noticed a tall engine-house with a big beam projecting therefrom busily at work. This looked like a mine of some sort; and feeling curious to learn what minerals were being sought for in this part of the world we pulled up and strolled to the spot; on reaching which we invited ourselves into the building. Here the measured throb, throb, throb, of the ponderous engine, the snorting of the steam, and the wash and rush of the water it had pumped up from the depths below at each power-suggesting throb, reminded us forcibly of the mighty force that this century has utilised for itself, and almost transformed the world thereby. At first we saw nobody; strangers were manifestly rare in those parts; there was not even the usual notice-board set up—"No one admitted except on business." Presently an engineer made his appearance, and we quite expected to be accosted with a "What do you want here?" for we were certainly trespassing; but he merely remarked, "Good morning, sir; it looks like rain a bit; I fancies as how we shall have some afore long." Then after the usual preliminaries about the weather, we ventured to ask if it were not a pumping-engine to a mine. "Mine—bless you, no, sir, this be a pumping-station of the Thames and Severn Canal; we are on the highest point of it here, and we need a biggish engine to keep up the water-supply; the beam goes up eight or nine times a minute and raises about two hundred and fifty gallons each time. You're close to the source of the Thames here, or rather what would be its source, only we pumps up all the water from the spring into the canal, and in a dry season like this we can't then get enough. Canals do use up a lot of water, to be sure. 'Tain't any water now as how the Thames gets from its source unless it gets down by the canal in a roundabout way." We had come upon the "Thames Head" quite unexpectedly.

As we retraced our steps along the towing-path we noticed how clear the water looked, and for the first time in our lives admired the scenery of a canal! The long winding line of silvery waterway, with its deep green wooded banks and dim dreamy distance far ahead into which it led, appeared very inviting. The one-arched bridge we had crossed was all ivy-grown, and added much to the picturesqueness of the prospect. I should fancy that a row in a boat or a paddle in a canoe along this canal from the Thames to the Severn, or *vice versâ*, would prove a pleasant aquatic expedition, as the canal passes through some beautiful scenery. I think that the picturesque qualities of canals are too much overlooked, though I must, in all honesty, confess I speak as a recent convert to their beauties, my acquaintance with canals, till of late, having been limited to those purely prosaic ones around London. We noticed, as we walked back, that there appeared to be milestones—or rather, to be absolutely correct, iron-stones—along the canal side ; at any rate we observed one inscribed as follows (and from this we presumed that there were others)—

Walbridge $11\frac{1}{2}$ | Inglesham $17\frac{1}{4}$

The miles were, we inferred, understood.

Remounting the dog-cart, as we sped along the good though hilly roads we noticed how red the soil was, like parts of Devonshire, and how effectively the warm red contrasted with the green of the trees, and in one large field with the blue of smoke from weed-burning. Suddenly we found ourselves in the outskirts of the cheerful town of

Cirencester, with its wide, sunny street or marketplace, bounded by quaint old houses. Several times, during our many drives through England, have we found ourselves in Cirencester, so that now it seems to greet us with a familiar friendly face. After all, there is something attractive in old acquaintance, whether of people or places. We felt pleased to be once again in clean and cheerful Cirencester, where we found what good old Dr. Johnson so much admired, and wisely, too, "a good inn." If "adventures are to adventurous," so good inns seem to come to the inn-lover!

We made up our mind that now we would steer a direct course to Ludlow in Shropshire, or at least as straight a course as cross-country roads would permit; with this point in view we decided that our next stage should be on to Cheltenham over the Cotswolds. Judging from our map this would take us through a wild bit of upland country, which is indeed the character of the Cotswolds. The sky still looked gray all over, the coming weather doubtful, the barometer had fallen since the morning, and when gently tapped, it fell slightly more—which was exactly what we did not wish; moreover, a slight rain was already falling; so we concluded (though we had not done our usual day's distance) that we would stay where we were overnight and trust to a finer morning on the morrow. Perhaps our comfortable quarters had a good deal to do with our decision!

During the afternoon, in spite of the rain, we set forth on a tour of inspection round about the town. First, the exceedingly fine old parish church attracted our attention; indeed, I should think that it is one of the finest in the kingdom. Over the richly-ornamented south porch are two large parvis chambers, doubtless in the pre-Reformation times intended for the use of the many officiating priests at the frequent services of the church; for there were several chantry chapels therein, endowed to support a priest, or even priests, to chant mass daily for the soul of the deceased donor. Presuming that things had gone on unaltered, and that rich people still kept endowing priests "to pray for my soul perpetually" (which was the usual form of endowment), what would have been the result in time, I wonder? The old endowments would have had in all honesty to be maintained in effect, new ones would have been made from time to time, so that the number of chantry priests would have gone on increasing indefinitely, till the arrangement must have collapsed by the very impossibility of continuing it. And how of the poor people who could not afford the luxury of their souls being perpetually prayed for? Surely it might be written as an article of faith of that very Christian church, "How hardly shall a *poor* man enter the Kingdom of Heaven?" Now, chantry chapels are forsaken, and priests are gone; the pious dead, who did their best to make sure of the other world, truly could not foresee this, and, let us hope, they are none the worse off, because events beyond their power have prevented their last testament being carried out. The interior of this church is very interesting, and we noted some well-preserved brasses on the floors. There is one to a Robt. Page, dated 1435, with a man and his wife engraved thereon; below the figure of the man are shown six sons, and below the figure of the wife eight daughters; so that Mr. Robt. Page appears to have had a fairly large family, as was the prevailing fashion, for we have observed from sepulchral monuments of the time that families of from fifteen to even twenty were not very uncommon. Whether on altar tomb, mural slab, or early brass, the sons are nearly always represented under the figure of their father, and the daughters under that of their mother, both generally being in goodly array, a sight that might drive a Malthus mad. Another brass close by, and dated 1442, was to a "Reg. Spycer, merchant," and his four wives, two being shown on either side of him. The head-dress of each wife of this much-married man was somewhat different. This brass, somehow, reminded me of a perfectly true story, which sounds too extraordinary to be a fact, yet such is the case, as I happen to know; and though I give it, I do not wish any of my readers to credit it, for if related to me, I honestly confess that I should not believe a word of it! Well, then, a certain old gentleman, who had buried three wives, chanced to be walking with a lady friend through the churchyard where his former spouses lay; coming up to the monument he had erected to their memory, he suddenly exclaimed by way of making a fourth proposal, "Miss Dash, how would you like to share the fate of the other three?" Perhaps he was rather nervous at the moment, and hardly knew what he was saying. Let us hope so.

Next, wandering about, we came upon a local museum, wherein we discovered so much to interest us that we spent an hour or so there quite contentedly, the more especially as it had begun to pour with rain outside. We found that the museum contained mostly Roman antiquities dug up in and around Cirencester, which seems a peculiarly rich hunting-ground for such relics, if what a gentleman we met at our hotel remarked to us be even approximately true: "You can hardly dig in your garden," said he, "without turning up some reminder of the old Romans." By the way he made the remark, one might almost imagine that he considered this a grievance! What interested us most amongst the treasures of the museum was the collection of bronze articles, one of which was a surgeon's probe. We also noted some Roman horseshoes, a key-ring, and an iron padlock, besides some very fine mosaic pavement, and two sculptural tombstones, the inscription on one being as follows, translated into English—

> Decius a Horseman of the
> troop of Albanus who had served sixteen years
> a citizen of Rauricum by the care of
> fvlviŭs Natalis and flaviŭs Bitvcus
> the heirs of his last will is here
> Buried.

Somehow, this old tombstone inscription seemed to bridge the long centuries past, and to make the Roman times a reality. The inscription is almost touching in its simplicity, and in the absence of any allusion to a future life.

Leaving the museum, as we walked along we observed the following notice in a shop window—"A Dark Room for Amateur Photographers." Thereupon it struck us that it would be a most excellent way of spending a wet afternoon to engage the room and develop some of our plates to see what they were like. For the benefit of my non-photographic readers I may explain that in the process of the development of a photograph, a dark room with only a red light is a necessity, a white light of any kind being fatal. Having secured the room we fetched our exposed plates—or, to be correct, films—and were conducted down a staircase, and along some mysterious underground passages to a dark and rather damp cellar; where, after lighting a dull red lamp, the owner left us to our own devices. We unpacked our films and had placed two of them into the developing dishes, when, after a spasmodic flare up or two, our lamp suddenly went out, and left us in utter darkness! We had not a match with us, and if we had, to have struck one would have meant ruining our films. Here was a pretty dilemma to be in! At last we managed to get the door open, and somehow found our way up to the shop and daylight again. This was our first and last experience of developing our photographs away from home. Certainly sketching has the advantage, that you know the result in open daylight and have not to trust to any dark room.

CHAPTER XI

The Cotswold Hills—"Posting" miles—A chat with a farmer—A twelfth-century churchyard cross—Old windows—A wooded valley—A picnic by the way—Cheltenham—Carriers' carts—Tewkesbury—Half-timbered inns—The Ideal *versus* the Real—Upton-on-Severn—A quaint church tower.

SOON after leaving Cirencester our road began to mount, and we entered upon that delightful old-world, primitive, and picturesque region known as the Cotswold Hills,—an elevated, lovely, railless tract of land where past traditions linger still, and things are to-day much as they were in the long ago. It is a bit of real old England set in the midst of the new: unprogressive, slumberous, slow, but full of infinite rest to the quiet-seeking pilgrim tired of the turmoil of towns. To travel through the Cotswolds is to turn back for centuries the hand of Time. On them you are away from the surroundings of the present; there one breathes as it were an atmosphere of the past; old churches, old homes, old hostelries, old villages, unaltered and unimproved, abound and give a genuine savour of antiquity. From rough measurement on our map we made out the Cotswold range to be some twenty miles long by about fifteen broad, so that here is an extensive district open to the lover of beautiful scenery, pure air, and interesting ancient buildings to explore—a district that, I believe, has not been touched by the modern tripper. The Cotswolds are not unlike the South Downs in their rounded forms and great hollows, but the outlines of the hills are more varied, and the sheltered hollows are in places well wooded.

Before we left our inn we asked the ostler how far it was on to Cheltenham, and he informed us that it was "sixteen posting miles, but fifteen driving ones." By which we understood that in the old posting days—and possibly in the present times if any one posts across country—they squeezed the distance out a little. Otherwise why should it be one more mile to post than to drive yourself?

Overnight, in the bar of our hotel, we whiled away a half-hour chatting with a farmer who had looked in "for a pipe and a glass of grog" before proceeding home. He had a good deal to say about horses and cattle, the weather, and the general state of agricultural affairs; the price of corn was of more import to him than home or foreign politics, and as he puffed away at his long churchwarden pipe we learnt how the world ought to be governed, and other things besides, more interesting to us. Of the latter he told us that, owing to the elevated position and open nature of the Cotswolds, the air thereon was "keenish," and therefore the crops were usually two or three weeks later than in the surrounding country; indeed there was a local saying doubtless arising from this circumstance, "As long a coming as a Cotswold crop." Then he related for our benefit a story " strictly true on my word, sir," which, as he was a total stranger to us, was naturally conclusive. "Some time ago a Yorkshireman took a farm on the hills" (Cotswold understood), "and the first thing he does was to get a lot of men and begin to clear the fields of loose stones. He said as how he were a going to show us how to farm properly: show us as had spent all our lives a farming in those parts! Well, it cost him a pretty penny a moving all them stones, and he got worse crops by a lot than we did after all. You see, sir, as how some people in the world be too clever. Now it's like this, the stones do more good nor harm; you could not do without 'em on the Cotswolds, leastways that's my opinion; they keep the land dry and warm. The sun heats the stones in the daytime, and they keep the heat in of a nights when it gets chilly on the hills." We had no idea before of the virtue of a stony field on the hills over a stoneless one, but one "lives and learns." Another local saying he told us of related to the cutting down of thistles by farmers to destroy them, which runs as follows:—

> If cut in May, it's before the day,
> If cut in June, it's still too soon,
> If cut in July, they'll surely die.

As we drove on from Cirencester the Cotswolds soon gave us a sample of their characteristic scenery; down to the right on the side of a hill was a picturesque, ivy-covered farmhouse with a quaint arched approach necessitated by the steep slope of the ground; then great bold rounded hills, rising out of deep, wooded hollows with white winding roads climbing over them, came into view, with a lengthened background of shadowed valleys and sunlit heights.

Presently our road began a gradual descent that took us into one of those charming, clean, and remote hamlets that are peculiar to the Cotswolds—North Cerney we made this out to be from our map. Just to the left of the village we noticed a quaint old church half buried in trees, with a remarkable tower of no definite type. Dismounting, we went up to the ancient gray fane with the intention of making a sketch of it. We found the door open, and walking inside discovered the rector there, who was about to ring the bells for a week-day morning service: the fact of the rector himself ringing his own bells struck us as delightfully primitive; yet why should he not? Pride in a Christian minister is out of place, and bell-ringing is a pleasant exercise.

Seeing the interest we took in the old church, the rector kindly offered, as there was ten minutes to spare before service, to show it to us: so, getting a boy to do the ringing, he placed himself at our disposal. First he took us outside and pointed out the very beautiful and well-preserved twelfth-century cross in the churchyard; this cross is supported on a tapering Early English shaft rising from some weather-worn steps and has a sculpture of the Crucifixion on one side. There are not many crosses of the kind and period in existence now in such good condition. Then the rector took us up to the curious tower which had in the first place attracted our attention. The base of this, we learnt, was of the original Norman masonry up to the string course; above this is a portion of an Early English belfry, all four sides being alike, only that the tops of two of the pointed arches are cut across by the peculiar and low roof. Our informant, who had manifestly well studied the matter, was of opinion that in former times there was a spire, possibly of wood; and as there are fire-marks in the belfry, this spire, he presumed, had been burnt down, most likely by the brasiers of plumbers doing repairs: whereupon, doubtless owing to want of funds, the belfry was simply roofed over regardless of style and wholly with a view of preserving the building for a period, the roof being adapted to the exigencies of the undamaged portion of the tower, which will account for its uncommon shape. It is certainly quaintly picturesque, and as it was the outcome of accident rather than design, the result is refreshingly original.

Next we were shown two most extraordinary and puzzling figures carved on the outer wall of the church; these were both alike, and resembled the fabulous centaur, excepting that they had no hind legs. What signified these mysterious figures? They were spiritedly drawn and manifestly by an experienced hand. The rector could give no explanation of their meaning, and we could suggest none. These figures interested us because they were so mysterious; we made a careful drawing of both, but my antiquarian friends can make nothing out of them. This old church has been restored; the buttresses of the chancel, having given way, were rebuilt, and in so doing all the original stones were used in their old places *excepting one*. This is real restoration, and an excellent example of how to do a thing properly.

Glancing round the hoary walls we noticed an ancient sun-dial near the south porch. The roof of this charmingly quaint and picturesque little church is of stone slabs, grown green and gray with age, splashed also with the silver and gold of the lowly but lovely lichen. Stone slabs certainly make excellent roofs and are most pleasing in colour, but alas! like many other good things, they belong almost wholly to a past age. The splitting of stones for roofing purposes used to be quite an art— of course only certain kinds of stones could be so treated, but considerable skill was required to split them properly; now this art seems about as dead as that of flint-squaring for the old-time flint-lock guns. In all my home travels I only remember having come upon one recent building with a stone roof, and this is on an architect's house, of all places in the world, in modern South Kensington!

Then we were conducted inside the tiny fane, and our attention was called to the pure Norman arch of the chancel, and to the finely-carved stone pulpit of the fifteenth century. But what interested us most in this gem of a church was an absolutely perfect fifteenth-century stained-glass window; the tinting of this is rich, yet restrained in a lovely harmony of quiet colour combinations, with a metallic un-glass like quality that I can only compare to the lustre of jewels. To such rare old work, modern stained glass is "as water unto wine," it is either garish or lifeless, and even with the sun streaming through, it never remotely reminds you of molten gold and rubies, and sapphires on fire! This little window is of three lights; the right-hand one is filled in with a figure of the Virgin Mary, the middle one with a figure of the diocesan bishop, pastoral staff in hand, and giving his blessing with the other,—below this figure is a crown, supposed to have belonged to the Virgin Mary, and to have got misplaced in the resetting of the glass; the left light also has the figure of a bishop with a crosier. It is presumed that this window was preserved by being taken down during the Puritan age and hidden away, and that in re-erecting it the figures got wrongly placed, it being manifestly intended that the Virgin Mary should have the central space, with the two bishops on either hand facing towards her. On the other side of the chancel is also another stained-glass window of the same period, but not quite so perfect; this has the Crucifixion in the centre, with the Virgin Mary on the left, and St. John on the right. Below the central light is the representation of a Benedictine monk with a full-sleeved robe, the tonsure clearly showing on his head. The glass is stained a deep purple for the black of the robe, there being no such colour as black in old stained glass. The rector believed this to be intended for a monk of Cirencester Abbey who probably had presented the window to his native parish; which window, he considered, was placed above the altar of the Holy Cross.

Thanking the rector for his courtesy and information, we left just as the congregation of three or four were making their way churchward, and by the surprised glance they all gave us, we concluded that strangers were somewhat of a rarity in this remote corner of the world. Then remounting our dog-cart we drove along a narrow wooded valley with the bare hills rising boldly above on either hand,—luxuriance in the lap of barrenness. The soft rounded forms of the foliage contrasted strongly and effectively with the pronounced outlines of the bleak hills beyond. It was a lovely stretch of road; the gray-green gloom of the overhanging foliage was a grateful change from the generally unsheltered country of the Cotswolds.

After a while the woods ceased, and our way gradually rose till at last we found ourselves in a well-built stone village set on the top of a hill; here we noticed a lonely but comfortable-looking inn. We hesitated as to whether we should call a halt here, but the horses seemed so fresh that we decided to keep jogging along; for ourselves, had we not ample refreshments with us, and for our gallant steeds a feed of corn in case of need, and was there not also always to be had a toothsome mouthful of fresh grass by the roadside for them? So we took an *al fresco* meal in the heart of the hills; and what can be more enjoyable than to picnic in the midst of beautiful scenery? It is one of the supreme delights of a driving tour that you are so thoroughly independent; it matters not where you stop, or for how long, your conveyance always waits your pleasure. So you may picnic, paint, photograph, or loiter by the way as much as you choose, with no anxiety as to how the time passes, and no haunting fear of missing a train. Is it not something to be able to travel from one end of England to another without ever having to look at a time-table, to say nothing of looking after luggage?

Proceeding on, the country opened out somewhat, the hills were farther apart, of greater height, and of grander form. From the elevated position of our road we looked down into a deep valley, and on the rough hillside opposite, that rose warm in the golden sunshine out of the cool gray shade below, were scattered farmsteads and cottages perched here and there where the ground was comparatively level, with steep roads leading up to them. The details of the landscape (or hillscape should it be?) are revealed in quite a Japanese manner; one road wound in and out in that curiously unexpected way that you would only expect to find on an Oriental blue plate. The scenery around had a quaint, uncommon look. Then we passed a fine park to our left, in which we noticed the fallow-deer resting under the shade of clumps of trees; on the other side of the road was a wild upland with a few wind-blown firs thereon. A stretch of fairly level ground followed, when suddenly we came to the end of our hilly stage; just beyond a cutting, crowned with pointed pines, the world in front of us seemed literally to drop down, and we looked over a vast expanse of level greenery that faded away into a mystery of far-off blue; half land, half sky. Our road now began to descend in real earnest; so much so, that even with brake hard on the carriage ran on the horses. As we drove down we had time to admire the grand scarped outline of the Cotswold hills, weather-worn into all sorts of fantastic shapes; from our point of view it seemed almost as though the level land below had once been covered by the sea, and that this side of the Cotswold hills had been mighty cliffs descending thereto.

We had a glorious run down into Cheltenham, where we took up our quarters at the old Plough Inn; the air there appeared warm and close after the fresh bracing breezes of the open elevated uplands, and the thronged fashionable thoroughfares of the town contrasted forcibly with the lonely and primitive villages of the sparsely-peopled Cotswolds. The traveller by railway from one town to another experiences nothing of these contrasts; indeed, so accustomed probably is he to being conveyed from place to place, that he little dreams how sudden these transitions seem to the traveller by road. The England of Cheltenham is the England of to-day, the England of the Cotswolds is that of the picturesque long ago.

Pleasant though the town of Cheltenham be, on this occasion it failed to charm us. Cheltenham is fashionable, the houses and shops are mostly modern; both the people and the place reminded us too much of the West End of London; we had not come out on a driving tour to see familiar scenes at second hand. However, we usefully employed our spare time in making a few needful and many needless purchases; the shops certainly were tempting after our rural wanderings.

The next morning proved wet, but the barometer was rising, so we delayed our start for a couple of hours in the reasonable hope of the weather improving; however, it did nothing of the kind, the rain poured down persistently. So we donned our waterproofs, and, prepared to challenge fate, started forth from our inn. The ostler prophesied that "we should catch it" on the way, which was not very kind of him as our tip was on a liberal scale. Certainly we did "catch it," for just after starting the rain came down in torrents, but with our mackintoshes, waterproof aprons, and buckskin caps, we effectually defied the elements, indeed I do not feel sure that we did not actually enjoy our wet drive. We laughed and joked as we drove along, as though to prove that nothing could damp our spirits, any more than it could our bodies. Come what may, we would be "jolly"; with that intent we started on our journey, and we determined that nothing thereon that fate might decree should daunt our good spirits. As to driving in the rain I may say that I found a buckskin cap with a big peak a real blessing, the wind would not blow it off my head, the rain could not hurt it, and the peak prevented the rain driving in my eyes. That cap made driving in the rain a real pleasure: the only weak point in our former touring outfit was the hat; one of tweed is useless in rain as it soon gets wet through, a hard felt hat gets sodden in time and is apt to blow off, but a well-shaped buckskin cap will turn any storm, and is comfortable to wear at all times, fair or foul. Except when entering or leaving fashionable towns, like Cheltenham, we wore no other on the journey.

Driving on thus, proof against any ordinary storm, we actually enjoyed the wild, wet weather. We looked at the wind-driven clouds above, the distant mists, and falling rain around with an artist's eye; and felt that the storm had its beauties as well as the sunshine. Rain it ever so hard, we had nothing on to be damaged, therefore we could observe, pleasurably and leisurely, the beautiful, ever-changing forms and soft varying grays of the water-charged vapours overhead; then as for a moment, now and again, a gleam of sunshine struggled downward, we noticed that the slanting lines of rain became golden and iridescent like falling opals; a very lovely effect, yet one to be often seen at the clearing up of a summer storm, as though the clouds were raining down gold and opals!

Yet how few people ever see, or even dream that there can be any beauty in a rainy day. Rather do they not deem it a disagreeable incident, causing them to put up an umbrella, call a cab, take a train, or stay indoors? Now, if you are properly equipped and use your eyes, a walk or a drive across country on a rainy day is a thing to be enjoyed; for the transient effects of a fine cloudscape are full of poetic mystery; and, as painters know well, such changeful conditions are infinitely more picturesque and paintable than a mere blue void of sky in which the sun simply rises and sets in an uninteresting monotony. For myself I must confess that I absolutely delight in a long country tramp on a wet day, provided always it is not one of those dull, dreary, east-winderly days with an unbroken stretch of gray leaden cloud above without form or change, that is the only sort of wet day I dislike; but wet weather generally comes from the west and abounds in revelations of sky scenery, which is just as well worth observing as that of the landscape below.

Our road now led us through a level land, level enough indeed to suggest, as before mentioned, that at some prehistoric period it had been the bed of a small inland sea, and that the broken, indented, cliff-like line of the Cotswolds, that descend so suddenly to the plain, had once been its eastern boundary, and the Malvern Hills had been islands rising therefrom. Indeed I believe many geologists have it that the Severn valley was in remote times a sea strait.

> There rolls the deep where grew the tree.
> O earth, what changes hast thou seen!
> There where the long street roars, hath been
> The stillness of the central sea.

As we drove along we noticed that the soil of the ploughed fields looked red and rich, and the great stemmed elms by the roadside told of a fertile land; for I have always found that where the elm grows big and flourishes thus the land is good. Here and there ample farmsteads showed a former if not a present agricultural prosperity; but times have sadly changed, and the burly, well-to-do, old-fashioned, corn-growing farmer has been almost entirely improved out of being by Free Trade. The picturesque old English farmstead, with its colony of rambling out-buildings and fat wheat-stacks around, is, alas! a rare rather than a familiar feature in the landscape. The disappearance of the yeoman farmer is a regrettable fact.

Driving through the little village of Uckington we noticed an open thatch-roofed smithy that made quite a picture with the cheerful warm glow of its furnace reflected on the damp roadway outside: here also we noticed one or two carriers' carts stopping at certain cottages. These old-time conveyances — that even the locomotive has not been able to drive off the road—serve a most useful part in the economy of country life, they are the poor people's carriage. The carrier calls at the houses on his way as he jogs along to the market, picks up passengers, goods, or receives orders to be executed in the provincial town. We once lived for a time in a farmhouse that was seven miles from anywhere, and then we realised the usefulness of the humble carrier: he called as he passed by to the local town, took our orders for groceries, books, paints, fishing-tackle, or whatever we might require, faithfully executing them and charging only the carriage of the articles as his commission: he daily delivered the London papers and kept us in touch with the outer world that seemed so far away. As he approached the farmhouse he blew a small horn as the signal of his coming, so that some one might be ready waiting to receive his parcels, but at some places where the farmhouses were at some distance from the road we noticed that he simply left any article by the wayside till they were fetched, which appeared a very primitive proceeding, and we could not help wondering how it was that tramps did not sometimes appropriate them. Such rural honesty was quite refreshing. As to travelling by a carrier's cart, we once ventured to make the seven miles' journey in that conveyance by way of a fresh experience; we found the progress to be slow, the constant stops by the way further delaying; in fine, the experiment was not a success. On the whole we deemed that walking was less fatiguing, and almost as speedy; but for the ordering and delivery of necessities, the carrier's cart we looked upon as a blessing to those country-dwellers who live in remote spots by or near to the roadside. I well remember how, our day's fishing, or painting from nature over, we used to wait in the weed-grown garden of the ancient farmstead watching for the arrival of the slow-travelling conveyance, that brought us our London paper of yesterday and other simple luxuries. It was the one apparent tie between our delightfully restful out-of-the-world life and modern civilisation—a civilisation that with all its advantages we are always so glad to escape from for a time as the sunny summer days come round.

As we drove on the weather gradually improved —it could not well have got much worse—the clouds lifted, patches of deep-blue made their welcome appearance, then watery gleams of sunshine came and went, the air grew warmer, and suddenly the rain ceased. But the clouds hung threateningly over the Cotswolds behind and the Malvern Hills ahead, both of which showed purply-dark under the gloomy, louring masses of aqueous vapour above. There is one advantage in a fickle climate, when it does rain there is always the chance of a favourable change and a clearance, and the blue sky and cheerful sunshine are all the more to be appreciated after the dulness of dun cloud-laden skies, which in their turn are a relief from the glare of the summer sunshine. Whatever abuse our climate may deserve it cannot honestly be accused of being monotonous; and, after all, change is the desire of the present century. Do we not travel afar for change? yet, as an American friend once remarked to me, "You Britishers need never go from home for a change of climate, you have it at home every day; within twenty-four hours you have a sample of all kinds of weathers." Well, so we may have, and let us be thankful for the fact! By the way, the same American said, "I never met any one like an Englishman to run his own country down; I don't complain of your climate, I rather like it, it does everything so gently. The rain falls softly, the sun shines softly, even your thunder-storms seem rather playful than dreadful." But he had not experienced the true delights of a London fog; I wonder what he would have thought of that.

Then, as we journeyed on, the great gray Norman tower of Tewkesbury Abbey came into view, with a flag flying from its summit, making it

OLD BELL INN, TEWKESBURY.

look from afar like some old feudal keep, and soon afterwards we found ourselves sheltering in an ancient inn almost beneath the shadow of the solemn walls of the hoary, majestic fane. Tewkesbury, we discovered, was *en fête*, there was a musical festival to be held at the abbey in the afternoon, and some of the artistes were lunching at our ancient hostelry. Hearing this, madame would attend the service (or musical treat), whilst I elected to remain without and sketch the old-time half-timbered Bell Inn, a well-preserved specimen of an English hostel built nearly now two centuries ago, for it bears the date 1696 on its weather-toned front. I also found time before the service was over to make one or two other sketches of quaint gables, windows, and rain-water-heads; for Tewkesbury still retains many a picturesque architectural bit whose beauty is emphasised by ugly modern surroundings.

Late in the afternoon we once more proceeded on our pleasant pilgrimage. Driving along the extended main street of Tewkesbury, just where it ended and the country began, we came upon still another quaint, old, half-timbered inn called the Black Bear. How homelike and eye-pleasing these half-timbered buildings are; they recall to mind the olden time when in many localities wood was cheaper than stone or brick. Their very construction leading to projecting upper stories, added to their convenience by increasing the upstair accommodation, and to their picturesqueness by the bold play of light and shade such projections caused. Oftentimes we have found quaint bits of carving introduced on the brackets of these ancient buildings, the wood lending itself readily to the carver's tool, and when near a sea-port we have been struck by the fact that frequently old ships' figure-heads are employed with a striking effect, generally on a corner support to the first overhanging story. I remember, when on a driving tour some time back, coming upon a "ship-knacker's" yard where there were several boldly-carved old ships' figure-heads for sale, and the sudden inclination I felt to bargain for some of them to make use of when I build my ideal half-timbered house in the country. I have the dream on paper, a long low two-storied building with great gables, clustering chimney-stacks, bell-turret, ample porch, bay mullioned windows, panelled rooms from floor to ceiling, and in oak too, a Haddon Hall terrace in front, with a sun-dial at one corner; the terrace looking down over a grand extent of English woodland, the garden close by being gay and sweet with old-fashioned, colourful flowers: a cottage built like a mansion,—we all dream dreams, it is less troublesome than reading novels!

Out of Tewkesbury we had a stiff ascent, near to the top of which we passed to our left an old house with an ivy-clad tower that looked romantic and suggestive of legendary lore. That at any rate was the poetic impression the distant glance of the place gave us; it is sometimes well to be content with a poetic impression—when you can get it: too close an inspection may rob you of all the romance. Richmond in Yorkshire, as seen from afar with its castle-crowned height, winding wooded river, old bridge, and bounding stretches of hilly moorland, looks like an artist's dream, but close at hand it becomes comparatively commonplace. When you have such a dream before you it is a pity to risk spoiling it. Do not inquire too closely, let the dream remain.

Then we had a pleasant stretch of level winding road that led us for a time through a very pretty and well-wooded country. Presently the bounding hedges ceased, and we drove through a stately avenue of elms with open sward reaching far away on either hand, as though we were traversing one vast park, but it was only the open country that chanced to be unenclosed. There was no feeling of nature tamed and patronised. It is a relief now and then to be free from the green hedgerows; they are truly most beautiful in themselves, a forest wilderness in miniature, with their tangled brambles, roses, honeysuckle, traveller's joy, and numberless other plants and wild flowers that flourish in their sheltered recesses; but they cut up the country into rectangular patches chess-board fashion, and so arrest the eye instead of allowing it to rove all over the spreading landscape unimpeded. It is certainly difficult to paint a pleasing picture of a panorama of hedge-enclosed fields.

Next we entered upon a wide far-spreading common, a rare bit of wild England, much as it was in the ages long ago. Here and there this was dotted with century-old oaks—rugged, gnarled, and picturesque. The lonely road, lengthening out far away over the wild waste, seemed to call for a knight-errant or a medieval pilgrim to complete its uncared-for picturesqueness; but not even a "knight of the road" did we see; you cannot get many adventures nowadays driving about England, but then I am not sure whether adventures on the whole are not a good deal more interesting to read about than to experience. Some of the giant oaks interested us; how many startling changes has this England of ours seen since they were young! They are aged now, yet seemingly strong in their decay. Many English oaks are said to be over a thousand years old, and to exceed all other British trees in longevity with the probable exception of the yew.

> The monarch oak, the patriarch of trees,
> Shoots rising up, and spreads by slow degrees:
> Three centuries he grows, and three he stays,
> Supreme in state, and in three more decays.

How grand a growth is an English oak that has had plenty of space to develop its roots and branches, and has been left free to disport itself as it will: its sturdiness is delightful to behold, and the ramifications of its mighty limbs a study and a perplexity to the artist, for they seem always to turn and twist about in a manner one would least expect. The English oak is full of character, and has a bold individuality; it is a glorious tree to paint owing to the grandeur and variety of its form, combining in a rare manner grace with strength.

Now to our left the Malvern range of hills rose grandly up from the level lowland, their summits raked by low-lying gray clouds that were being driven before the wild west wind. Ever and again the amber glow of the setting sun showed above the dark hills as the clouds lifted for a moment only to descend again, and at the same time warm streaks of light were thrown athwart the landscape, giving a cheerful glimmer to all they rested on, and bringing into prominent relief solitary church tower, lowly cottage, and leafy tree; turning also the leaden waters of the gliding Severn into a streak of gold. The sudden transition from gray gloom to golden glory was wonderfully effective and surprising. Such effects are only to be witnessed during the clearing up of stormy weather when the sun is setting low and lurid, and hill and dale permit of a powerful display of light and shade: then Nature becomes for the nonce almost theatrical in her scenic display.

Crossing the Severn on a swing bridge, so constructed as to allow masted ships to pass up to Worcester, we entered the ancient town of Upton-on-Severn and pulled up, and sought a night's lodging and entertainment at the old White Lion, an ancient hostelry made mention of by Fielding in his *Tom Jones*. A former landlord of the house also advertised himself by an epitaph on his father in the churchyard, wherein, after stating he was "resigned unto the heavenly will," the mourning and dutiful son proclaimed that he kept "on the business still." The White Lion of our inn was very mild of countenance, and, when we were there, had grown somewhat gray with age; his left paw was resting listlessly on a golden ball, though why a lion should be so occupied we could not imagine.

Upton-on-Severn proved to be a small town picturesquely located on the banks of the river and surrounded by a lovely country. Quite a feature of the place is its prominently situated old church going fast to decay, like all uncared-for things in this world; the tower of this forsaken edifice is slowly crumbling to dust, and is capped by a curious looking cupola, that gives quite a character to the otherwise commonplace town. The windows of the old church, we noticed, were nearly all broken; possibly they had served as targets for the youthful population—at any rate we saw a goodly number of small stones lying at the foot of some of them. The Upton people, we discovered, had provided themselves with a new place of worship, a Gothic church boasting a tall steeple of the approved type, a well-designed building, perfect as a whole, and perfect in its parts, but somehow it looked ordinary and uninteresting to us after the ancient, neglected fane, which may have every architectural fault (it has a good many), but it has the bloom of age upon its crumbling walls, it has grown—if I may be allowed the expression—into what it is, and its unique, cupola-crowned tower is a special and picturesque feature in the surrounding landscape. Even ugliness is forgivable at times, when it is quaint, distinctive, and has the savour of age—if a thing that is really quaint can ever fairly be deemed ugly, of which I am not sure.

The bridge over the river at Upton-on-Severn

appeared to be a sort of open-air club for the inhabitants of the place, where, the day's work over, they meet of an evening to discuss the affairs of their little world. Late at night, as we strolled about, we noticed quite a gathering there and much smoking and conversation going on. I have often noticed in country towns that wherever a bridge exists, thereon the townsfolk assemble in the summer evenings : great is the attraction of a winding river, for there is generally some kind of life by the waterside to look at or for, and the long lines of the stream vanishing away in curving parallels have a certain fascination, often even for the unimaginative, for unknowingly they lead the eye into the far away, into the dreamy distance, where all things seem possible. There is more poetry in everyday people than one would imagine, and day-dreaming is not a costly luxury.

CHAPTER XII

An ancient home—Old customs—A haunted room—A "Powder Chamber"—An old coach bill—The Malvern Hills—A country of orchards—Worcester—Old sayings—Knightsford—A picturesque spot—Inn yards—A quaintly-clipped yew tree—"Far from the madding crowd."

WHILST at Upton we learnt that there was a picturesque and an interesting old house called Severn End only about two miles off. It was uninhabited, but the landlord did not know whether we should be able to see over it. From the description of the place we determined to risk a disappointment and drive there as the distance was not great. Severn End was difficult to find as it is not to be seen from the highway. A road across some meadows that doubtless of old formed a park, leads to it; and at the end of the road low down in a sheltered hollow lies the ancient deserted home, so that you do not notice the building till you are close upon it. The exterior is very picturesque with its age-mellowed, half-timbered, and many-gabled front, ornamented brick chimneys, and carved barge-boards. Some little way from the house stand two stone pillars, gray and weather-worn, each surmounted with a sculptured heraldic dog—or what we took to be intended for such—that face each other in grim silence; the pillars support a rusty, wrought-iron gate, which was locked when we were there, so that strangers are kept at a respectful distance from the entrance porch. We rang the ancient bell, and after a considerable time an aged caretaker made his appearance; he was doubtful at first if he could allow us to see over the place, as he had no instructions to show it, but after a long palaver we eventually managed to overcome his scruples and gained the coveted admission. Opening the iron gates, which creaked on their hinges as though resenting the intrusion of a mere modern tourist, we followed the caretaker across the enclosed grass-grown court and came to the entrance door, where we stopped a moment to copy the crest and motto of the Lechmeres that is engraved above, to which family the property was granted by the Conqueror, and who have retained it ever since—not a bad record of long possession! The crest consists of a pelican " proper "; the motto is "Christus pelicano," one word on either side of the crest. The family now reside in a more modern and possibly more convenient, if less romantic, house not far away.

We were first shown the oak-panelled hall, around the walls of which hang specimens of ancient armour: the ceiling has big moulded beams, and from the centre one we noticed suspended a great bunch of mistletoe; this we were told was put up on St. Thomas's day and left there undisturbed till the same day on the following year. At one side of the hall is a large open fireplace with a stone hearth and old-fashioned dog-irons on either hand; the ashes of the burnt wood, according to ancient custom, are never removed; this is all very well in a carpetless hall, but a modern house-wife might raise objections to such a system; it is convenient, however, as I know from experience of such fires in old country homes and farmhouses, for the ashes retain a glow all night, and a fresh supply of wood in the morning placed on them soon becomes a blazing fire. Peat will do the same, and is an ideal fuel, being clean to handle even with one's fingers, noiseless to put on, and the gases from it being antiseptic and healthy rather than sulphureous and injurious like coal. I always burn peat now—when I can get it. A peat fire will keep in all night without any looking after, nor will any sparks fly out therefrom. Our guide told us that if we would look up the great chimney we could see the sky above, but we were content to take his word for it. This olden chamber, with its deeply-recessed windows, and dark panelled walls with the gleam of medieval armour around, is a veritable picture; standing there, for the moment, the past seemed very near, the present far away.

Next we were conducted to the withdrawing-room, which has a ceiling of enriched plaster between great beams that cross one another. The walls of this room are also panelled from floor to ceiling, but have been unfortunately painted over, just to show how modern taste and refinement can improve on that of the past. All the woodwork of the house, we were informed, was of "heart of oak." I only wish that the woodwork of my house were! The speculative builder who runs up "desirable residences" to sell does not, however, see any beauty in solid construction; an ostentatious age, alas! preferring cheap show and glitter to more substantial benefits—and it gets its desire. A speculative builder, who had made his fortune, once told me in a moment of confidence that he found it did not much matter how he built a house so long as it looked "taking" and had plenty of cupboards, and a pretty porch, "it's these as the ladies fancy, especially the cupboards; and, after all, the ladies settle the matter. I always put plenty of cupboards in my houses."

Then we came to the great staircase of solid oak with massive carved newels; ascending this we were shown "the haunted room," for of course an ancient home like this must needs have its ghost. It appears that a servant murdered his master there, but further particulars of the ghastly deed we could not gather. The caretaker had only been a few months in the place, and so far had not seen the apparition; possibly the ghost was a little shy of the newcomer.

After this we were ushered into a small apartment called the "Powder Chamber"; here the ladies of the family in past times had their hair powdered. Several rings were pointed out to us fixed in the ceiling from which curtains were suspended to protect the ladies' dresses during the process. We have seen over many ancient mansions, each with its own unwritten history, but never before had we come upon a "Powder Chamber," nor till then were we aware that such things ever existed. But one travels and learns!

Another room was pointed out to us in which Prince Charles slept one night during the civil wars; he arrived, we were informed, with a hundred and thirty men, uninvited and unexpected, for the Lechmeres were on the side of the Parliament and Prince Charles threatened them that when he was king he would turn them out of their property. By the way, the number of rooms that have been shown to us during our driving expeditions across country in which either Queen Elizabeth, King Charles I., or Prince Charles is reputed to have slept is quite astonishing : I do not think we have made a single journey without coming upon one or more of such chambers.

Hanging in a frame on the wall of a passage upstairs we discovered an old coaching bill which we deemed of sufficient interest to copy in full as follows :—

YORK FOUR DAYS
Stage Coach
Begins on Friday the 12th of April 1706.
All that are desirous to pass from London to York
or from London to any other Place
on that Road : Let them repair to the Black Swan in
Holbourn in London, and to the Black Swan in Coney
Street in York.
At both of which Places they may be received in a
Stage Coach every Monday, Wednesday, and Friday
which performs the whole journey in Four Days (if
God permits) and sets forth at Five in the morning
and returns from York to Stamford in two
Days more, and the like stages on their return
Allowing each passenger 14l. weight
and all above 3d. a Pound.

Performed by { Benjamin Kingman
Henry Harrison
Walter Baynes.
Also this gives notice that the Newcastle Stage Coach sets out from York every Monday and Friday and from Newcastle every Monday and Friday.

These old coaching bills are getting rare now, and I hear that collectors set great prize on them: I wonder whether, in the dim, dim future, our remote descendants will collect railway posters, and if ever they will sigh for the good old slow railway-travelling days; for Time manages very successfully to throw the glamour of romance over the never-returning past.

From Upton to Worcester we had a pleasant drive through a prettily-wooded country. The air was clear and cool, and filled with fragrance after the rain of the previous day, whilst the sun shone softly down from a fair-weather, cloud-dappled sky. The wind coming from the south wooed us with a gentle caress. It was one of those inspiring days that make the fact of mere living a luxury, and driving through a pretty country a supreme delight. There was neither dust nor dirt nor any glare; and we fell into an enviable mood wherein everything seemed beautiful, and this "the best of all possible worlds." We passed through one or two small villages on the way, that appeared to us delightfully picturesque in their primitive homeliness, with their tidy cottages set in their own colourful flower gardens, that suggested rustic contentment and cheerfulness; but we were in the frame of mind to see all things in a roseate hue that day, perhaps another time we should not have been so much impressed with their charms. A good deal of the poetry of a scene consists in what we put into it; it may exist to us and not to others, and it may not exist to us to the same degree, or at all, on a different occasion. Smile on the world and it will smile back on you, frown on it and it frowns in return.

As we drove along we had a fine view of the whole of the isolated Malvern range of hills, their gray-green rounded summits being sharply defined against the light summer sky. Small wonder that the highest point of this range was selected in the pre-telegraphic days for a signal beacon station; its position, rising as it does right out of a vast level plain, must have made a fire thereon noticeable far and wide—as on the occasion of the approaching Spanish Armada, when "Twelve fair counties saw the blaze, from Malvern's lonely height."

The country around us abounded in fruitful orchards, which must appear a perfect sea of white in the early springtime when the trees are in full bloom. Different portions of England have their own special seasons of beauty. The beauty of Worcestershire is, I take it, most revealed when Nature bursts forth into buds and blossoms. Here and there, peeping above the wealth of spreading woods, we caught sight now and again of a quaint gable, or the red chimney-stacks of some ancient home. The buildings, we noticed, were mostly of the black-and-white half-timbered style that is so picturesquely assertive, and pleasantly suggestive of the ideal old England known to us in story and song.

Excepting the quiet beauty of the landscape

there was nothing that called for particular note till
"the ever-faithful city" came into the prospect, of
which we had a strikingly effective view from an
elevated upland to the left of our road, which showed
us the silvery Severn winding in and out far below,
and the great cathedral rising in a solemn mass of
gray above the surrounding buildings. The humility
of the Christian religion is certainly not expressed
in its lordly cathedrals. Entering Worcester we
passed close by the ancient edifice, which, however,
has been so restored as to look almost like new, for the
whole of the exterior has been re-cased in stone (the
interior has also undergone a thorough process of
renovation); the result of this was to afford us an idea
of the appearance that these majestic fanes of ancient
worship had when they were first raised in the
Pliocene period of church-building. The new look
of the old cathedral is disappointing and displeasing
to the lover of the antique; the beautiful, suggestive
bloom that age alone can give is gone for ever. You
may restore an ancient building till it ceases to be old
in all except name, and it becomes to the antiquary a
mere meaningless mass of masonry. Of such, money
can give us any day; but the charm of age, the
weather-tinting of centuries, the very chisel-marks
of the old-time builders, these nothing can replace.
The work of the modern contractor is of necessity
mechanical and without feeling; the craftsman of
old put himself into his work, it was individual.
There is as much difference between the two as
there is between a machine-produced oleograph and
a painting by an artist.

In the spacious courtyard of our hotel at Worcester, where erst the old mail coaches used to start and arrive, we discovered, as we drove in, a number of conveyances standing, of all sorts and conditions, from the nobleman's carriage to the small farmer's tax cart—for it chanced to be a market day; but what struck us as a novelty was that on almost every conveyance we observed a label with the owner's name plainly painted thereon. The ostler explained the use of these. It appears that the country people of all degrees drive into the city upon market days and make sundry purchases, which they order to be sent to their carriage at the hotel, and these labels were placed thereon so that the tradesmen's boys might know where to put the parcels. As we judged there were thirty or more conveyances standing in the yard and most of these contained packages readily removable, we thought that the arrangement spoke well for the honesty of the Worcester people. But why the local clergy and gentlemen should elect to drive in to town on a crowded market day puzzled us. We once spent our holiday in a farmhouse and every now and then drove in to the nearest town to make sundry small purchases, but we were careful to avoid the market day there, when the inn yards were inconveniently full, the streets thronged, and the shopkeepers unusually busy. Possibly, however, there are a number of people who live quiet, uneventful lives in the country who rather enjoy, by way of change, the moderate bustle and activity of a market day in a provincial town.

During the evening, in the smoke-room of our hotel, we came upon two jovial Roman Catholic priests who smoked their pipes, drank their whisky, and cracked their jokes like any ordinary sinners. Very excellent and entertaining company we found them to be, apparently not given to look too seriously upon the world's pleasures, but perhaps they considered themselves "off duty" for the time. The elder of the two was manifestly a bit of an antiquary, and he enlightened us upon many early Catholic customs and traditions, and he quoted freely for our special benefit, from his goodly store of local folk-lore and sayings. He said that in the part of Gloucestershire he came from, the following distich was formerly employed to express the supposed peculiarities of certain places—

> Beggarly Bisley, Strutting Stroud,
> Mincing Hampton, and Painswick Proud.

The question that occurred to us was whether truth was in any way sacrificed to the manifest craving for alliteration. Of another village (the name of which I have forgotten, and which perhaps does not much matter) it used to be said

> Thatched roof, and wooden steeple,
> Drunken parson and wicked people.

Speaking of the old days when England was Roman Catholic we were told that we had then

> Golden Bishops with wooden crosiers,

but now we had

> Wooden Bishops with golden crosiers.

One remark that this enlightened priest made *apropos* of some modern publications, and especially of certain works by Professor Huxley, which appeared very wicked to him, fairly startled us; said he vehemently, " I verily believe that printing was invented by the Devil." Had we not actually heard this exclamation we simply could not have credited that any one could have made it in this present year of grace and progress!

At Worcester we consulted our maps as to our next stage, for we learnt that there were two ways of reaching Ludlow from there—one by Bromyard, the other by Tenbury. We eventually selected the Bromyard route, for the reason that by so doing we found we should be enabled to follow up the prettily-wooded Teme valley for some miles. A river is always pleasant company; the fisherman wanders by its side, there the artist lingers, the rustic youth tarries, thither the cattle wend their way to slake their thirst or cool themselves in the flowing stream, the birds haunt it all day long. There is always life by a river; its banks are refreshingly green, and nearly every old bridge that crosses it forms a picture, to say nothing of an occasional weather-stained mill with its great gray-green droning wheel and gleam of glancing water. A river lends life to a landscape; it brings down a portion of the brightness of the sky above to the world below, and gives an added touch of beauty to even the fairest scene. There is, too, a certain amount of poetry about a flowing stream; as it winds away from you it directs the eye into the unknown distance, and takes the thought to the far-off sea, for every river leads eventually thither. Of all things in inanimate Nature the most companionable and suggestive of life (except perhaps the sea) is a gently-flowing river; and what an indescribable melody, a wordless song that knows no end and yet is always fresh, is there not in the plashing and gurgling of its gliding waters! The wild music of the waves may be grander, but it is not half so restful.

We also found from our map that by taking this line of country we should cross the Teme at a hamlet amongst the hills called Knightsford. Did this name imply, we wondered, that there was formerly a ford at the spot by which those ancient warriors crossed the river? Anyhow the title suggested to us the days of old romance—a good deal more desirable to read about than to live in, I should imagine. The names of many country places have arisen from past associations, and thus are reminders of other times and ways. In nothing is rural England more conservative than in the retaining of the old names of places. I have visited at an ancient country home, which over two centuries ago was an important inn known as the Lamb, and though it has been converted into a charming residence all that time with a new name to suit its changed estate, yet to this day some of the rural folk around speak of the house as the " Lamb." So tenaciously are old titles, even when inappropriate, held in the land.

We had some difficulty in finding our road out of Worcester, for in the confusion of streets our map was of little use. Eventually, however, by dint of constantly asking our way, and after being misdirected once, we managed to get on the right road and so out of the city. Reaching the open country once more, we had a fine view looking south of the north end of the Malvern range, the Beacon showing a grand purple-gray in the dark shadow of a heavy overhanging bulging rain-cloud, which happily confined its aquatic attentions to the distant hills. It is astonishing how the colour of a hill or mountain changes with the passing clouds above. I have seen Snowdon look inky black and weirdly impressive during the clearing of a thunder-storm, and in a short time afterwards, when the sun was shining, the peak and the whole range appeared almost too ethereal to be real. So much does the effect of scenery depend upon atmospheric conditions.

About a mile on the way we pulled up to inspect the picturesque little church of St. John in Bedwardine—as we made it out to be from a parish notice attached to the doorway; this church possesses a quaint open-timbered porch with a carved barge-board over, having representations of lions thereon, though why lions should be chosen as a subject for church adornment we could not quite make out. The single-light windows, we noticed, were filled in with plain plate glass, which looked painfully out of place; they gave one the feeling of mere holes in the wall; like fire, plate glass is a good servant, and perhaps desirable for shop windows, but it is a very bad master, and unfortunately the modern architect is frequently mastered by it. We noticed that the quiet God's acre was situated apart from the sacred edifice, being separated from the churchyard proper by a yew-tree hedge.

Then as we drove on the country began to give us a taste of its scenic capabilities, which were of no mean order. A sudden dip in our undulating road revealed a glorious panorama over a vast portion of wooded Herefordshire,—we had now proceeded so far westward as to look upon the Hereford side of the Malvern Hills. A most entrancing prospect it was, even to our eyes grown accustomed to scenic revelations; our vision ranged far and wide over a sea of many-tinted woods—a sea of green that rose and fell with the rise and fall of the ground, and that faded away to the south in a horizon of indigo blue; to the left the Malvern Hills rose out of it like a great island, and to the right the dark, rugged outline of the Welsh mountains showed stormily forth. In driving westward the first distant glimpse of the wild Welsh mountains is always a delight to me, there is something so characteristic about their clear-cut profile, their dark-purple hue, their wild tumultuous aspect, and the bold assertiveness of their prominent peaks. I know no mountains so beautiful in colour or so noble in form as those of Wales; they are infinitely more paintable than the Alps.

From a spot where we pulled up to admire the view, in all the miles upon miles of spreading landscape—woodscape, if I might coin a word, would better express the outlook—neither far nor near was there a house, cottage, or even a building of any kind, however humble, visible; only waving woods bounded by distant hills, with here and there the silvery gleam of water,—and this was in the heart of thickly-peopled England! We might almost have imagined ourselves in some western American territory, the solitude could not have been more seemingly profound.

After admiring the distant prospect we gave attention to the minor attractions of the country side, and soon discovered that the tangled hedgerows close by abounded in big, luscious-looking blackberries. The instinct of our school-days was at once called forth, and we neglected the scenery, which we had come so far to see, for the blackberries! Then we sat down to attempt a sketch of the spot and distant view, made beautiful by hill and dale, rock, wood, and winding river. Elizabeth Barrett Browning thus describes the charms of this her native shire:—

> Green the land is where my daily
> Steps in jocund childhood played,
> Dimpled close with hill and valley,
> Dappled very close with shade;
> Summer-snow of apple-blossoms running up from glade to glade.

As we neared Knightsford the country became more hilly, whilst the valley beyond narrowed romantically. The sloping sides of the hills were clad with thick woods and dotted here and there with homelike half-timbered houses and cottages. It was pleasant to come once more upon signs of human occupancy; there is a touch of sadness about a lonely country, however lovely it may be; to the moors and mountains solitude and silence properly and rightly belong, but hardly to the lowland English country.

About half a mile before Knightsford one of the most pleasing prospects of the journey opened out before us. Looking down upon the secluded little hamlet sleeping peacefully at the foot of the wooded heights, with the winding Teme brightly gleaming here and there between overhanging trees, we looked upon a perfect picture. It was one of those scenic gems that cannot fail to impress the mind by their rare natural beauty. Truly our journey revealed to us countless lovely rural scenes, picturesque places, dreamy out-of-the-world spots, ruined castles, romantic homes, comfortable and cosy inns of the coaching days that still open their doors to the traveller, all of which we have added to our mind's gallery of pictures to be recalled to memory at future times as a pleasant relief from the commonplace affairs and surroundings of everyday existence,

> For oft when on my couch I lie,
> In vacant or in pensive mood,
> They flash upon that inward eye
> Which is the bliss of solitude.

Knightsford is one of nature's beauty spots, and let us hope that, unlike lovely Lynton in Devonshire and other places I could mention, it may not become famous and half spoilt. At present the genus tourist does not appear to have discovered it, the primitive wayside inn there has not blossomed forth into an hotel, and there are no attractions in the neighbourhood except for the pedestrian artist in the fine scenery around, and for the angler in the pleasant reaches of the river.

At Knightsford we found sufficiently comfortable quarters for our mid-day halt at the homely Talbot Inn. We determined to rest a while there, attracted by the picturesque surroundings of the spot, and to make a late start on to the little town of Bromyard, about six miles farther westward, where we proposed to spend the night. After a frugal repast, but the best the inn had to offer us, we set forth sketch-book in hand to explore the locality, and to make, if the mood took us, a hasty sketch or two of any special points of beauty or interest. We reserved our camera more for purely architectural subjects, where there was a wealth of detail to be reproduced beyond the power of the pencil in a limited time. The advantage of photography is its faithful rendering of all things; it does not scamp any work, indeed in less than one short minute it will give you all the elaborate carving on the front of a cathedral down to the most unconsidered trifle, even to the accidental details of the chipped and weather-worn stone: as an unprejudiced recorder of facts and in mere speed photography can easily out-rival both the brush and pencil. Yet a photograph is seldom or ever a picture, it is too precise, too mechanical, it leaves nothing to the imagination, it faithfully renders all things, trivial as well as important; one can hardly ever sit down to make a sketch under the most favourable circumstances but there will be something in

TALBOT INN, KNIGHTSFORD.

the view that spoils the subject as a picture, but which the artist conveniently ignores, or, when that is impossible, hides as far as may be in shade. On looking over the numerous photographs that I took during our journey I cannot find one that is not so ruined pictorially. Sometimes it is an ugly bit of straight wall that will come in the foreground, sometimes it is such a simple thing as a new chimney to an old cottage (which, though a trifle, utterly spoils its picturesque qualities); oftentimes, of late, I have found telegraphic poles and wires sadly in the way; many a quaint street corner in some quiet country town too has been spoilt to me by advertisements on the walls. Once or perhaps twice only have I had what I consider a perfect picture before me when employing the camera, and on both of these rare occasions something went wrong with the plate during the process of development! As a handmaid to art photography is invaluable: but as an enthusiastic amateur photographer I am fain to confess—at least as far as my own work goes—that a few hasty pencil lines and washes of colour, though not so accurate in form, and sadly wanting, of necessity, in detail, give a better general impression of a place and a truer feeling of a scene than the camera can possibly do. And, after all, it is a general broad impression of a place that we carry away with us, not the detail thereof, which we could not possibly remember, even if we would. The comparative value of an accurate photograph and the impression of a place as rendered by a rapid, though, as far as it went, fairly accurate water-colour sketch was revealed to me some time ago when I showed to a friend a photograph and a painting I had done of Boscastle in Cornwall. On seeing the photograph he exclaimed, "Whatever place is it? I seem to know it, yet cannot call it to mind"; but on showing him the sketch from nearly the same point of view he at once exclaimed, " That's Boscastle!"

Now after this over-long digression to return to the point from where we started. The first object that attracted our pencil at Knightsford was the court-yard at the rear of our inn, which was the oldest and most picturesque part of the building, so we forthwith proceeded to make a drawing of it. The courtyards of these old country inns generally make capital subjects for water-colour sketches. They are, as a rule, delightfully rambling and spacious, and abound in odd nooks and corners that cause a charming effect of light and shade; quaint old sign-boards find a resting-place there, as also do ram-shackle vehicles long past duty, and of curious con-struction, at least to modern eyes. In one of these yards, on a former outing, we discovered the body of an old mail coach with the names of the places it passed through still plainly figuring thereon. They also nearly always possess sundry queer tumbledown outbuildings, some of which are approached by out-side steps, others apparently going into disuse and profitless, if picturesque, decay. Altogether the courtyard of an ancient hostel frequently forms a delightful sketching-ground, and is of interest to the antiquary as well as attractive to the artist. With the many tokens around, the history of an old-time hostel may frequently be read from its olden courtyard: the long range of stabling where erst the mail changes were kept; the postboys' room; the faded and weather-worn signboard that greeted our ancestors' eyes; the brew-house; the pack-house; the old coach office where the places on the coach were booked and the like, all have their story to tell, and to him who can read them they tell it as plainly—or plainer—than any printed page.

The front view of our inn was less interesting, but we were tempted into making a sketch of it, as we got a peep of the hills beyond in our drawing and also a quaintly-clipped yew tree that stood at one end of the building; this, we were told, was intended to represent a peacock. The fashion of trimming certain trees into the shapes of birds and animals (though mostly birds) we noticed prevails a good deal in Worcestershire, Herefordshire, and Shropshire.

Then finding our way to the river we wandered a short distance along its banks till we came to a spot where the translucent waters of the Teme foamed and tumbled over a weir into a quiet pool below: there were steep banks on the other side crowned with trees, and sheltering under these was a gray stone-built mill with its great wheel slowly revolving round and round. In a country where streams abound the picturesque windmill is seldom found, the water-mill takes its place, which though equally pleasing to the eye does not boldly proclaim itself from a height like the former, but has to be sought out in some unexpected hollow. The tranquil pool in front of us reflected the old mill and wooded banks beyond on its smooth surface, the musical murmuring of the weir delighted our ears, whilst the rustling of the trees in the summer wind soothed us with a sense of untold rest. The liquid melody of gliding and falling water, and the gentle, indescribable " sur, sur, sur," of wind-stirred foliage, are two of the most peace-bestowing sounds in nature. We wandered no farther, but simply sat there and dreamed the soft summer noon away, idly doing nothing; and for a busy man to successfully do nothing for a time is a blessed thing both for mind and body in an age when over much is attempted.

Long we rested in that delightfully cool and retired nook; we had an entrancing picture ready-made before us, but we were too lazy to sketch it. Even the subdued hum of the mill, mellowed by coming across the water, failed to rouse us from our reverie; it too seemed to take life and even labour in a leisurely fashion, as though there were no such thing as hurry in the world. We were rest-seeking pilgrims, and this quiet beauty-spot, enclosed by wooded hills from the intrusion of the outer world, suited well our listless mood. Then it suddenly occurred to us that the day was slipping by, and that unless we would be benighted on an unknown road it behoved us to be moving. So, reluctantly, we retraced our steps to our inn, and after paying our modest reckoning, ordered the horses to be put to, and once more proceeded on our way.

From all we saw of Knightsford during our brief

sojourn there, we imagined that the country around would well repay leisurely exploring, especially the lovely valley of the Teme, both up and down stream. The few houses that compose the village are neat and clean; and the wheelwright's cottage, with its open forge, together with the felled timber lying on the grassy margin of the road in front, presented to us a pretty picture. Roses, we noticed, were growing over the walls of the little church instead of the usual ivy; it is perhaps a matter of sentiment, but we prefer the ivy on the church wall from old association's sake; Gray's "ivy-clad tower" would surely have lost all its poetry had it been "rose-clad!"

We should have imagined that Knightsford was the favourite haunt of the fisherman, the surroundings seemed so suggestive of him; but no angler was visible there at the time of our visit, nor were there any signs at the homely inn of his past presence, as usually prevails at the hostelries he frequents, in the shape of odd rods and creels; stuffed fish of phenomenal size (always an incentive to the amateur, and an excellent advertisement to the inn); or angling pictures on the walls, or angling literature in the rooms. It appeared to us an angler's paradise, without the angler!

CHAPTER XIII

An old-fashioned garden—Amongst the hills—A steep bit of road—Storm and sunshine—Bromyard—Prosperous farmers—Twelve miles from Anywhere —Epitaph-hunting — Country life — Leominster — A quaint old home — A curious inscription—Nature's many moods.

LEAVING Knightsford we crossed the Teme by an ancient bridge that has taken the place of the still more ancient and inconvenient ford. Then we had a stiff climb up hill, to which succeeded a fairly level stretch of country made homelike by pretty cottages and frequent farmsteads, whose mellow-toned walls and lichen-encrusted roofs harmonised well with the soft tints of the landscape. One unpretentious home by the roadside—built in the picturesque half-timbered style that happily prevails in this part of England—attracted our attention on account of its tranquil garden of old-fashioned, sweet-scented, and colourful flowers ; the present system of bedding out garish greenhouse plants does not seem somehow half so productive of beauty. Possibly my judgment may be prejudiced by old association, for the flowers that our forefathers loved are to me like familiar friends, their names constantly greet one in story, legend, and poetry. To them belongs the magic glamour of the past, as well as that of inherent beauty; they have nothing in common with the delicately-nurtured and pampered products of the greenhouse — products that are too often valued according to their difficulty of rearing; whilst even the hardy gorse, or wild purple heather, growing untended and uncared for on the poorest soil, is oftentimes infinitely more lovely. Indeed anything more beautiful than the gorse or heather in full bloom I cannot conceive; there is a quality about the golden glory of the first and regal purple of the latter, when beheld in mass, that no hothouse flowers I have ever seen can at all approach. It is the beauty of common things and of our everyday surroundings that the present over-luxurious age fails to see to its great loss—unless an artist first reveal it. So we neglect our natural hardy flowers in spite of their rich colours and sweet perfumes, and grow, at vast trouble and great expense, less lovely exotics in our greenhouses. It is not always the most costly things that are the most to be admired; rarity need not mean beauty. Nature is more lovely than any artist's dream on canvas, for which the wealthy pay great prices, yet the glories of the sky above and the charms of the landscape below are free to all. Fortunately, unlike pictures, scenery cannot be bought and sold.

After a time our road began to mount again and in good earnest; up and up we went, leaving the tilled fields and green meadows far below, till we found ourselves traversing a wild, wind-swept upland, on which even the hardy thorn had a severe struggle to maintain its stunted existence; in truth, had it not been for stray patches of the "ever-blooming" gorse which showed like spots of sunshine here and there, the prospect would have been a gloomy one. Yellow suggests light, red colour, and blue shade; and these are the primary tints of the artist's palette practically if not in theory.

Resting for a while on our ascent we glanced back and had a grand view over a wooded country bounded by the western side of the Malvern Hills; it was to us an object lesson in the geography of our land; a certain portion of Great Britain lay spread out below us like a living map,—hill and plain, river and valley were there revealed with a reality and a meaning that no amount of rapid railway travelling could have made known. Were it only feasible for the latter-day schoolboy, what a pleasant way it would be of learning the history and geography of his country to drive through it, stopping at the most memorable places. Our driving tours have taught us a good deal more of English geography than we ever learnt at school.

Then as our ambitious road climbed still higher so our horizon rose and increased in extent, till we came to a point from which we looked down upon and over a vast expanse of rolling country bounded in the distance by a range of rugged moorlands. We were getting now amongst the hills, and we rejoiced in the fact. The bold bare outline of a mountain, or a bleak moorland range, rising from a wooded plain or valley, enhances the beauty of the soft sylvan scenery by the contrast of form and colour. But we had no time for loitering; not only was the day growing old, but dark threatening clouds were gathering around; they might mean mischief, or they might not, but an unsheltered upland is no place to be caught in a storm. Sudden gusts of wind came and went, big drops of rain were blown into our faces, so that we deemed it wise to don our waterproofs; the bulging clouds drove by apace overhead, the wind increased and howled eerily, everything pointed to our getting a thorough drenching; there was nothing for it but to brave the weather and make what haste we could. Fortunately, at the crest of the hill we were crossing was a cutting, and a few Scotch firs and other trees of the hardy mountain tribe grew there, and afforded some slight shelter; this, however, was very welcome, for just as we reached the spot the storm burst forth in all its fury, and I do not think I was ever out in a heavier downpour; it could hardly have rained harder at the Flood, we thought. The sides of the road were quickly converted into miniature torrents, and the outlook was decidedly dark, damp, and depressing.

Whilst stopping there in comparative shelter waiting upon events, a brewer's dray with four big burly horses appeared coming from the opposite direction; the driver also pulled up close to us for shelter. "Bad weather," exclaimed we, and he agreed with us, only he emphasised his opinion thereon by an expressive though unparliamentary foreword; "and a —— bad road too, it's like the side of a house; it's the worst hill in the county, and I don't think as how any other county 'as got a worser anyhow, it wants a lot of beating. I've been five hours getting over it in the winter time. They calls it Clater pitch. I was hung up here one frosty day and couldn't get on nohow: you should just try it in the winter time." We duly sympathised with him, but declined his invitation; we were quite satisfied with our present experience. Then we admired his sturdy horses and ventured an opinion that they were quite capable of taking him anywhere, even with his heavy load. "Yes," replied he, "I owns the horses is good 'uns, but it wants a traction engine, this 'ere hill do. I likes a flat country to drive in. Why, I've a friend at my business down in Essex and he never even needs to use a skid, think of that."—" Well," we remarked, " but consider what fine scenery you've got." Even this did not satisfy him. "Scenery!" he responded, "why, you don't surely thinks as how I drives about to see scenery?" This was rather hard on us, we felt, who did drive about to see scenery, but we kept the peace. Every man looks on the world from his point of view; the mere driver likes a level road; to the average Dutchman a mountain is simply a hindrance to the view, and a nuisance as causing an obstruction to travel.

Whilst we were chatting a sudden change came over the weather, the sky above grew light, and a gleam of warm sunshine more felt than observed at first followed, the rain fell less heavily, and the wind lulled. Soon afterwards the downpour ceased; the storm had made amends for its severity by being short, and our spirits once more rose to their accustomed height. Then we proceeded on our way and the brewer's dray did the same.

At the other side of the cutting we looked down upon a world of brightness; the storm-clouds had blown over, and before us the sun was setting in a glory of melting rubies and gold. It was like driving out of Hades into Paradise. Below us lay spread out a wide prospect of hill and dale with the little town of Bromyard set in the midst, the wet roofs of its clustering houses gleaming in the light; the ruts in the road were liquid gold, the moist herbage, the shrubs, and trees, all reflected the brightness above, and we even felt the glow of colour on ourselves. The sudden transition from a world of gray gloom to one of golden glory was an experience long to be remembered.

Driving down over a far-spreading common we came in time to Bromyard, where we drove up to the Hop Pole Inn, the landlady of which came forth to welcome us, and, observing our damp condition, set to work, as soon as we had reached our sitting-room, to make a large wood fire therein "to warm the good lady after her wet drive." It was a homely inn, with a homely landlady, and, thanks to her kind-hearted attentions and thoughtfulness, we soon forgot our temporary and trifling discomforts, indeed they served but to enhance our present ease, and made the crackling fire, that was soon all ablaze, seem the more cheerful still.

As she laid our evening meal the landlady provided us with unlimited gossip free of charge, and we were very glad to have it, for if she were garrulous she was given to look on the bright side of life, and on some matters her talk interested us. Asking her about the place, she said that Bromyard was twelve miles from any town, and that some one had suggested that she should paint on her hotel,

Stop Here
Twelve Miles from
Anywhere!

Times were very prosperous for the farmers round about; they had plenty of money to spend, and they spent it, and that was a good thing for the innkeepers. Where she had been staying some time before, the farmers were all badly off, and went home from the market without even calling for a glass of ale. It was quite a relief, as well as an unexpected pleasure, to hear of uncomplaining, not to say contented and money-making agriculturists. The last season, we learnt (though very bad indeed over the rest of England), had been a most propitious one there. All the crops were exceptionally heavy, those of hops alone being three times as large as was expected, and of prime quality. One farmer had told her that he cleared several times his year's rent by his hops alone. Then, perhaps thinking that we might scarcely credit such unusual prosperity without some confirmation of her statements, she went out and presently returned with the week's local paper, namely, *The Bromyard News* of 21st September 1893, and asked us kindly to read the following paragraph, which we did and copied as follows: "It has been estimated by an official who was supplied with the acreage under hops in the parishes comprised in the Bromyard Union (taking the average price per hundredweight at £6) that no less a sum than £165,000 will this season be received by the growers in this district." Taking into consideration that this related to one crop alone, and that all the other crops, especially that of hay, which was fetching high prices, were far above average, it did not seem wonderful that the farmers round about Bromyard were flourishing and "had nothing to complain of." To read such cheery news was a pleasant relief from the generally gloomy articles in the country papers, when they referred to agricultural affairs. Moreover, it came to us so unexpectedly, we had been so accustomed to hear of and read about the acute depression of the farming interest, that the reverse of the medal seemed almost unreal. I think that it was in the same paper we noticed an amusing printer's blunder by which he had very considerably forestalled old Father Time; writing of an inhabitant of the place the remark was made that "he only came here in the year 18900!" These local papers, other things failing, often afforded us amusement in the evenings; they gave us, too, an insight of the world from a local point of view and helped to show "how the town was served." On the whole, perhaps, the inevitable "Poet's Corner" was the most amusing; who ever reads these productions seriously, I wonder—except their composers?

Bromyard struck us as being a somewhat uninteresting little town; set in the heart of a very lovely country, it stands on high ground, so that from different points therein we obtained fine panoramic views over the richly-wooded and undulating country around, through which the narrow river Frome winds in and out gleaming in the sunshine like a streak of silver. On every hand the distance is bounded by finely-shaped hills that rise gracefully and gradually out of spreading woods, fruitful orchards, golden cornfields, hop-gardens, and rich green meadow lands. The landscape has an essentially English look of mellowness and contentment that comes alone of long human occupancy and the careful cultivation of centuries. There are few towns so happily placed in regard to surrounding scenery as Bromyard; this is truly not of a striking type, there is nothing wonderful about it, no special features for the guide-book compilers to rave about, it is simply, unpretendingly beautiful, the sort of scenery to live in and to love; its quiet charms appeal more to the true admirer of Nature than to the average tourist.

Wandering round about Bromyard we came in due course to the old church. Somehow in country towns all roads seem to lead naturally thither; the right of way to the ancient place of worship was always beyond dispute; along it the population of a place went to be baptized, to pray, to be married, and along it they took their last sad journey to rest in the churchyard's hallowed ground. God's acre at Bromyard has grown to two or more, and we searched amongst the numerous ancient and moss-begrown tombstones in the hope of coming upon some quaint or interesting epitaph, as it appeared a likely spot to find one; but our search was unrewarded. Father Time is slowly but surely destroying the old epigrams of a past age; dreary verses, ending with the inevitable moral, were plentiful, but such doleful reading is apt to be depressing, as the following example may show—

> Stranger, if thou canst read,
> Think on this line :
> The grave that's next opened
> It may be thine.

After this we gave up our hunt after epitaphs; we searched for wit and only discovered trite morals; we preferred to do our own moralising. So we turned our attention to the church, which possesses a massive Norman central tower with a stair turret embattled at the top, and two well-preserved Norman doorways with good and characteristic zigzag mouldings; one of these is on the north and the other on the south side of the edifice. The northern doorway is built up; over the southern one is a curious figure of St. Peter holding the keys, carved in stone,—the church being dedicated to that saint. The interior of the structure is uninteresting, and glories in a plaster ceiling, done doubtless in the era of whitewash, that dark age of ecclesiastical building and re-edifying.

Out of Bromyard our road at once began to mount as though it meant business, and continued its ambitious career for some miles. However, hilly roads generally afford fine views, and in such a lovely country we could forgive the steepness of the way for its scenic rewards.

At the first village we passed through, called Bredenbury, we noticed a stone by the roadside, which in the distance we innocently took to be one of those now rare articles a milestone; but it proved to be simply erected there to record the fact that that particular spot was 715 feet 3 inches above the sea level, for which valuable information we felt, I trust, duly grateful, though not being in a scientific mood just then I fear we should much have preferred to know how far it was to the next town. However, it is to be hoped that the rural population duly appreciate the fact of the elevated position in which they live! We were glad to find that whoever raised this stone was so particular as even to record the inches,—there is nothing like being exact in statements; but this was by no means the highest point of our road, which still kept climbing till we wondered when it would cease.

Then we reached what we took to be a small wayside hostelry, which had inscribed thereon—

New Inn
&
Coffee Tavern

———

Licensed to Sell
Ale, Wine, and Spirits.

———

Post Office and Grocery Stores.

A Coffee Tavern licensed to sell ale, wine, and spirits, with a Post Office and Grocery Store attached, struck us as a delightfully unique combination. Moreover, by the side of the inn was a butcher's shop with a notice above stating that it was open "every Friday." Housekeeping must be carried on with some difficulty in these parts, we thought. We had previously passed through a village where we learnt from a brass plate on a door that "Doctor Dash attends here every Wednesday"; we could only trust that the rural folk had the good sense to be taken ill on the right day! But the absence of a doctor for six days in the week did not appear to trouble the people, judging from what an old body said to us : " Lor, sir, we don't mind ; we don't bother the doctor much, we physics ourselves, it comes a good bit cheaper nor the doctor ; he's a luxury for the quality, but he's useful to draw teeth o' times. We dies from old age in these parts, not from doctors. What I says is this, there's t'old parson, he's only wanted once a week on Sundays, why don't they make parsons doctors too so that they might be of some use o' week days for those who likes being doctored?" This was quite a new idea to us, and after all we thought, on giving the matter consideration, there would be no harm if the clergy in remote and poor country districts did possess some slight knowledge of medicine. Would it be feasible, I wonder, to combine the cure of souls with the cure of bodies ?

Then at last our climbing came to a welcome end, and we had a long and glorious run down hill for some miles with the brake hard on nearly all the way into Leominster—or Lemster as it was written on the sign-posts and pronounced by the natives.

As we descended, we had grand views ahead

over a well-wooded country extending westward to the rugged Welsh mountains, and northward to the softer-featured Shropshire hills. It was a lovely sight to watch the gleams of sunshine and patches of cloud shadow following one another in ceaseless succession over the far-spreading landscape, whilst the play of light and shade caused the hills to assume ever-changing aspects; now they showed as a dark mass of purple-gray, then as the sunshine raked their rugged sides the mass of gray revealed an unexpected detail of crag and hollow, of rocky ravine and wooded slope. The darkest object in the panorama was the pine woods, whose deep and gloomy tints gave a value to the lighter greens of the fields and leafy woods.

Reaching Leominster we drove up to the first hotel we came to, which was plain to ugliness without, but exceedingly comfortable within, so that we felt inclined to pardon its unpromising exterior in virtue of the proverb "Beauty is as beauty does."

Leominster is a town that improves on acquaintance; it contains plenty of commonplace buildings, but it also contains some old houses of more than passing interest; these, however, require finding out, for they are hidden away in odd nooks and corners and so do not proclaim themselves to the public gaze. Rambling around the outskirts of the town we had a most delightful surprise; just as we were imagining that there was nothing architecturally noteworthy to be seen in the place we came upon one of the quaintest houses imaginable, more like an artist's invention than a veritable English home.

Yet there it stood, no dream, but a happy reality. I shall not readily forget the thrill of delight I had when the gray gables and ornamental half-timbered front of that old building first caught my eyes. It was another of the many "finds" of our journey.

We learnt that the house was called the Grange, and that it had a rather curious history, having formerly been the old market-hall of the town, which it had graced for over two centuries. But in 1853 the enlightened inhabitants of the place, having been bitten with an improving mania (which, alas! appears to come sooner or later to all corporations), sold the rare old building at auction for the large sum of £95, it being then one of the most beautiful and well preserved in the county, in order to make more room in the market-place. Fortunately, however, instead of being ruthlessly destroyed, the picturesque structure was purchased by an art-loving gentleman (to whom all archæologists and antiquaries owe a debt of gratitude), and by his orders the unique old building was carefully pulled down and as carefully reconstructed on a fresh site and converted into a charming and most uncommon home by the simple process of walling in the arched recesses below and making the enclosed space into rooms.

The building is supported on a series of substantial oak pillars, joined together on the top by graceful arches; from these pillars also spring a number of boldly-carved brackets that help to carry the projecting upper story of well-designed half-timber work; above all is a high-pitched roof with a bell-turret in the centre surmounted by a weather-vane. On the front of the house we observed the date 1633, plainly carved; and running along the big oak beam is the following inscription, a line between each pillar :—

> Like Collvmes doo vpprop
> the Fabrik of a Bvilding
> So noble Gentri doo Svpport
> the Honor of a Kingdom.

It struck us that in giving this the clever architect might have had an eye to please the "noble Gentri," with a view to further commissions, and as he designed so picturesquely and so well, let us hope that he got them.

Then continuing our rambles we eventually found ourselves in quite another part of the town called the Bargate. There we discovered some ancient Alms-houses, in a niche in the front of which stood a curious carved and painted figure of a man with a cocked hat upon his head and a real hatchet in his hand,—at least we presumed that it was originally intended to be so placed, but as a truthful chronicler I am fain to confess that at the time of our visit it was simply tied to his hand by some string; on a tablet below was inscribed this singular legend :—

> He that gives away all
> Before he is dead,
> Let 'em take this Hatchet
> And knock him on ye head.

On reading this it struck us that possibly there was some history or tradition attached to the figure, so we looked round for any likely person of whom to make inquiries, and observing a native leaning over his cottage gate close by indulging in an evening and non-fragrant pipe, we ventured to ask of him. "Ah!" exclaimed he, "that figure do puzzle strangers. It's like this 'ere, you see; the lady as built them Alms-houses spent all of her money on the building and endowing of 'em, and died in the workhouse herself, so I suppose they set up that figure as a warning to other folks not to do the same. It seems to me, though, as how folks nowadays don't want any warning of the kind. Leastways that's my idea," whereupon our informant smiled sagaciously, manifestly deeming that he had made a witty remark; and he recommenced puffing at his pipe in peaceful satisfaction, and we returned to our inn well pleased with our little tour of discovery.

We left Leominster on a warm morning of low-lying mists, so that at first our views of the country around were circumscribed, but soon after our departure the mists dispersed and the day turned out all that we could desire. We had a good level road to start with that led us through a pretty and treeful country. Through the rising mists we could just catch a glimpse of gently-sloping wooded hills to our left, picturesquely indistinct. The hazy atmospheric conditions lent that charm of mystery to the landscape which gave room for the imagination to play. The country we passed through was pleasing but uneventful; here and there on either side of the way the gray gables of ancient farmsteads and stone-built barns peeped out from amongst the trees. All things had a mellow, dreamy look, half revealed as they were, that gave us a most poetic vision of the country-side. Nature that morning was in a suggestive mood, as though in league with the impressionist school of painters. After all, Nature seldom wears one aspect long, so artists represent her in that mood which appeals to them the most.

There are no progressive manufacturing towns in or near this corner of England, so the air is sweet and pure, and the landscape bears that restful old-time look that is so peace-bestowing to the jaded mind. Age has beautified the homes of man therein from the mansion to the cottage, it has tinted their walls with many hues, has decorated their roofs with green and gray and gold of moss and lichen: how differently age treats the buildings of our large towns, which simply become smoke-stained into a dirty sort of brown. That day, however, we were far from any smoky city, and we drove on through the fresh beautiful country in quiet contentment, rejoicing in the spreading loveliness around.

Presently we passed on our left a fine park of considerable extent dotted with big elms and stalwart oaks, which cast great circles of shadow around them; the beauty of the ancient trees and the sunlit stretches of green sward was emphasised by the ugliness of the mansion that was visible from the roadway. Ugliness, however, may serve a purpose in enhancing beauty—when beauty exists in proximity. Even artists have found out the value of the commonplace by way of contrast. Too much sweetness is apt to cloy.

As we proceeded slowly on, for it was no country to hurry through, our attention was attracted by a quaintly pretty cottage built of rough unhewn timber; this showed us how easily and cheaply picturesqueness may come; it is generally more effective too when it comes naturally thus and is not too much sought after.

CHAPTER XIV

The Teme valley—A romantic town—A quaint old hostelry—Round about Ludlow—The Whitcliff—Ludlow Castle—We come upon a character—A round chapel—" Buried history "—Old proverbs —A huge fireplace—Ludlow church—An ancient dole—Tales in carving—A pleasant land.

As we drove on our road dropped down into, and led us up the well-watered Teme valley,—surely one of the most lovely in the land,—and whilst we were admiring its many charms of sunlit hill and shady dale, of shaggy wood and sparkling silvery stream, straight ahead of us suddenly came into view the ancient and romantically situated town of Ludlow clustering around an isolated hill, with its gray-towered church and ruined castle keep dominating the top.

So romantic did the town appear from our standpoint that we felt quite prepared to be disappointed with it on arriving there, remembering the poet's warning that "'tis distance lends enchantment to the view." But happily there was no disappointment in store for us in Ludlow; the real, for once again, came up to our ideal. The old town simply delighted us; it is one of those charmingly unprogressive places that seem to be imbued with the repose of centuries, — a town of many-gabled, irregular-roofed houses and architectural tit-bits that any antiquary would revel in and every true artist love to paint.

We entered Ludlow by the ancient Ludford bridge, which crosses the Teme at a most picturesque point. Looking up stream, the river flows and falls through a romantic rocky ravine; looking down, it ripples over stony shallows and glides over stilly deeps to a spot where it tumbles and foams over a broad weir with much musical murmuring, a sound delightful to listen to with its indescribable liquid melody; so both ear and eye were pleased. Here the right bank of the river is overhung with trees, through the thick foliage of which may be seen peering the high-pitched gables of some charmingly picturesque old half-timbered houses that form a part of the little hamlet of Ludford. On the doorway of one of these old houses we noted as we passed by the date of 1614, and a more delightful-looking abode we had not come upon during the whole of the journey. Farther still down stream stands an oddly-built weather-stained old mill of stone and timber backed by shady woods; this mill, with the quiet stretch of stream above, the rushing river below, and the splash and sparkle of the tumbling weir, makes an ideal subject for the painter's brush.

Ludford bridge in itself is an interesting structure, and forms a pleasing object in the riverscape. It is manifestly of ancient date, is massively built, and bears signs, we imagined, of Norman workmanship. On either side of the roadway over the piers are great recessed spaces in which foot-passengers may stand well out of harm's way from passing wheel traffic, and, if so minded, can admire the view at their peaceful leisure and in safety. Like the bridge at Bradford-on-Avon this one of Ludford had a mass chapel erected thereon, but an unromantic age had it improved away. Leland writes of it thus : "There be three fayre arches in this bridge over Teme, and a praty chapel upon it of St. Catherine. . . . Men passed aforetime by a ford a little below the bridge." When the river was in flood, we should imagine, from its present appearance, that the ford must have been a dangerous one. The nearest approach we have ever had to a disaster during our numberless driving tours was when crossing a ford in Wales at a time when the river was swollen with heavy rains, a thing that we ought not to have attempted possibly, but we were eager to get on our way, and it is tedious work waiting upon the pleasure of a river to subside.

Having crossed the Teme we entered Ludlow by a hilly street, in the centre of which we passed under the Broad Gate, which spans the roadway with one deep arch and marks the site of the ancient town wall; thereupon we found ourselves in the crowded market-place lined with curious old houses and alive with picturesquely-clad country folk, for it chanced to be market day. The crowd, for some undiscoverable cause, chose the roadway instead of the foot-pavement to walk upon, or loiter about in groups, so that our progress was somewhat slow. At last, however, we reached the ancient Feathers Inn, erected in 1603, a rare old three-gabled building of richly-carved ornamental timber-work, one of the finest structures of its kind in the kingdom. Not every day does the modern pilgrim come upon such a wonderful old inn. There are, however, I rejoice to say, still a few such charming hostelries left to us in the land,—all the rest I know are far from the railway,—but perhaps, for sundry reasons, it would be wiser not to catalogue them or give their precise whereabouts, the best way to discover them is by driving about country.

Within, the "Feathers" is almost as picturesque as without, to a certain extent even more so. It possesses two fine panelled oak chambers, one of which forms the coffee-room,—and I make bold to say that it is the most charming coffee-room in all England; this is panelled from floor to ceiling and has a wonderful chimney-piece of oak upon which the royal arms are carved in bold relief with the letters I.R., possibly intended for Jacobus Rex. The ceiling is adorned with enriched plaster work, and has also the royal arms modelled in the centre; altogether this chamber, with its ample bay window of lozenge-shaped leaden lattice panes, is the most charming one imaginable and entirely delightful. The adjoining room is also panelled in oak, and around the top of this runs a quaintly effective frieze of carved dolphins, a scheme of decoration worthy of the attention of modern architects when designing new houses on old lines. There is a certain warm look of cosiness and solid comfort about a panelled room that no papered walls can ever give, however artistic the pattern of the paper may be, or however costly.

As it was only mid-day, after a light lunch we hurried off with sketch-book and camera to explore the town and its immediate surroundings. We hardly knew which way to turn; look in what direction we would, some quaint bit of old-time architecture, an odd gable, a carved doorway, an ancient hostelry, a pargetted house-front beckoned us first here, then there, so we trusted to fate, and fate eventually led our footsteps towards the castle. But we determined to reserve a detailed inspection of this and the grand old church near by till the morrow morning; for the present we felt more inclined for rambling out of doors. The most notable things in a place always keep; they proclaim themselves, too; it is the picturesque "bits" hidden away here and there, which you come upon ever and again unexpectedly, that we always make a point of searching after; things that never get mentioned in the guide-book except by the rarest chance; things that you must discover for yourself, for, as you do not even know of their existence, you cannot ask your way to them.

So, skirting the castle walls instead of going within them, we made our way along the top of the wooded height on which the ruined feudal stronghold stands, and glorious peeps of the distant country we had looking down through the trees; then we descended by a winding path to the Dinham bridge, which crosses the Teme about half a mile higher up than the one we entered the town by. Having reached

LUDLOW CASTLE.

the opposite side of the river we turned first to the right, and, strolling on, were struck by the charming views of the castle we had from different points. From one of these we made a sketch, which is engraved and given herewith. This is only one of the many views of Ludlow Castle that were presented to us, each fresh view seeming more effective than the last. Not only was the general outline of the prospect pleasing, but the colour also; the solemn gray mass of the castle walls, the many tints of the trees below just touched with their autumn glory, the fresh green of the grassy slopes, the warm and cool contrasting colours of the rocks, the silvery gleam and sparkle of the river in the light and its deep rich tones in shade, the warm reddish hues and creamy whites of the cattle lazily cooling themselves in the water heedless of the beauty of the scene or of their own effectiveness therein,—all went to compose a most charming picture, and one that will long dwell pleasantly in our memory. There is a certain advantage about sketching a scene; the very fact of so doing impresses it more or less upon the mind, so that its chief features are not afterwards readily forgotten.

Then we strolled along under the Whitcliff, a steep wall of craggy limestone that rises above the river in a most romantic fashion; from the summit of this, to which we climbed by a rough rocky path, fine views open out of the country around, and the town with the river stretching far away is well seen. This Whitcliff is an extensive tract of open common, and belongs to the citizens of Ludlow;

rugged, wild, and picturesque, it forms delightful wanderings; here Nature is unspoilt, and this public recreation ground left to her care costs nothing to maintain. Beauty and economy, for once, are happily and successfully combined.

Then we descended from our elevated position by another rocky path to Ludford bridge, and re-entered the town on foot by the same way we had driven in, halting first a long time at and about Ludford to make some sketches. Then in the town we sought out a photographer's shop, and so discovered by the eye of the camera what a wealth of picturesque old buildings there is in the vicinity of Ludlow, and scenery that better deserves to be called romantic than some which is much more thought of and written about. I think that in all England there is not another place that would so well repay the amateur photographer to visit as Ludlow; for it is just in the representation of old and beautiful buildings that photography nearest approaches to picture-making; in such subjects we do not so much feel the loss of colour, and can best excuse the superabundance of detail, which latter, in a pure landscape, simply distracts the eye.

We were up next morning early, and started off to see the castle. This grand pile of time-rent, storm-stained, ivy-grown ruins, as beheld from the courtyard, with the grim, tall, square Norman keep rising over all, its base deep down in the now dry moat, is both impressive and picturesque, two things that do not always go together. With the possible exception of Raglan, I consider that the ruins of

Ludlow Castle are the most picturesque in England. The drawbridge has been replaced by one of stone, which itself is ancient now, crumbling and ivy-covered. Ludlow Castle has arrived at that precise state of decay—sufficiently but not too ruinous—as to be beautiful and poetically suggestive of the romantic side of the undesirable days of old. Its sternness is a thing of the past, the harsher features of the ancient feudal stronghold are all toned down by age, its jagged and broken walls are gently touched by soft mosses and enlivened by silvery lichen, where not half hidden by green growing and trailing ivy, that ruin-loving and decorating creeper. Only the massive Norman keep looks at all frowning now.

> There is given,
> Unto things of earth which Time hath bent,
> A spirit's feeling ; and where he hath leant
> His hand, but broke his scythe, there is a power
> And magic in the ruined battlement,
> For which the palace of the present hour
> Must yield its pomp, and wait till ages are its dower.

Passing under the heavy arches of the hoary gateway, which bears the crumbling coats of arms of Queen Elizabeth and Sir Henry Sidney carved in stone above, we entered the inner court of the castle and found ourselves on a grass-grown space with stately buildings all around. Here we were charged a small fee, upon payment of which we were made free of the building, and graciously permitted to wander about where we would and at our leisure. "You don't require a guide," said the custodian, "there's printed particulars hung up in each room of the castle as tells you all about everything. You can go where you likes, and stay as long as you likes; only please be careful as how you don't climb on the tops of the walls, for they's dangerous in places, and you might tumble down and get killed, and that might be awkward for me." We could not help thinking that it might be a good deal more awkward for us, but we kept our thoughts to ourselves.

After all, however, the fates decreed that we should not wander about altogether guideless. An old talkative gentleman—whom we at once put down to be an antiquary, and rightly so as it afterwards proved—came up to us and pointed out the round Norman chapel that stands in the centre of the court. We could see it quite well, for there it stood straight before us; but the old party seemed such a genial enthusiast that we had not the heart to repress him. He thereupon attached himself to us during our explorations, and proved to be a most interesting companion. This curious round chapel is now roofless, windowless, the pavement has disappeared, and the doors are gone; it is a mere shell, but the two round-headed stone doorways remain with their fine mouldings fairly well preserved. Here our newly-made antiquarian friend pointed out to us an ancient and broken tombstone, which, unless he had called our attention to it, we should certainly not have seen; this had a cross rudely sculptured on the top, and at the foot of the cross was the representation of a battle-axe or hatchet. The interior walls of the chapel are arcaded in stone, the en-

closed panels being of old filled, we were informed,
with painted coats of arms of the various Lords of
the Marches of Wales; then followed a long history
of these warlike individuals, which I do not remember. But it seems that these Lords did pretty
much as they liked, and ruled supreme in these parts,
even to the appointing of their own sheriffs, for the
King's writ did not run in the Marches; in return
for which privileges and independent jurisdiction they
were expected to keep the lawless Welshmen at bay,
and were allowed to steal as much territory from
them as they could,—indeed they formed a small
kingdom within a kingdom.

Then taking a place in the centre of the round
chapel our antiquarian friend suddenly gave two or
three jumps (for the moment we thought that he must
be mad), then after more jumps he exclaimed in a subdued and impressive tone of voice, "Listen! Do
you hear how hollow it sounds?" We duly noticed
the fact. "I believe that there's a crypt or vaults
below, otherwise there would not be that sound."
Then continued he in a most solemn manner, "Who
knows what rare relics of the past might be discovered if the ground were only opened! I have
long wished to open it, but have not been allowed.
There's buried history there; mark my word.
Buried history. Tombs have tales to tell." Then
he became meditatively silent, which was more
expressive to us of his feelings than even words.
Our friend began greatly to interest us; we had
manifestly come upon a genuine character, and as
it appeared to afford him considerable pleasure

to act as an amateur guide and to relate some of his antiquarian lore for our especial benefit, why, we made him happy, and provided entertainment and information for ourselves free of tips.

Then we wandered into some chambers, from which a spiral stone staircase at the side led to some sleeping-rooms above. On the walls of the former we copied the following printed and framed information, thoughtfully placed there for the benefit of visitors. This struck us as a decided improvement on the usual loquacious guide or tiresome handbook, for at any rate there was no doubt as to the exact room to which the information related. When chambers much resemble one another it is not always easy to discover this from guide-books, which are frequently provokingly indefinite, and you may romance in the wrong spot, or rejoice where you ought to sympathise. This, then, is what we copied: "Apartments occupied by the two princes, sons of Edward IV. By order of their wicked uncle Richard they were taken to the Tower of London and cruelly murdered there."

Next we inspected the Watch and Beacon tower, which rises grandly from the rocky crags below. The very title of the tower suggests the "stormy days of old," and we tried to picture to ourselves the medieval watchman on the lonely summit keeping his outlook over the vast tract of country that stretches away far below on all sides. On the wall of this commanding tower is hung the following little history in connection therewith: " From a window here the grap-line was thrown which forced the Royal Prince of Scotland from his saddle. King Stephen fled to his rescue, cut the rope with his sword, and disentangled his royal youthful hostage."

Then we came to the great hall, or Council Chamber, where our friend pointed out with glee "the very original oak shutters to the windows" that still stand *in situ*. Here in this now roofless hall the Court of the Marches was held, and here also Milton's *Mask of Comus* was first performed in 1634 before an appreciative audience of nobles. Adjoining this is the chamber in which Prince Arthur of Wales, son of Henry VII., died.

The state apartments next attracted our attention. "In these," said our friend, "kings and queens were entertained." On the walls here we noticed the remains of two fine stone hooded fireplaces; why will not modern architects sometimes give us these instead of the usual monotonous mantelpieces? Above where we stood we noticed also some stone corbels, carved to represent women's heads, treated in a decorative way; these corbels evidently of old supported the main timbers of the roof, but that was in an age when the construction of a building was shown, gloried in, and then decorated. The thin, cheap rafters of the present-day speculative builder would hardly stand this mode of treatment; plaster and putty "cover a multitude of sins" in the way of scamped work, so at least a man, who had made his fortune by running up rows of desirable houses to sell, once confessed to me in a confidential mood. Certainly the old proverb, "Fools build houses for wise men to live in," in no way applied to him, or most of his tribe. I am afraid that this and sundry other old proverbs will have to be altered to suit modern developments.

But to return to ourselves. From the state apartments we found our way to the ample kitchen; this, with its huge fireplace fifteen feet wide, suggested feudal feasting; here our antiquarian friend pointed out a mighty oven, in which, he informed us all, the bread for the necessarily large garrison was baked, as much as eight sacks of flour being used every day; manifestly he had made this old castle his special study. The floor of this kitchen still retains its original stone slab pavement. We next, in passing, glanced at the well close by; this is three yards wide, and was originally over one hundred and twenty-five feet deep, but it is now more than half filled up with rubbish, it having at one period suffered the indignity of being converted into a convenient sort of dust-bin.

Then we mounted to the top of the old Norman keep up innumerable stairs. On reaching the summit we felt that our toilsome ascent was more than rewarded by the truly magnificent all round and unimpeded view that was revealed to us, a prospect extending over a vast expanse of well-wooded country, enlivened in the west by the silvery Teme and in the north by the winding Onny. Again we had to confess to ourselves our limited knowledge of the geography of our own land, the name of the latter lovely little river being unknown to us till we came across it on this tour. At the foot of the keep are some damp and dismal dungeons that suggest the unromantic side of the days of chivalry, a stern medieval reality that takes away a good deal from the glamour and the poetry of the past. On the whole, I rejoice that I live in the prosaic present; I prefer my romance in the printed pages of Sir Walter Scott and other old-world dreamers. Nothing earlier than the coaching days would, I fear, have suited me, and perhaps even they would not have been so pleasant as I fondly imagine.

Leaving the Castle Palace of Ludlow, as it was called in the ancient days of its glory, we discovered, by accident, that there is a very fine echo from the entrance gateway, as from that spot, when we shouted "good-bye" to our antiquarian friend, the outbuildings around twice repeated our farewell.

We now bent our steps towards the grand old church. The exterior of this is much weather-worn; and its lofty tower, that rises boldly from the centre of the building, shows signs of age in the crumbling of its delicately-carved stone adornments, but not of weakness; it is truly storm-stained and weathered, but looks strong and substantial enough to still outlive unborn generations of worshippers. The sculpturing of countless winter storms has only given an added history and interest to the handiwork of man. Time has chipped off a corner here and there from the square old tower, has rounded hard angles, has crumbled some of the softer stone away, has tinted it with the green of moss and gray and gold of lichen, and given, in fine, to the art of the past the priceless bloom of age.

Entering by the south porch we found the clerk's wife within, and on seeing us look round she at once volunteered her services as guide, and forthwith took us in hand and bade us follow her,—and we meekly followed. First she conducted us to "Prince Arthur's tomb," but as this had no inscription upon it, it might have belonged to any one. Tradition, on what ground I know not, has, however, assigned it to him, and in all such cases my experience is that the onus of proof lies not upon the guide, but upon the stranger who dares to query any old-established tradition. On the top of this tomb is a flat stone slab whereon an effigy might have been, but at the time of our visit there was nothing there but a goodly quantity of bread crumbs, that appeared to us strangely out of place. Observing that we noticed these our guide said, "That's the remains of last Sunday's dole. I dare say as you may be strangers in these parts, and so don't know about it. It's like this, every Sunday after morning service, twelve and a half pecks of bread is given away to twelve poor widows. The bread is placed on Prince Arthur's tomb, him as died in our castle." We noted the expression "*our* castle," as showing a kind of feeling of personal pride in the place which pleased us. "His body is buried here, but his heart is buried at Worcester." Then she began a long account of the history of this Prince, which, however, we diplomatically managed "to nip in the bud" by forestalling the inevitable tip, and calling attention to a fresh body of strangers who had just entered the church, whereupon she asked if we would excuse her for a minute,—we did! and, as she conducted the new arrivals to the Prince's tomb, quietly slipped away and inspected the church by ourselves, carefully avoiding, as far as possible, the personally-conducted party.

As we walked towards the chancel we noticed. on our way the high lantern tower, and stopped a while to admire the finely-carved and massive oak rood screen. Then, without any special order as to what to inspect, we proceeded to view the glorious east window, which contains much well-preserved fifteenth-century stained glass, and is a marvel of translucent loveliness. There is a rare gem-like quality about the glass of this fine old window that fascinated us. There are few things more beautifully striking than to behold the sun shining through a window of good old stained glass, making it glow like molten jewels — a very miracle of glorified colours. This lovely east window of Ludlow church illustrates the legendary life, the miracles, and the martyrdom on the gridiron of St. Lawrence, the patron saint of the place.

Then we inspected the fifteenth-century stalls in the wide choir, which indicate that the church was collegiate; some of the miserere seats belonging to these are finely carved,—a few unfortunately are much mutilated,—many of the carvings are grotesque, and all are interesting. These seats lift up so that the aged and feeble ecclesiastics might lean upon them, whilst seeming to stand, during the long services of the church. A number of the carvings have a story to tell, though one not always easy of interpretation. The medieval carver was a man of humour, he loved to have his joke in stone or wood, even apparently sometimes at the expense of the church, as in one instance here where we noticed a mitred bishop represented with the head of a fox, and a cunning fox, too, preaching from a pulpit to a congregation of geese!—a startling satire on the priesthood of the period told in wood by one of themselves. On a previous journey we discovered at far-off St. David's Cathedral a somewhat similar carving on a miserere seat there.

Perhaps the finest carving of all amongst the Ludlow seats is one of a mermaid with a glass in her hand and a fish on either side of her. This is a work of art; it is purely ornamental and has no tale to tell. Another ornamental one represents that fabulous animal the cockatrice, which, however, the clever medieval craftsman has made to look as though it might have being. Another seat is adorned (?) by an ugly cross-eyed woman wearing a wonderful horned head-dress; on either hand of her are two grinning boys holding up a glass for the woman to see herself in,—it appeared to us that this was intended for a skit on the prevailing fashion of the period. Another represents a beer barrel with two men kneeling down before it, possibly meant for the worship of Bacchus. Still another shows a woman being carried off by the Devil and being thrust into hell; another demon reading a list of her wrongdoings. These are only brief outlines of a few of these curious carvings; many of the rest are too complicated, and their meanings too obscure, to be described without the aid of illustrations, and more space than I can afford. The miserere seats at Ludlow are well worth seeing, for those interested in such things; a few of them will repay careful study, without which they will not readily reveal their hidden meaning. On examining some of the more detailed ones, which I have not ventured to describe, I quite felt that they had a deep purport, but time is required to unravel these enigmas in wood.

In the church we observed some interesting altar-tombs with effigies thereon showing the details of the dress of lord and lady, knight and dame, as worn in the long ago. One of these tombs to Edmund Walter, dated 1592, "Chieffe Justice of three shiers in Wales, and a Councill of the Marches of Wales," is surrounded by the original wrought-iron railing, having quaint-looking and perfect pennons of iron at the corners, in which the initials E. W. are shown in open work.

Close to the church, and facing it across the churchyard, is a most picturesque building, partly of hewn stone and partly of carved oak and plaster; this was of old the official residence of the Reader, and is still called the "Reader's House." On the front of it is inscribed—

A.D. 1616.   Thomas Kaye

and a charming bit of old-time building it is.

The churchyard itself is on a high terrace, which is supported by a portion of the old town walls; from this elevated spot there is a glorious view looking towards the north; standing there our eyes wandered over a goodly portion of the pleasant land of Shropshire, rich in sylvan beauty, our prospect being bounded in the far distance by the broken outline of faint-blue hills. Long we lingered there enjoying the tranquil loveliness of the scene, till at last hunger got the best of our poetical, dreamy mood, and we returned to our inn.

CHAPTER XV

Bromfield Priory Gateway—Craven Arms—A flourishing village—Stokesay Castle—Relics of a forgotten fight—A medieval hall—A fortified manor-house—Corve Dale—A quiet corner of England—A curious church tower—Munslow—A picturesque church—A ghastly tomb—A seller of tracts.

FINDING that there was a good inn on the road some eight miles from Ludlow and only half a mile from Stokesay Castle, to which place we proposed to proceed next, we determined to drive there in the cool of the afternoon, for the day was hot. And a most delightful drive we had. We started just when the shadows were beginning to lengthen, and the low golden lights were spreading over woodland, meadow, and hill, making the beautiful Onny valley look its loveliest.

For the first mile or so oak trees lined our way, forming quite a shady avenue; then we reached the small and pretty wood-embowered village of Bromfield, consisting chiefly of picturesque, half-timbered and thatch-roofed cottages. Here we noticed by the roadside a quaint bit of old-world architecture, which, we were informed, was Bromfield Priory Gateway. This consists of a timber structure of black and white, supported upon a lower story of massive masonry that has a wide archway in the centre; on either side of the archway are big buttresses. Truly those old builders were very generous of their material; solid and strong, seems to have been their motto; look at the thickness of the walls they raised and the substance of the timbers they used.

Near to Bromfield we came across an old, chipped, crumbled, and moss-encrusted milestone, the lettering upon it almost undecipherable, but we could just manage to trace the words "To Ludlow Cross" thereon. How old was that milestone, we wondered, and how long ago was it since Ludlow Cross stood in Ludlow and the distances were reckoned to it? Had we, in the year of grace 1893, asked the way to Ludlow Cross, I fancy people would have looked at us with wonderment.

Then as we journeyed on, admiring the lovely, leafy landscape with its background of far-stretching fir-clad hills, half lost in a delicious day-dream, suddenly to our left we espied the weather-beaten walls and gray towers of Stokesay Castle bathed in the warm light of the setting sun, and standing out sharply defined against the shadowed hills beyond. It was a scene to delight the heart of a poet or painter; a romance in stone, a picture rather than a place. Stokesay Castle is one of those perfectly beautiful spots that seem almost unreal because so beautiful. Moreover, it is set in the heart of a lovely country, and the setting is worthy of the gem. Stokesay Castle is situated only a short distance from the highway, but as the gloaming was coming quickly on, we reluctantly decided to make for our hotel, and devote the next morning to a leisurely inspection of the place.

A few minutes' more driving brought us to the Craven Arms, a comfortable inn (which that night we chanced to have all to ourselves); in the coaching days it was a famous house, we were told, being the only one in the locality; now, however, there is quite a large modern village gathered around, and curiously enough the name of the hotel has been given to the village. Craven Arms is becoming quite a little town, and the collection of houses is no improvement to the scenery. The railway has made the place; for there is a busy junction close at hand, and the roar and rush of the expresses, the whistling and shunting of the goods trains, have quite robbed the lovely and erst secluded valley of all its ancient tranquillity, besides some of its beauty. Opposite the hotel stands a tall stone obelisk with the names and distances of thirty-six towns inscribed thereon, a relic of the old road-travelling days. Does any one ever consult it now, I wonder?

Early next morning we set out on foot to see Stokesay Castle, not neglecting to take our camera and sketch-book with us. The footpath that leads to the castle from the high road goes through the churchyard, from whence there is a good general view of the building, embracing its timber and plaster gateway, its massive keep, the gables of its great hall, and its curious Priest's Tower with a projecting top story of timber. We made a drawing of this view, which is reproduced in the illustration herewith. The quaint and unique Priest's Tower is also shown separately in the frontispiece, as we deemed this interesting bit of building worthy of a special sketch. But no reproduction in black and white can, of course, give the charm of the mellow time-tinting of its rugged walls, painted as they are every imaginable hue by the winter storms and summer suns of six hundred years. At least, we had it on good authority that the stone-work of this tower dates from 1291, the more modern gate house itself boasting of the very respectable antiquity of four centuries.

To call Stokesay a castle appears to me somewhat of a misnomer, for it seems to have been more of a fortified manor-house than a castle proper; a house prepared to resist a sudden attack, not a regular stronghold. Indeed the large Early English windows of the hall that overlook the moat bespeak a peaceful abode, and hardly one intended for warlike purposes, or to resist a siege.

To reach the gatehouse we crossed the now dry moat by a wooden structure that has taken the place of the drawbridge. On approaching it we noticed that the massive oak timbers of which the house was constructed were richly carved in places; over the doorway are the figures of Adam and Eve shown with the forbidden fruit tree and the serpent. The big brackets, too, that support the slightly-projecting upper story are boldly carved with grotesque figures.

Passing through the gateway we reached a grass-grown inner court, whereupon an old woman

STOKESAY CASTLE.

presented herself to us as the guide, and a very good show-woman she proved to be, not given to much talking, but answering all the questions we put to her plainly and to the point, which, according to my experience, few guides do—or perhaps can. Crossing the courtyard we entered the great baronial hall by a heavy and very thick oak door studded all over with big-headed iron nails; here our guide pointed out six or seven bullets that were embedded in the oak, the relics, doubtless, of some forgotten fight.

Entering the hall the first thing that attracted us was its magnificent and well-preserved roof of open timber-work; the massive arched beams that uphold this, spring from stone corbels on either side of the grand apartment. At the top the beams are blackened with smoke, for in old days the fire was made in the centre of the hall, a brazier or andirons being used; and, according to the primitive fashion of the period, the smoke had to find its way out as best it could, no special aperture being provided for it. The hall is lighted by a series of Gothic windows, some looking over the moat and some over the courtyard.

From the hall we descended by a flight of stone steps into a cool and gloomy chamber lighted with narrow loop-holes or arrow-slits; this our guide called the buttery, and in the floor of it she pointed out a well, which was made square and not rounded as usual; it was also provided with stone ledges to descend by. The walls around were originally covered—I had nearly written decorated, but I am not sure if that is the right term—with rude-painted representations of animals; these, though much faded and otherwise damaged, can still be traced in parts. We made out what we presume to be intended for a bull, also a deer, besides many birds of a nondescript kind.

We now retraced our steps to the hall, and, ascending the original staircase that occupies one end of it,—the steps of which are formed of solid blocks of oak,—we reached an apartment called the Priest's Chamber. The floor here is interesting, being paved with ancient tiles of various devices. On one we noticed a man with a bow and arrow, on another the Prince of Wales' feathers (or what we took to be such), besides a number of quaint heraldic designs, ornamental patterns, and animals decoratively treated; some of the animals, by the way, appeared to us to be of a new species, and certainly unknown to Natural History. The medieval artist, however, was not above inventing new animals upon an emergency; we noted and copied on some gargoyles elsewhere very curious creations of his in this respect.

Ascending more stairs we came to a large apartment of irregular form situated above the Priest's Chamber; this appears originally to have been divided into three or more rooms; it is constructed of timber and plaster, and a portion of it projects on a number of wooden brackets over the stone tower below. The reason of this quaint and exceedingly picturesque arrangement is somewhat puzzling. It appeared to us that it must have been an after addition, and built for light and cheerfulness, and to gain space at a time when defence was not so imperative, and comfort more considered. It is certainly the best-lighted apartment in the castle, and the comparatively large windows with the pleasant and wide view they afford, give it a more livable look than any of the rest. There certainly is no medieval gloom about it. Opening one of the ancient casement windows of diamond-shaped leaded lights, we looked down upon a smiling sunlit landscape; the ever-fresh life of the immutable country struck a strong note of contrast with the decaying castle, so did the modern railway that runs now close beneath its rugged walls. Anything more picturesquely peaceful than this relic of the warlike past I cannot imagine. Within its undefended time-rent walls the harmless daisy grows, and the artist paints in a tranquillity undisturbed—except by the songs of birds, or the tread of some infrequent stranger, for Stokesay is no regular show place, and so the tripper cometh not to it. Whilst we were there we saw not a soul but our guide the whole day long, and a farmer's boy in a field close by.

In this quaint upper chamber are preserved a rusty cannon ball, of about 6 inches in diameter, that was found in the moat, a few coins, and fragments of china, also a curiously-shaped stone of about 5 inches long and $2\frac{1}{2}$ inches wide by guess measurement, with a hole bored through the centre, and seven holes round the outside leading to the centre one. Its use is by no means easy to make out. Our guide suggested that it might have been the head of a hammer, but this hardly appears probable, as the transverse holes would be needless for such a purpose. We imagined that it might be some sort of a charm, or possibly a portable dial, the central hole being intended to receive the gnomon.

We next descended to the hall again, and, regaining the courtyard, ascended a staircase now open to the weather, but probably of old covered in, to the withdrawing-room, a fine apartment panelled from floor to ceiling, and possessing an elaborately carved chimney-piece of oak resting on a massive stone arch.

Then we proceeded to the South Tower or keep; the form of this is peculiar, and, I imagine, unique, being in fact two octagonal towers joined together, which gives, of course, considerably more wall and window space than a simple round or square tower would. This marked departure from the usual mode of castle-building is interesting; doubtless the designer had good reasons for what he did, but it is not easy to discover them now. The arrangement certainly gives the tower, as seen from the south-west, a most picturesque appearance; but I very much doubt whether the element of picturesqueness ever in the remotest degree entered into the designer's head; rather, I fancy, was he striving for strength, and possibly deemed that the irregular wall space would give more opportunities for defence, by increasing the number of loop-holes for the archers of the garrison. This tower is embattled on the top, and has a staircase built in the thickness of the walls that leads from one story to another, and to the roof above. The apartments here are not over-cheerful, as may be imagined; their narrow windows, deeply recessed, open obliquely from the interior, doubtless to prevent, as far as possible, the entrance of arrows or other missiles that might be shot from without. From the top of this tower fine views of the country around are to be had, and if the medieval sentinel were an admirer of scenery, his eyes should have been gratified.

Stokesay Castle does not seem to have had a very eventful history, much possibly to the quiet enjoyment of their fortified home by its owners. Of it, as well as of a kingdom, it may well be said, "Happy is the castle that has no history."

Stokesay Castle does not appear to have ever possessed a chapel, as nearly every building of like character did at the time. This exception to the prevailing rule may possibly be accounted for by the proximity of the church, a plain Norman structure, whose chief interest appeared, to us, to lie in its history. However, even romantic history will not make a plain building beautiful. On the other hand, I know of one old English home, a veritable ancient picture in gray gables and mullioned windows, with ghost-like panelled chambers, a hall with the gleam of knightly armour on its walls, with a moat in front over which the house is approached by a hoary stone bridge, having great stone pillars on either side, from which look down crumbling, heraldic lions; around this past-time home is an old walled garden, in which peacocks may be seen proudly strutting about; and a moss-begrown sun-dial stands in the centre of a lawn that is centuries old. On the other hand, as I have observed, this dream of architecture, this ballad in building, that seems to speak aloud of past legends, family ghosts, and romantic love affairs, *à la* Dorothy Vernon, has positively neither legend nor history (except of the mildest family, and, therefore, private description) connected with it.

Having finished our inspection of the interior of Stokesay Castle, we spent the rest of the day in the delightful occupation of sketching and photographing its picturesque exterior. From almost every point of view it makes a charming picture, and I cannot call to mind an ancient building of like kind of which this can be honestly said. From the west, the aspect of the old pile is especially effective; in the foreground is a large tranquil pool of water that reflects the gray walls and towers of the time-worn castle, and the wooded hills beyond form a fitting background to a scene of rare beauty,—and this was the last view we had of ancient and deserted Stokesay, one of the most picturesque spots in all Great Britain.

That evening, in the comfortable sitting-room of our hotel, we got out our maps and well-used copy of *Paterson's Roads*, and had a lengthened consultation over them as to where we should drive on the morrow. We had already, during our roundabout progress, travelled close upon 300 miles (282 miles we made it out, to be precise), and we thought that it was about time to turn our horses' heads homewards. After due deliberation we determined to make for Bridgenorth, going up Corve Dale as far as Munslow, striking from thence across country, as best we might, to our destination, as no direct road was shown on our map.

What chiefly caused us to select this route was the fact that by so doing we found that we should pass through a remote tract of country well out of sight and sound of the railway, and so, possibly, we thought we might make some discoveries; there is always a pleasure in such anticipations, even though they be not realised. At any rate, we should traverse a part of England that, we imagined, was little known, or seen except by its inhabitants. Judging from our map, we should have hills to the right and to the left of us, and the little river Corve for company, more or less, as far as Munslow.

In the morning early we sought out the ostler and inquired of him about the road. His replies to our inquiries were not exactly encouraging. It was a hilly and a rough road, he said; the distance was about 21 miles, as far as he knew, but it might be more; we could bait our horses, he thought, at the inn at Munslow, but he believed that this was the only place on the road where we could, people did not often go that way. Indeed he did not seem very sure about anything excepting that the road was very hilly—on that point he had no doubts. From all of which we concluded that it would be advisable to make an early start so as to have a long day before us.

It was a lovely morning, the sun was already

shining warmly down out of a nearly cloudless sky; our aneroid had risen steadily during the night and appeared inclined to keep on rising; our horses would be fresh and fit after their day's rest, so we started forth after breakfast under the most favourable of auspices, in the best of spirits, and in a state of delightful expectancy and uncertainty about everything. If we were compelled to picnic on the way, well that would be an enjoyable thing, and if we could not put our horses up anywhere, had we not a reserve supply of corn for them in the dog-cart?—and possibly they would enjoy a picnic too with a dessert of freshly-plucked grass as a special treat. We were always prepared to picnic out provided the weather were fine, and this it promised to be for the next twenty-four hours at any rate, and he who would prophesy longer ahead of British weather would be a bold man.

Upon leaving Craven Arms, hotel and village, our road forthwith commenced to mount gently but continuously, and led us upwards between wooded heights. As we proceeded a prospect of hill and dale was gradually revealed to us that suggested pretty, and possibly even romantic, scenery to come. Our spirits seemed to rise with our road; every mile of the way the country, if possible, became more beautiful, and our road so far, though narrow, was of excellent surface. We had not proceeded far when to our right, through a dip in the hills, we caught a charmingly poetic view of Ludlow in the distance, with its prominent church tower and old castle standing out a tender gray against the sunlit sky.

Corve Dale is well worth exploring; it is a corner of old England whose beauty seems to be quite undisturbed by modern progress. During the whole of our day's delightful stage we did not come upon anything ugly; quaint old churches that have escaped the restorer's hand, picturesque homes of the past, cottages built long years ago, sleepy-looking, weather-stained farmsteads with their colony of rambling outbuildings, ancient water-mills, and rustic foot-bridges abounded, and these more than sufficed us. The country all around had a mellow, restful look; and a peaceful, uneventful life its rural inhabitants seemed, to us, to lead. How eye-pleasing and heart-gratifying is such natural home-like scenery; it appeals to one's feelings in a way that mere grandeur never can, it is not astonishing, there is nothing to rave about in it — it is simply lovable by its birthright of beauty!

There are endless Societies nowadays for the protection of almost everything at home or abroad, I would that there were a Society for the Protection of Beautiful English Scenery! I write this feelingly, having just returned from a short drive in the lovely Lake District, and found, to my horror, one of the most beautiful peeps of Windermere at the lake-head built out, for ever probably, by a row of commonplace houses. I wish it were only feasible that some small areas of England that have "the fatal gift of beauty" could be held sacred from being further despoiled by the hands of the railway contractor, the speculative builder, and the money-making manufacturer. One eyesore in building, it must be remembered, if at all prominent, may so assert itself as to wholly ruin a lovely prospect. This does not point to the moral that there should be no erections in a beautiful country, for a building in harmony with a scene may be harmless, and, under certain circumstances, indeed, it may even give an added grace to a landscape.

After a time, when we had reached high ground, the vale opened out before us, and we had a glorious prospect looking up the secluded Corve Dale bounded by green hills gently sloping down. Amongst the spreading woods the gray gables, big chimney-stacks, and uneven-tiled roofs of many an old home, both large and small, peeped out every here and there; and at one point, rising right above a wood, we saw what appeared from our standpoint to be a very quaintly shaped—not to say an exceedingly eccentric—church tower, as far as we could judge of no known type. Owing to its distance, however, we were not able to make it out as clearly as we could have wished; and we had a too long and uncertain day's stage before us to deviate so far from our course as to inspect it close at hand. The position of the church in question corresponded with a village marked on our map as Culmington. Here I may remark that on future journeys I intend to provide myself with a good field-glass, as it would add greatly to the interest of a tour like ours to be able to examine more in detail any special feature in a distant view.

Munslow proved to be a picturesque and an attractive village, consisting mostly of old half-timbered houses and cottages, one old cottage that we noted on entering the village being especially picturesque, and of this we made a sketch, which sketch the owner was gracious enough to admire, and informed us that " I drawed a little myself when I were a youngster"; then he began a long history of his "fayther and grandfayther" that was not in the least interesting — except to himself. These country people, how they do love to talk!

At Munslow we pulled up at the "Crown and Hundred House Inn"—why "The Hundred House Inn" we could not discover—and found that there were stables attached, and though there was no ostler on the premises, we soon had the horses housed therein, and procured them some corn. Then, after attending to our animals' needs and comforts, we sought the interior of the rural inn on our own behalf, for we were healthily hungry after our long drive in the keen morning air, and thirsty also. Mortal man, we found, needs plentiful refreshment on a driving tour; of a truth it is appetising work, whereon, moreover, " good digestion waits on appetite," and well that it should be so, for on the road the fare is sometimes of necessity primitive. You cannot expect first-class cooking in remote country villages far from any town, or if you do there are many chances to one against your getting it. We always endeavoured to secure comfortable quarters of a night; for our mid-day halt and meal we gave no thought, and accepted contentedly whatever the Fates decreed; and, be it known, generally the Fates were good to us. The interior of the Crown was a pattern of neatness and cleanliness, but bread and cheese, with a bottle of Bass's ale, was the best that the inn could do for our entertainment, and a very good best, too, under the circumstances. There is one advantage in a bread-and-cheese lunch, it entails no waiting for anything to be cooked, and for a man who is *really* hungry this is a consideration.

Munslow seemed to be a very sleepy place, and our inn had a sleepy look to match; the door of it was carefully closed when we arrived, and we had even some little trouble in rousing any one; but we supposed that Munslow folk do wake up at times, for we read the following notice hanging up in the bar :—

> Be merry, my friends,
> And drink your beer:
> But do not swear
> Or gamble here.

The landlady said to us as we were leaving, "You're never going away without seeing our church, surely, sir. It's most interesting, and the most beautiful in the country, and it's only five minutes' walk up the first lane to your left. You really ought to see our church, it's well worth seeing." When the wife of a publican recommends one to go to church, we felt that we must go—and we went. Moreover, in such an out-of-the-way place, it struck us that just possibly we might discover some noteworthy old monument or ancient brass, quaint inscription that ecclesiastical prudery had not obliterated, interesting architectural feature, or curious bit of carving.

The approach to the church was up a very pretty, narrow, tree-embowered lane, and the church itself proved to be a most picturesque building externally, and interesting internally. Besides the frequent yew trees, there were a number of Scotch firs in the peaceful God's acre, and amongst the many moss-grown tombstones therein we noticed one to a Rev. W. Read having a great superstructure of timber, roofed on the top, raised over it, and covered with creepers. This protecting a tombstone from the weather appeared to us somewhat peculiar.

Within the church what interested us most was a very beautiful and ancient stained-glass window, manifestly a relic of the old Roman Catholic days. On the top portion of this little gem of a window the Virgin Mary is represented as crowned; below, the lights are filled up with figures of what we presumed to be a mother and her four daughters kneeling, with the words over their heads, *Sancta Maria ora pro Nobis*. We imagined that this window had been taken down at some period, possibly during the Commonwealth, and had been hidden away to preserve it, for we noticed that some of the glass had apparently got a little mixed in re-leading. We could not help wondering also, when this window was whole, whether the father of the four daughters might not have had a place therein opposite to his wife, with perhaps his sons kneeling beside him, provided he had any; if so, possibly this part of the window was lost or broken in the removal. It looks, however, fairly complete as it is, allowing for the slight displacement of the figures inevitable in the resetting. In the chancel we noticed a stone slab to a priest, the figure being incised thereon in black lines; but it was not of particular interest except for its age.

On the north wall, nearly opposite the porch we had entered by, we observed a very curious, but a very ghastly, mural tablet to a William Churchman, bearing the date of "Septr 23.—Ao. 1602." The inscription on this began, "Sonne of Man can Hese Bones live. O Lord God thou knowest." Then the body was represented as wrapped up in its shroud, the form plainly showing; below this was an hour-glass on one side, and a Death's head on the other. Should the wandering eyes of any worshipper chance to alight upon this monument during an over-long sermon, they would not find it especially enlivening; possibly the sermon in stone, however, would be more powerful than the sermon in words! At the foot of this tablet are the following lines:—

> I In the Hovver of His povver
> By Christ doe Rise
> And vve vvhose Bones rot under stoanes
> Our Dust Heel not despise.

This quaintly-ghastly monument fascinated us in spite of its gruesomeness; it was repulsive, yet it compelled attention. It will be noticed in the verse that for the letter "w" two "v's" are employed side by side.

Leaving the church we walked back to our inn. On passing through the village we met a man actually dressed in a shabby black frock coat, and with a still more shabby tall hat on. To find a man dressed thus in this remote old-world hamlet did astonish us. He had a portfolio under one arm, and held an umbrella in his hand. What could he be, we wondered; but before we had time to come to any conclusion, he came up to us—and begged! This act of his took us fairly aback, it was so totally unexpected. We thereupon asked him why he did not work instead of begging. "Work!" exclaimed he in quite an injured tone of voice. "Work! I do work; I'm selling illuminated texts and tracts, and it's precious hard work selling tracts, I can tell you." We believed him. Then he opened his portfolio, and showed us a selection of gilt and illuminated texts that he was willing to sell us for a shilling apiece, together with a supply of tracts at a penny each. I think that of all the curiosities of begging humanity we have ever met on or off the road—and we have come across a goodly number of peculiar specimens—this man beat the record. I am afraid we did wrong, but he managed to wheedle a sixpence out of us, in return for which we received his blessing and the solemn assurance that our money would be returned to us a thousand-fold. We made that out to be £25, nevertheless I am willing to part with my interest in the investment for a very moderate sum; the blessing was, I presume, purely personal, and therefore "not transferable."

CHAPTER XVI

The Wrekin—A Shropshire toast—Bridgenorth—A leaning tower—Thirsty souls—Abbreviation of names—Romantic and picturesque towns—Quatford—A curious effect—Kidderminster—Round about an old coaching inn—Hills and clouds—Droitwich—Satire in stone—Buildings with characters—Pleasant company—On the road.

On leaving Munslow we had a long stretch of level road, and we began to wonder when the bad hills were coming of which the Craven Arms ostler spoke. Some way ahead, at a bend in the road, we came upon a quaint old church with a curious wooden bell-turret set on the top of its gray stone tower; and just beyond the church we espied an ideal-looking old Tudor home, with mullioned windows and a lichen-stained roof; this ancient house stood out well against a background of dark fir trees. We did not, however, call a halt for a nearer inspection of either of these picturesque structures, for at the moment we felt in a lazy mood, so we simply glanced at them and passed by.

We had now reached what we presumed to be the head of the charming Corve valley, and had a long pull uphill out of it; but though the surface of the road was a little rough here, the gradient was not severe. There was nothing to complain of in either respect. From a point on our road, after reaching high ground, we had a view of that famous Shropshire "mountain," the Wrekin. "To all friends round the Wrekin," is a familiar toast in these parts, and without which no banquet is considered complete. It is to this part of Shropshire much as is "Auld lang syne" to Scotland.

We had now a long and glorious run down hill, with the traces slack, and the brake hard on. We did this downhill stretch at our best speed. At the foot of the descent we noticed an ornamental stone pillar carved as a sign-post. Here and there in remote districts one comes now and again—though rarely—upon such artistic sign-posts, erected by generations long since departed, who had some thought for beauty. Then we passed through a neat little village with a very pretty and clean-looking inn by the wayside. Our road still kept good till we came into sight of Bridgenorth, when we had a steep dip down, followed by a short ascent into the town. On the whole, we found our cross-country stage that day a very good one; from what we had been told we had expected a rough journey, and were agreeably disappointed; here were we at our destination without having encountered any really serious hill. So little can you depend, in the present railway-travelling age, on the correctness of any information as to a road far afield from your starting-point. Besides, the goodness or the badness, the hilliness or otherwise of a road, is, after all, a comparative matter. A hilly road, according to an Eastern Counties ostler, most probably will be found to be a very different thing from a hilly road in the estimation of his North country compeer. What a Yorkshireman might consider a fairly level stage, an Eastern Counties man might deem a hilly one, and *vice versâ*.

At Bridgenorth we were fortunate in finding a most comfortable inn, and a quaint old town to explore, romantically perched on the top of a cliff, round the foot of which the silvery Severn winds; at least the river looked clear and silvery to us there, whatever it may be in its lower courses. As we had still two hours or so of daylight left, we set forth to inspect the old castle, and some of the quaint buildings we had observed on driving in.

The ruins of the castle consist of a massive keep a good deal out of the perpendicular, so much so indeed as to appear in danger of toppling over altogether some day. This leaning tower of Bridgenorth, standing as it does in a prominent position at the edge of a high cliff, is a characteristic and notable landmark from far around. At the foot of the keep is an elevated terrace which affords charming and extensive views over a well-wooded country. The Bridgenorth people, however, do not seem to prize the possession of the prospect much, for on that lovely summer evening, though the streets of the little town were fairly crowded with groups of chattering Bridgenorthites, we had the terrace, the view, and the golden sunset all to ourselves.

On the way back to our inn, we stopped a short time in the High Street to make a sketch of the ancient Swan hostelry, an exceedingly picturesque and interesting specimen of a black-and-white half-timbered building. This old hostelry looks legendary, every inch of it. A native to whom we spoke said he believed that there was some story or another connected with it, but what it was he did not know; this was tantalisingly indefinite, and merely served to raise our curiosity. Further inquiry of another native only elicited the remark, that "it be a rum old place. I have heard say as how several coaches used to start from it"; then he suggested that he was thirsty. By the way, I have found that many of the country people I get into conversation with suffer from sudden thirst; and the number of total strangers I spoke to on the road, from time to time, who were anxious to drink my health was surprising. My health ought certainly to be excellent considering the quantity of twopences that I have parted with, on this and previous journeys, for the special purpose of drinking it. Still, now and again, I have had good worth for my money thus expended, in the shape of local information imparted, not readily to be gleaned otherwise.

We next made a hasty sketch of the quaint old market-hall, another picturesque building of black-and-white half-timber, supported on a lower story of brick arches; from a date thereon we learnt that this was erected in the year 1652. Then the light failed, and we sought the shelter of our hotel. In the coffee-room there we found a jovial, ruddy-faced farmer installed, with whom we had an interesting conversation upon the agricultural outlook. "Times are bad truly," he said, "but they might be worse. 'Tain't the prices, I say, so much as the bad seasons in succession we've had that beats us. Prices might be better certainly; I don't make a fortune at farming, but I make a living, and that's something. Just pay my way, but put nothing by at the end of the year for a rainy day, or old age. But what's the good of worrying? Things may change for the better, and if they don't, worrying won't make 'em; besides, it takes a lot out of you. That's my way of looking at it." Philosophical farmer; manifestly he was a born optimist, and optimists are pleasant people to talk to, their cheerfulness is inspiring. The optimist is to the pessimist as sunshine is to shadow.

On studying our map during the evening, after the departure of our "jolly" farmer, and when we were left alone, we determined to drive next to Droitwich *viâ* Kidderminster. It was always a pleasant part of our programme to have our maps out every evening, and to study our route. We never planned our stages for more than a day ahead, and even then we sometimes changed our plans on the way; so that when we started forth in the morning it was by no means certain where we should eventually arrive. It frequently happened, in truth, that we did not arrive at the destination we had agreed upon over-night, for the excellent reason that we changed our course during a consultation at our mid-day halt. The very essence of our tour was absolute freedom.

Sauntering into the stables early next morning

to see our horses, as was our wont, and whilst chatting with the ostler about the road on to Droitwich, we were struck by his abbreviating Kidderminster into "Kiddy." "It's fourteen good miles into Kiddy," said he in reply to our query as to the distance ; and we told him that we were glad to hear the miles were "good" ones, as we never liked bad miles. Whereupon he took the needless trouble to explain that he meant, "it is fully fourteen miles, rather more than less ; as for the road beyond Kiddy, I don't know anything about it." This was honest, and far better than imparting wrong information, which some ostlers are inclined to do, rather than own their ignorance.

Our road out of Bridgenorth led us past the castle and down by a steep descent to the river-side. Here we crossed the Severn on an ancient bridge; looking back from the opposite bank of the river we had a very effective view of the gray old town, perched high on the rocks above. Some of the houses of the lower town had stables and other outbuildings hollowed out in the steep side of the cliff. Bridgenorth, from across the Severn, makes a charming picture. Many far less romantic old towns are frequently painted by artists, but I do not remember ever to have seen a representation of Bridgenorth on the walls of any picture gallery. Yet, under certain conditions of light, Bridgenorth possesses all the elements that go to make a most charming composition and a poetic picture, and has, besides, the advantage of not being a familiar subject. I am rather tired of seeing "the old stock places," as an artist once called them to me, everlastingly painted from this and that point of view, as though those towns (picturesque enough in themselves) were the only romantic or paintable ones in all England. It is a good thing for an artist, now and again, to break fresh ground, and it is a bad thing to get "groovy" in art. "Paint what you love," truly; but is it necessary to love only one or two localities?

Proceeding on our way, we had the wide and winding Severn to our right, and refreshingly green its meadowy margins looked on that hot summer morning. In about a mile we reached Quatford, a small hamlet, with a fourteenth-century church; hamlet and church being situated on a rocky eminence overlooking the river; a second edition of Bridgenorth on a small scale. The church door was open and we glanced inside, without, however, discovering anything of interest.

Then our road led us up and down hill, through rocky cuttings, past waving woods and rich meadowlands, and as we drove on we caught peeps of the shining Severn ever and again over the fields and through the many-stemmed trees. The silvery sparkle of the river in the sunshine was enlivening, for, after leaving Quatford, our road became somewhat desolate, we met no one thereon for miles, excepting three sturdy tramps walking together, who, strangely enough, did not beg. At one spot we passed through a large wood, mostly consisting of Scotch firs, with a lonely little mere in a hollow where the road dipped down. The water with its reedy banks, and encircling trees reflected on its still surface made quite a pretty picture, and we were tempted to rest awhile in this cool retreat, not in idleness, however, for we both photographed and sketched it.

On the sign-posts, as we drove along, we noticed the words "To Kid." and "To Brid.," meaning, manifestly, to Kidderminster and to Bridgenorth, thus reducing the names of those places to an amusing minimum, and even outdoing the ostler's attempt in that direction. From Kidderminster in full, through "Kiddy" to "Kid." abbreviation could hardly farther go!

The first village we came to after and some distance on from Quatford was Quatt, an exceedingly pretty and clean hamlet. The resemblance in the names of these two villages points to a same origin for both. One is by the Severn-side, the other on high ground and well away from the river.

As we drove on through this wooded land we noticed another village of irregular-roofed houses with a very fine church in the centre, some half a mile to the right of our road; the place had quite a Düreresque look, as though it had stepped out of one of his quaint woodcuts. It is strange how some old towns, villages, and scenery, as you drive by, call to mind some painter. Bridgenorth, seen across the river, suggested Turner to us; portions of Ludlow recalled Prout; some of the moorlands we passed through made us think of David Cox; many a country-side picture brought Creswick, as well as Birket Foster, before us, and so on with other painters of lesser renown.

Then we came to a decayed old mansion, apparently converted into a farmhouse, with an avenue of elms leading up to it, and some moss-grown stone pillars in front, that once, doubtless, supported a great gate, which mutely bespeak the former importance of the ancient home. There is something very pathetic about these erst stately homes that are scattered over the land, in their old age doing duty as farmsteads, or given over to slow decay.

Still keeping on high ground, from our elevated and breezy position we had grand prospects over a wide extent of hilly country. Hills beyond hills rose and fell in a confused array, strongly outlined near at hand, but hazy with mists on the high horizon. At one spot, far away out of a wide and deep hollow, a mass of blue-gray smoke arose; this came from some manufacturing town, we presumed, that lay hidden from sight, which from our map we took to be Stourbridge. The effect of this uprising smoke, from our point of view, was as though we were looking down upon the crater of some vast volcano; now and then, to heighten the illusion, there was a ruddy glare on the smoke, caused probably by some ironworks. Portions of the Black Country, rightly so called, are weirdly picturesque at times and under certain atmospheric conditions, when beheld at a suitable distance.

We had now a long and steep descent of two miles or more all the way into Kidderminster, and

ROADSIDE ENGLAND.

as we descended we had an extensive panorama before us, looking right over that town and southward beyond on to a great stretch of level country bounded by the circling blue. We got our map out here, and tried to find thereon the names of the towns, villages, rivers, and streams that we saw spread out before us.

Entering Kidderminster we came upon smoke-stained houses, a feature of modern civilisation that had been distinguished by its absence since we left London on our rovings. But for its smoke-begrimed buildings, parts of Kidderminster, we thought, might be considered almost picturesque. Smoke is the curse of our modern cities, and is responsible for a great deal of their ugliness and sad want of colour; it reduces our house-fronts to one uniform and depressingly dull gray. What is the good of raising fine buildings only to have them blackened by the filthy compounds we allow to escape from our chimneys? When we have put a stop to the smoke nuisance we may have beautiful towns; now we can only have grand ones.

At Kidderminster we drove into the ample courtyard of the Lion Hotel, intending to rest our horses a while there after their long and hilly fourteen miles' stage, and to proceed on to Droitwich in the cool of the late afternoon. But the Fates ordained otherwise. The Lion was an old coaching inn with its own little history; our modest lunch there was cooked to perfection, and served by the neatest of maids; the stabling was excellent; the landlord was good-natured and interesting, and we enjoyed a long chat with him as he conducted us over the rambling stabling (of which more presently). Kidderminster might be smoky, but our hotel was "comfortable exceedingly." It was, moreover, delightfully cool, and the day was oppressively hot, the result of the combined circumstances being that we proceeded no farther that day. We were touring purely for pleasure, and after an excellent lunch our present pleasure was to stop where we were.

Rambling about the ancient and extensive stableyard, whilst we smoked a meditative afternoon pipe in solitary peacefulness, we found our way to the top of it, for it rose steeply at the back. From this point we had a fine view right over the busy town, and also of its many smoky chimneys. Here the cheery landlord joined us, and after a talk about the coaching days and past times, he kindly offered to conduct us over the rambling place. First he took us to the old booking office for the coaches; here he pointed out the ancient desk and stool, "just as they were when the mails travelled by corn and not by coal." Here also he showed us one of the old posting books, and a letter that very day received addressed—"The Lion, Coach Office, Kidderminster." This envelope we begged for as a curiosity, it having the date 1893 thereon. Then we were led into a large room that was used by the coachmen and postillions. This had the original wooden seats or forms around. We next inspected the stables, where the mail changes were kept. All of which made us realise more than any word-pictures or drawings could the days of old road travel. The coaches, the landlord informed us, used to drive right through the yard, entering by the archway and departing at the top, or *vice versâ*, as the case might be. At the end of the yard, though now converted to other purposes, is a building that in years past formed the Kidderminster theatre. Here several famous actors and actresses from time to time appeared, but whose names I forget, not having made a note of them. In this old building there still remains a relic of its early use and greatness in the shape of the faded remains of the original curtain. The old brew-house was also pointed out to us, where long ago all the ale sold in the inn was brewed. Nowadays it is almost impossible to obtain a glass of home-brewed ale anywhere in the land. More's the pity!

During the evening we found our way into the cosy bar of the Lion for a last smoke, and also for a chat with any inhabitant of the town who might drop in and prove interesting. Plenty of people did drop in certainly, and a deal of talking was done, but neither the people nor their conversation greatly interested us, so we were left to our own resources. On looking round we observed on the wall a design for the lion that does duty as a sign over the porch of the inn, and below it we read—

A statue for a Ligne
for Mr. Woodward.   Kidderminster.
March 1785.

The unique spelling of the word lion amused us. In the last and earlier centuries there appears to have been a great latitude allowed in the matter of spelling (a grand period, surely, for schoolboys!). Indeed, we have noticed on several fine altar-tombs to noble and famous men of a bygone age, the same word quite differently spelt in the same inscription. In former times everybody appears, more or less, to have been his own orthographist.

We started off next morning early, bound for Droitwich—and elsewhere, but where that elsewhere would be we had no idea. Leaving Kidderminster and our entertaining landlord with regret, and passing under a high and long railway viaduct, we once more found ourselves in the pleasant open country, and rejoiced in the light fragrant atmosphere. The day was cloudy and inclined to be showery, but there was a freshness in the air that was delightful as well as inspiriting; and if we had no sunshine, neither had we any glare. The soft south-west wind that was gently blowing was very soothing, it rustled musically the leaves on the trees, and made mimic waves of the long grass and growing corn in the fields as we passed by. There was a sense of movement everywhere. A gray day has its charms when the gray comes from the west or south, and not from the east.

On our road we noticed that the abbreviated spelling of the towns still held place on the signposts, "To Wor." and "To Kid." being inscribed on several of them—"Wor." being intended for

Worcester. Even Bradshaw has not arrived at this!

Now to our right our old friends the Malvern Hills loomed up grandly gray, looking indeed almost mountainous, so much does the effect of height depend upon atmospheric conditions; the low-lying clouds just raked their summits as they were hurried along by the wind, and made them look strangely big. Even a low hill may look high when the clouds stoop down to it. Clouds give, generally, an impression of height, so that one does not readily realise how low they descend at times. The Malvern Hills, rising out of a vast level plain as they do, are a landmark for miles around. They lie, too, in the centre of some of the most beautiful of English scenery; little wonder, therefore, that Malvern has become such a popular resort.

It was a very pleasant, homelike country we drove through that day—a country of old orchards, green meadows, big elms, and pretty cottages. Some of the cottages were especially pretty, with their rose and honeysuckle-covered porches, and little gardens gay with the varied colours of old-fashioned flowers. The Englishman seems to have an inherent love of flowers. They are the poor man's luxuries, with which he can happily decorate and make cheerful the small room of his lowly abode on some equality with the rich man; the latter may have real paintings, whilst the poor man has to be content with trashy oleographs; the rich have silver, the poor, cheap plate or pewter; but the poor cotter's flowers, if not as rare, at any rate are as real, as colourful, and as sweet-scented as those of a nobleman. It amused and interested us to note the way these thrifty rural folk had utilised in their gardens old preserved meat and fruit tins, bottles, packing boxes, and sundry other little-considered articles of a similar nature. The old tins were made to do duty as flower-pots. An old tub set on end at the top of a pole with some holes and compartments constructed therein made a really effective and even picturesque pigeon-house; another tub with the end out formed a very fair dog-kennel; a number of bottles stuck in the ground bottom upwards were placed round the flower - beds as borders. One cottager had pressed some tea - chests into service as hen-coops by the simple expedient of removing one side and covering the opening with some laths of wood.

The south-west wind did not bring up the rain as we expected, for the clouds blew over and the sky became a deep blue, the sun shone out in his glory, and our gray world changed to one full of colour and varied by light and shade everywhere; the transition was surprising by the rapidity with which the clouds cleared away. The English climate is always doing something wholly unexpected, and therefore is ever interesting.

Then, driving on through that truly lovely land of orchard, meadow, and distant hill, we passed by a lonely public-house rejoicing in the uncommon title of the " Live and Let Live," where we learnt that we could buy home - made cider. We quite believed this, for cider-making was going on at the time there. It was something, anyhow, to know that we could get a home-made article somewhere.

The country retained the same characteristic features till we came into sight of Droitwich, famous for its salt-works, brine baths, and tumble-down houses, the latter due to the subsidence of the land owing to the continued extract of brine from below. On entering Droitwich we had to drive under two railway bridges and over a canal bridge, all close together. There were locomotives letting off steam on the railway, and a steamboat of some kind on the canal doing the same thing; and as this hissing of escaping steam at high pressure is just what our horses have a special objection to, we had an enjoyable five minutes of it, the more so as just as our horses began prancing about, the inevitable baby-child ran and tumbled down in front of them, right in the middle of the roadway, as though in all Droitwich he could not have chosen a more suitable place to run to and tumble down upon! Then followed a long narrow street of old houses. On the keystone to the archway of one of these a curious bit of carving arrested our attention and we pulled up to inspect it. This carving represented a man's face with his tongue projecting, and a toad jumping out of his mouth. Not a very elevating work of art truly, but it struck us as curious, and we could not help thinking to ourselves that "thereby hangs a tale." So we looked round to see if there were anybody about of whom to inquire, when we noticed an intelligent-looking youth close at hand, and this is the explanation of the strange carving he gave to us. "Oh! that's intended for a portrait of the bloody Judge Jeffreys, and the toad is the lies coming out of his mouth. I don't think the judge would have liked it had he seen it." And the youth laughed at his mild joke, and we drove on to the Raven Hotel, a half-timbered building that possesses a pleasant homelike look that caused us to take a fancy to it at once; for buildings—and I now refer to inns in particular—have their characters as well as human beings; some, like the Raven at Droitwich, seem to greet you at once with a welcome, some have a forbidding look of stately dignity as though above receiving a travel-stained guest. I do like an ample porch to a building, it looks hospitable and friendly; it is also so essentially English as opposed to the open Italian portico; it ever seems to me to speak a welcome without words,—perhaps it was because the Raven at Droitwich had a porch that we were so pleased with its outward look. Just over the road, too, were some picturesque stables (in the same style of building) belonging to the hotel; one does not indulge in the luxury of picturesque stables every day!

At the Raven we fared well and were made very comfortable; moreover, we found there a pleasant and sociable company gathered round the lunch table, and you do not always find the company particularly sociable at an English hotel. However, it chanced that most of the guests had seen us arrive, and knew that we were on a driving tour; and here, as elsewhere, this simple fact appeared to break down all the usual British icy reserve, so much so that everybody at once appeared to take a deep interest in our journey. One old gentleman proclaimed that he had driven across country when he was younger, and had never enjoyed anything so much in his life; another said he had always intended to do so, as it was such a delightful way of seeing the country; a lady and her two daughters forthwith became enthusiastic on the subject, and commenced planning a tour similar to ours, and asked so many questions about this and about that, that we found it hard work to answer them all. We felt, indeed, more as though we were at a friendly luncheon party than mere road wanderers just arrived at a strange hotel. Speaking from my own experience, I must own that if you travel by railway nowadays you are simply one of a crowd; your comings and goings matter to no one, except always, of course, to the waiters at the hotel, and then only when the time for your departure and their "tipping" arrives. But if you travel by road (possibly because it is such a novel proceeding, or from some other cause), I have always found that everybody takes a special interest in you,—you are no longer merely one of the crowd; perhaps you are considered peculiar, or, like a piece of odd china, unique; perhaps, and let us hope honestly, you are simply interesting. However it may be, the special consideration shown to you (without any extra charge) is very pleasing, and adds vastly to the enjoyment of a tour by road in the good old-fashioned way. With the railways all the discomforts, the pleasures, and the romance of travel have departed, except to the favoured few whom time and opportunity allow to drive about country; to them the discomforts of old-time travel are unknown, and only its pleasures and romance remain. Much-to-be-envied mortals they!

CHAPTER XVII

Salwarp House—A paragon of perfection—Droitwich brine baths—Up and down hill—Alcester—Changeful weather—Histories in Monuments—A veritable Arcadia—"Shakespeare's Town"—Beneath the sign of the Red Horse—Washington Irving's Parlour—Geoffrey Crayon's Sceptre—A storied chamber.

ONE lady who joined in the conversation at luncheon remarked to us, "As you are at Droitwich you ought really to walk over to Salwarp; there's a charmingly picturesque old half-timbered house there, built, they say, early in the fourteenth century. It is only about two miles off and is well worth seeing." And we further learnt from another of the company that not only was the old house picturesque, but that it was of considerable interest, being the birthplace of no less a personage than "the king-maker," Richard Beauchamp, Earl of Warwick. After this we decided that we would see Salwarp (or Salwop, for it is spelt, we found, both ways), and proceed no farther that day. Possibly our comfortable hotel, and the pleasant company we had so unexpectedly come upon, had something to do with our decision; however that may be, early in the afternoon we started forth with our sketch-book in search of the old historic home. We had no trouble in finding our way there after we got clear of the streets; as usual, the difficulty was in getting out of the town in the right direction.

We had a very pleasant walk along a narrow elm-bordered lane, shaded with over-arching foliage, musical with the songs of birds and the rustle of leaves in the wind; so pleasant, indeed, was our way that the two miles seemed like one. As we strolled slowly on, there was a rush and a roar to our right, followed by a long trailing line of white steam, that told of the railway and a passing train hidden in a deep cutting; just where the scenery was so lovely the unfortunate railway traveller saw nothing of it!

Salwarp House stands near to the road, and its long black-and-white timbered front is readily seen from it. We half feared and were prepared for a disappointment on reaching the place, for one cannot rely with safety on the recommendations of strangers. Salwarp, however, delighted us the moment we caught sight of it. We were charmed with its picturesque appearance. The old home is now apparently converted into an almost ideal farmstead. We walked across a meadow to the ancient house, and set to work to make a sketch of it. There was nobody about, otherwise we should have begged permission to do this, as we do not see why, because a person chances to live in an interesting old home, people should feel entitled to trespass in order to see it. Yet after this saying be it owned that we frequently did trespass first and ask permission afterwards, so much easier is it to preach one's duty to one's neighbour than to practise it!

SALWARP HOUSE, NEAR DROITWICH.

Salwarp House makes a capital subject for a water-colour drawing. We had, however, only our sketch-book and pencil with us, so we did the best we could with these. Truly, we made that sketch under difficulties; first, the wind blew in fitful gusts and kept turning our leaves over in a most temper-trying way; then a big dog took a sudden fancy to us, and was disagreeably demonstrative in his friendliness, for he would keep jumping up and knocking our sketch-book with his head; this he appeared to consider great fun. Still, in spite of wind and dog, the sketch was finished at last. Salwarp House is long and low and many-gabled, but the illustration I have given of it with this chapter will convey a better idea of what the old place is like than pages of printed description. We should much like to have seen the interior of the building, but we could not see our way to beg such a favour of utter strangers.

Before returning to Droitwich we took a stroll round about the locality, as the country there was exceedingly pretty. Crossing a canal—whose banks were overhung with trees—over a high one-arched bridge, we found ourselves in front of Salwarp church, an ancient building gray with years; here we noticed a modern tall cross in its quiet God's acre, and an aged yew that looked strong and flourishing. The interior of the church is interesting; we observed several arched recesses on either side of the nave; what these might be for, we could not say, but they suggested to us the idea that it would be an excellent arrangement if modern architects would leave such recessed spaces in the walls of their churches for future monuments, so that the effect of the interior of a fine building might be disturbed as little as possible by these after-additions.

There are one or two altar-tombs in Salwarp church, but of no special merit, and on the wall a long inscription to the memory of a gentleman of the name of Trymnell, according to which he seems to have been a paragon of perfection. We took the trouble to copy this as an excellent example of the fulsome and sycophantic epitaphs of the period. One could hardly help wondering what the actual man was really like in his non-glorified everyday life. If all our ancestors were as noble, true, and good as their tombstone panegyrics proclaim, what perfect creatures they must have been! This, then, is the inscription we copied :—

> Though hee be dead and gone yet fure
> His name for euer will indure.
> Others may boast in words heer's one
> Made faith appeare by good workes done.
> A sauour sweet he left behinde
> Shall keep his memory in minde;
> That neither time nor enuy shall
> Raise out his name perpetuall.
> You that are riche and minde to giue
> May see a patterne who did liue.
> Not like the world he euer made
> Eternall friends of things which fade.
> Loe happie change blest Trymnell makes
> Leauing poor earth Rich Heauen hee takes
> In this yeare 1661.

How a man could make "eternal friends of things that fade" puzzled us, but that is a trifle to the epitaph writer. The two lines commencing "Not like" appeared to us also as possibly conveying two opposite meanings. There is one thing notable about this eulogy to the dead, the name of the man it is designed to perpetuate is not at all prominent, and does not appear till the last line but one. Then leaving the interior of the sacred fane we made search amongst the sad colony of graves around for any quaint epitaph. We traced, with some difficulty, the inscriptions on many a moss-grown tombstone, but without discovering one. Some journeys we have come across quite a number, on this tour none.

On one side of the churchyard we found that the land drops down suddenly to a level country, and from the churchyard a long flight of rough stone steps leads to a stream of water at a spot where it widens out into a broad pool. Descending the steps we discovered an old mill. The church, set high above on the hill, the unruffled water reflecting the steep slope, together with the old mill, made a very pretty and uncommon picture.

Then we retraced our way to our hotel. During the evening we made the discovery that most of the company, if not all, were supposed to be invalids, and were staying there for the purpose of taking the brine baths, and a very "jolly" and robust-looking set of invalids they were. The baths, from what I could glean, are pleasant to take; the waters indeed are so buoyant that the merest tyro could swim in them with ease. In fact, it seemed to us from the cheerful gossip that an exceedingly agreeable way of spending a holiday would be to invent some malady as an excuse for taking the brine baths and to go to Droitwich. There is a very pretty country around the town to explore, affording plenty of opportunities for the amateur artist to try his skill, with a number of interesting old houses to see, and historic spots to visit; and when a wet day comes, or you are at a loss to know what to do, why there are the baths ever ready.

In the large staircase window of our hotel we noticed some old stained glass, a jumble of portions of sacred and heraldic subjects much mixed in a former re-leading; one fragment remaining perfect had on it "Mr. George Winter, 1580." This glass, we were told, belonged to a window of an old manor house that still forms part of the hotel. At dinner that evening the lady upon whose recommendation we had gone to Salwarp told us that on the porch of St. Peter's church in the town is painted this awful warning, "Remember Lot's Wife." We did not seek the church to verify her statement, as she wished, next day, for, after the pleasant experience of our Salwarp expedition, we placed implicit confidence in her statements. But when she told us of some more picturesque and interesting old houses in the neighbourhood "that we really ought to see before we left Droitwich," we had to explain that did we stay at every place on our way long enough to inspect all of interest around, our tour would not be completed till the winter time, if then. We were bound, of necessity, on this as on every outing to leave something unseen, and we did not regret the fact; for it is pleasant to leave room for fancy pictures of spots and places that seem so romantic in description. The reality might rob us of our ideals.

The following day we awoke to a beautifully fine sunshiny morning, so that we were tempted to make an early start, intending to sleep the night at Shakespeare's town, as our American cousins love to call far-famed Stratford-on-Avon. We were loth to leave our comfortable quarters at the Raven, and the entertaining company we found there, but it is the lot of the road traveller to ever be making, and parting from, fresh friends. Several of the guests at the hotel came to the door to see us off, and to wish us a pleasant journey. Said one of them to me, " I do envy you; I cannot imagine anything more enjoyable than your way of travelling."— " Then why don't you do likewise ? " we replied. " Oh, I will, next year," he said ; " perhaps we may meet somewhere on the road, who knows ? " It struck us, as we drove away, that we had made a good many converts at Droitwich to our mode of seeing the country.

At first we had a level stretch of highway alongside of a canal, then our road began to climb, so did the canal by means of a series of locks. For the next four miles or so we passed through a pleasant wooded country abounding in oak trees, but with nothing of particular interest on the way, except a picturesque blacksmith's shop with some clipped yew trees in front, which showed that even a blacksmith can have artistic feelings of his own, and this, we presumed, was his mode of giving expression to them. Now came a stretch of open, treeless country with fine views in all directions, for we were on high ground; then we dipped down into a large village with some old and picturesque half-timbered cottages by the roadside. These we photographed, and the inhabitants thereof also and unwillingly; for, as usual in such cases, they came forth "to be taken," and taken they had to be, every one of them looking straight at the camera and standing stiffly upright, very effectually spoiling our photograph as a picture. Amateur photography has its trials as well as its pleasures! Why should all those people so desire to be included in a photograph which there was not the remotest probability that they would ever see? Once I desired to take a very pretty cottage without its ugly owner; perhaps I was not very diplomatic over the matter, anyway I could not get rid of that owner, "If you takes my house, you takes me, so there I tell 'ee!" At the end of the village was a small rustic hostel with an ancient yew tree in front, to which was affixed the sign of the house, the tree, doubtless, giving its name to the inn, "The Yew Tree."

Again our road began to climb, and continued doing so till we reached an elevated tract of land, from which we had wide views ahead over a vast stretch of fertile and undulating country, dotted with old churches, old homes, and old hamlets. Here we pulled up for a while to admire the spreading landscape all bathed in unclouded sunshine. The far away has always a peculiar fascination for me. In the vague distance all things seem possible; where mystery reigns the poetic imagination has full play. It is well to dream for ourselves now and again in this prosaic age, and not to let the poets and painters do all the dreaming for us at second-hand.

Now began a steep and long descent through thick woods and sloping fields, that eventually brought us to the neat and clean little old-fashioned town of Alcester, which the ostler of our inn there pronounced Alster. After a very satisfactory lunch of roast beef, fresh salad, and cool clear ale, we set out for a stroll round the town whilst our horses rested. Just as we were starting, a small party of cyclists made their appearance, apparently wet through, indeed the water was then dripping from their clothes. Their peculiar condition mystified us, as we had no rain and the sun was shining. At the inn door the cyclists dismounted, and forthwith demanded whether we had not had a heavy downpour, as they were drenched through in a thunderstorm only a few miles back. They could hardly credit that we had not had even a drop of rain, as we could hardly credit that there should have been such a storm so comparatively close at hand whilst the sun was shining so brightly with us, and the roads were even dusty. However, the ostler said that he thought he had heard thunder rumbling in the distance during the morning. The weather reports manage this sort of weather very well. "Thunderstorms locally," they prophesy, only the trouble for the driving tourist is to locate them!

Alcester appeared to us to be a prosperous little market-town, with perhaps a rather large proportion of public-houses to other buildings. Some of the old houses have retained their ancient carved timber fronts, and this fact gives the streets a picturesque look. Rambling about, we eventually found our way to the church. In these old country town churches something of the history of a place and its inhabitants may at times be discovered. Many of our old churches have local histories writ in monuments, and form interesting museums, as far as they have preserved for us relics of the past. On entering the church we noticed a quaint oak cupboard fixed to the wall, the doors of which opened, and revealed some curious and crude paintings inside. Outside of the doors was a painted list of benefactors to the poor of the parish, with the date 1683. There are some fine monuments in the building, notably one by Chantrey to a Marquis of Hertford. But what interested us far more than all the rest was a most beautiful and elaborate altar-tomb, gorgeous still in gilt and colour though over three centuries old, and so well preserved that even the recumbent effigies in alabaster thereon, of a knight in full armour and his wife by his side, are perfect, even to their noses! which in most old monuments of the kind are more or less damaged, when not wanting altogether. The details of the armour are most faithfully rendered; so accurate indeed are they that the helmet on which the knight's head rests is carved inside to represent the leather lining with which most helmets were provided to make them more comfortable—or, should I not say, more endurable—to wear! So truthfully are all the details, even to the smallest trifle, of the armour rendered, that were a craftsman sufficiently skilful to be found, he might, from the effigy, make a perfect reproduction thereof. It is interesting also as showing the exact mode of wearing the armour, about which many learned antiquaries have hotly disputed, and wasted much good ink and paper to no purpose, when it seems to me, as a humble outsider, that an appeal to some such well-preserved effigy as this would at once have authoritatively settled the matter; but I verily believe that antiquaries oftentimes find much pleasure in argument. If you have a hobby it is a great part of its charms to discuss it, upwards from a schoolboy who simply collects foreign stamps.

I may remark that this gallant warrior is shown with his moustache carefully curled, and his beard as carefully combed out and cut into a point, from which we judged that he was quite a "masher" in his time. His wife is by his side, and her dress is as painstakingly rendered as is her consort's armour. These ancient effigies are truly works of art, and prove how picturesque were the fashions of the sixteenth century; possibly, however, undoubted picturesqueness was gained at a certain loss of comfort. Above this very interesting and stately monument the good knight's,—it is a pleasant fiction to presume that all old knights were good and brave, though I gravely doubt the first quality as always prevailing,—but good or otherwise, the knight's original helmet hangs suspended over him on an iron bracket, and his coat of arms, just below the helmet, on a painted wooden shield. The inscription, which runs around the tomb, commences—" Here lyeth the bodyes off Noblle Gervile, Knyght, and Elizabeth his wife." Reading farther on we noticed that Alcester was spelt "Alincester," and on another tomb we found it spelt "Alnecester." I do not know whether these old spellings may give any clue to the origin of the name of the town.

In the churchyard we had another vain search after any quaint epitaph. We were, however, somewhat amused by an inscription on an old tombstone, which, after recording a long list of the many virtues of the underlying dead, ended somewhat strangely and inconsistently with the quotation—"Praises on stones are vain words idly spent." Another old tombstone had inscribed thereon—

Sacred
to the memory of

and
of Elizabeth his Wife.

As the husband's name was left blank we concluded that the stone was put up during his lifetime, and that possibly he consoled himself with another wife, and lies elsewhere. This, at any rate, was more intelligible than an epitaph we came upon on a previous journey to the effect—" Here lies Thomas Woolner, who was drowned at sea and his body was not recovered!" Or of a certain knight who, according to an altar-tomb in Hereford Cathedral, lies by the side of his wife there, and who, according to another tomb in another church, lies there also by the side of his wife. The explanation being that the first tomb was erected just after his first wife died, and the worthy knight ordered his name to be inscribed thereon as buried beneath, doubtless intending to be so in the fulness of time; but he married again, and was interred with his second wife, which accounts for his body apparently being in two places at once.

Discovering nothing more in Alcester to interest us we returned to our inn, and ordering the horses to be "put to" were soon once more on the pleasant country roads, and we found the green fields, the sunlit foliage of the trees, and the songs of birds a good deal more inspiriting than churchyard exploring. Then in time we came to signs of the storm of which the cyclists had spoken, for the dry, dusty roads became wet and muddy, and pools of water still stood in the ruts formed by the carriage wheels. Gray gathering clouds around suggested a repetition of rain, so that we deemed it advisable to make what haste we could. I find from my notes that we had a delightful drive that afternoon through a prettily-wooded country on to Stratford-on-Avon, where we proposed to spend the night if all the inns were not overcrowded with American tourists to their English Mecca.

On approaching Stratford-on-Avon the weather changed again. The clouds gave place once more to the cheerful sunshine; whilst the scenery, to our mind, grew even more beautiful. Softly sylvan and sweetly rural the landscape looked; a happy mingling of woods and meadows, of time-mellowed homes and red tilled fields, with low-lying hills of green between, the landscape stretching away into a distance of hazy blue nothingness. Upon all this spreading panorama the soft sun of that quiet afternoon glinted down, throwing long blue tree-shadows across our road and upon the verdant grassy slopes around, and suffusing a tender warm glow over all things else. As we drove on through the fragrant hedgerows it verily seemed as though at last we had come to Arcadia. Here were we in the heart of England, in the midst of scenery essentially English, inasmuch as there is no scenery like it in the world. All around was full of that dreamy beauty, that peace-bestowing restfulness, that is so soothing to " world-weary souls "—a beauty utterly beyond the power of mere words to communicate, for it possesses a subtle charm that cannot be analysed.

Reaching Stratford-on-Avon we alighted at the Red Horse Hotel, an ancient coaching-house with ample stabling, so that we were fortunate in our choice of an inn. This is, I believe, the first time during all our road wanderings that we have sheltered beneath the sign of the Red Horse, nor do I remember to have come across this title on an hotel anywhere before. Could it possibly, we wondered, have been in the days of old a Red Lion, and the village painter have represented that animal (which probably he had never seen) so badly as to look like a red horse, and so the name got changed? At any rate the Red Horse is as unfamiliar a sign as the Red Lion is common.

Stratford-on-Avon has become renowned the English-speaking world over by the happy chance that nearly now three centuries ago Shakespeare was born there; that fact is the glory of the town. Shakespeare has made the name of Stratford-on-Avon "as familiar in our mouths as household words"; but for the accident of it being the place of his birth, Stratford would probably have been to this day a sleepy out-of-the-world place as unnoted and unfamed as Alcester or Kineton, or any other small neighbouring town that boasts no illustrious poet's origin. The history of Shakespeare's life for so great a genius is strangely obscure; but this for certain we know, that at Stratford-on-Avon he was born, and that there he was buried; and thither, drawn by the magic of his great name, each year come pilgrims by thousands even from across the stormy Atlantic, and from far-off Australia. I am not going to weary you, kind reader, with any description of Shakespeare's birthplace, his reputed haunts, or his grave in the grand old parish church which was ancient when he was young; that would be but to repeat a thrice-told tale. It would be a shame for any travelled Englishman to confess that he knew not these. But two traditions, that were told to us by an old antiquary whom we met and had a pleasant chat with in the smoke-room of our hotel, I must find room for, though, of course, I cannot claim for them better authenticity than that they came to us from a stranger at a strange hotel. We all know the oft-quoted lines that are inscribed on the stone that covers the poet's grave, the appeal "for Iesvs sake" not "to digg the dvst encloased heare," and the curse on the man who should do so. Well, it appears, according to the tradition that was told to us, that both Shakespeare's wife and his daughter Judith greatly desired to be buried in the same grave with the poet, as seems only natural; but so dreaded was the curse upon the tomb, that no one could be found who would dare to disturb it. The other tradition may have been invented to account for the disappearance of his plays in manuscript. It must be remembered that Shakespeare died at a time when the Puritan spirit was beginning to assert itself in the land, and that the Puritans looked upon the play-house as a den of iniquity; now this tradition has it that his daughter Judith, who outlived her father many years, was a Puritan, the inference being that from a strict sense of religious duty she destroyed all the "wicked" play writings.

At our comfortable inn that evening we found our way into a small sitting-room known as "Washington Irving's Parlour." Here the chair in which that great American sat and pondered as related in the *Sketch-Book*, is carefully preserved in a corner recess of the room, or perhaps I should say a cupboard with a plate-glass door in front, so that the historic relic may be plainly seen and yet be protected from the touch of profane hands. Here, too, is preserved "Geoffrey Crayon's Sceptre"; and hung framed on the wall is an extract from a letter of Washington Irving's, dated 20th January 1832, which we copied as follows:—"We next passed a night and part of the next day at Stratford-on-Avon, visiting the house where Shakespeare was born, and the church where he was buried. We were quartered at the little inn of the Red Horse, where I found the same obliging little landlady that kept it at the time of the visit recorded in the *Sketch-Book*. You cannot conceive the fuss that the little woman made when she found out who I was. She showed me the room I had occupied, in which she had hung up my engraved likeness, and she produced a poker which was locked up in the Archives of her house, on which we caused to be engraved Geoffrey Crayon's Sceptre." Strange enough, it appeared to us, that the English pilgrim to old-world Stratford-on-Avon may muse there upon the relics of one of new America's greatest writers. So Stratford-on-Avon delights to honour and keep green the memory of the illustrious American author as well as of her own immortal dead! It cannot now be said of Shakespeare as of the prophet, that a poet "has no honour in his own country!" In this same storied chamber, in one corner, stands an old "grandfather's" clock, on which is inscribed:—

The
Old Sexton's Clock
Mentioned in the
Sketch-Book
by
Washington Irving.

We rejoiced that chance had brought us to this old inn. And as we sat in Washington Irving's

Parlour, the glamour of its associations took possession of us; it is well and a relief to give way to sentiment sometimes in this matter-of-fact and seriously intellectual age. It is not every day that a traveller, whether by road or rail, finds at his inn such a storied chamber.

CHAPTER XVIII

Stratford-on-Avon from the old coach road—Charlecote Park—On the wrong track—Nature's music—Driving for health—An old Roman fossway—The unexpected in scenery—Kineton—Architectural details — A puzzling date — Edgehill and battle-ground—A stiff ascent—An evening drive—Banbury cross—Horses on the road.

FROM Stratford-on-Avon we decided that we would drive on to Banbury, passing through the site of the battle of Edgehill on the way, making a day's stage of about twenty-one miles. The weather next morning left nothing to be desired; had it been specially supplied to order we could not have had it more to our wishes; overhead was a bright blue sky, across which great white rounded clouds were slowly sailing before a gentle south wind, and gleams of golden sunshine came and went as the clouds passed by. It was one of those bright, inspiriting days that make life worth living, and driving through a pretty country a supreme delight; the atmosphere was light and buoyant, it was simply exhilarating to be out in the open in such weather. I certainly think that a perfect English summer day, when it does come, is the best thing of its kind that the world can produce.

Crossing the smooth and silvery Avon on an old gray many-arched bridge we reached the country side of the river, and turning back to take a farewell glance at "Shakespeare's town" a charming vision of it was presented to us. Above the houses, and above the trees in its churchyard, soared the tall tapering spire of Stratford's ancient church, its gray and weathered stone being brightened and warmed by a gleam of sunshine that rested on it, and around and below the spire the irregular roofs of buildings were scattered in picturesque confusion, their broken outlines being hidden here and there by the foliage of trees, whilst the river and bridge in the foreground completed the picture. This was the first view of Stratford that was presented to the pilgrim of past days coming from London by the old coach road; the modern pilgrim, alas! travels by rail, so that the poetic prospect is lost to him.

Shakespeare, during his walks, must frequently have wandered by the beautiful and broad Avon's side; the bridge we crossed was built long before his birth by "Sir Hugh Clopton, maior of London," in the reign of Henry VII. With little doubt Shakespeare frequently crossed it and came naturally to the spot on the road where we pulled up, and therefore he must on returning home have looked upon the same view of the church, town, river, and bridge that we looked upon. The prospect has, of necessity, changed somewhat in the course of time, but in general features it remains probably much as it was in Shakespeare's day. The church still stands as it did, there were possibly trees around it as now; the river glides tranquilly past its peaceful God's acre just as of old; the bridge of many arches is still there; only some of the buildings in the town may have had a newer appearance. But taking a broad look at the prospect, leaving minor inconsequential details for the photographer, the general impression it conveys to an ordinary observer is probably much the same now as it did three centuries ago.

Having taken our final glance at pilgrim-haunted Stratford we once more proceeded on our way, and a very pleasant way it proved to be that sunny summer day—I say summer, though, truth to tell, it was a warm September morning. We had a level road at first, wide and winding, with grassy margins to the right and left, and great elms on either hand; along this we rattled apace, for we guessed from our map that there were stiff hills in store for us farther ahead, and we did not know how soon slow progress might be compulsory.

In about four miles we came to Charlecote Park, in which, according to tradition, Shakespeare shot one of Sir Thomas Lucy's deer. It may be that tradition for once is true, for Shakespeare did not profess to be a saint, and he makes a coarse punning allusion on the Lucy name in the "Merry Wives of Windsor," that seems to point to the fact that the poet had some grudge against that knight. Poet and knight are both now at rest; and what matters it, except for those who love to dispute about trifles? The park is a very beautiful one, with its great trees, and vast stretches of sloping sward that lead to its grand old genuine Elizabethan mansion—for it was built in the first year of the reign of good Queen Bess. An ideal English park and an ideal English stately home are these. As we passed by we noticed some timid deer sheltering beneath big branching elms, possibly descendants of the very deer that were there in Shakespeare's time.

The country still maintained much of the same character as it had from Stratford—tall elms on either side of the roadway, in rows in the hedges, and here and there in clumps of two and three in the fields, with now and again a stretch of park-like ground. Soon after leaving Charlecote we arrived at the large and straggling village of Wellesbourne Hastings—a long name in keeping with the place. Here we found a number of roadways converging; and being in doubt as to which to take for Kineton, where we proposed to make our mid-day halt, we asked of a stranger, as less trouble than consulting our map, besides saving time; he pointed out the right-hand road, and said, "Straight on." So to the right we went, which, alas! proved to be all wrong. We had proceeded some way, when, in the absence of any milestone, we asked of another stranger how far off we were from Kineton. "How far from Kineton!" exclaimed he, with a look of astonishment; "why, bless me, you a bees a-coming as straight aways from it as you can; that you bees." This information took us quite aback. We had been driving on, trusting to that young man's direction at Wellesbourne, expecting at every bend of the road to find

Kineton in sight, and now we were told that we were driving right away from it. Oh, for the good old days of plentiful sign-posts and milestones, with the names and distances of places legibly inscribed thereon! But neither sighing nor regrets will make them come again. Then our last guide continued, "Your only way is to go back through Wellesbourne. You've come a goodish bit out of your way; that you have." And thereupon the man lighted his pipe afresh and chuckled to himself as though it were a good joke. "Small things amuse country people," we muttered to ourselves; manifestly we were rapidly losing our tempers. Every man has his weakness. My special detestation is being sent out of the way when on a driving tour, particularly when I have a sufficiently long day's stage before me without making needless detours. Returning to Wellesbourne, and getting on the right track at last, we took advantage of a good level stretch of road to spin along apace, so as to make up a little for lost time. But soon our trotting ground came to an end at the foot of a wooded hill up which we had to climb; the foliage of the overhanging trees afforded us a grateful shade, whilst the soft wind just swayed their many branches and rustled their multitudinous leaves, making a soothing sound, suggestive of some half-heard, mysterious melody. The music of Nature, how tranquillising it is! whether it be the wordless song of a mountain stream splashing over stones and boulders, or chattering along a pebbly shallow; or the liquid, silvery melody of a gliding and gurgling lowland river; or the wandering winds making a grand harp of the forest trees; or the majestic tones of the sea as it breaks against some rock-bound coast, or the sweet harmony it makes when in a more peaceful mood it ripples on some sandy shore or dallies with the shingle.

After a stiff mount we reached level ground once more, and our elevated position afforded us lovely views over the country all around. We were not very high up in the world, yet the air was perceptibly fresher than on the lower ground. Coming up through the woods the shade they gave was acceptable; here we were glad of the warm, unclouded sunshine. You may have plenty of changes of climate in a day's drive in England: you may sleep in a town or in some country hostelry one night that lies snugly sheltered in a hollow where the air is warm and soft; and the next night fate may ordain that you sleep at an hostelry on the top of a hill exposed to all the bracing breezes of heaven. Indeed you may travel from the south coast to the extreme north of Scotland and not find so much change. The body as well as the mind likes variety, it gets tired of breathing the same air as the eye tires of the same scene. It is the constant combined change of air and scenery that makes a driving tour such a health-giving as well as an enjoyable mode of spending a holiday; and the mere fact of having to be out so much in a pure atmosphere vitalises the blood. I should imagine that sufferers from anæmia, chronic indigestion, and sundry nervous disorders begotten of overwork, would reap great benefit, if not an absolute cure, from a prolonged driving tour; at any rate, it is a harmless remedy to try—and not a disagreeable one.

Possibly the soil on this high ground is not so good as in the valley, where farming looks outwardly flourishing, for we noticed at least one field apparently gone out of cultivation altogether—a sad sight in the centre of densely populated England; this was given over to thistles and rabbits, the old gate opening to it from the road broken down and fast going to decay, and the hedge that bounded it growing as it would—wild, wayward, and tangled, just as we love, and careful farmers equally dislike, to see a hedge. But whatever the quality of the land, it could grow a famous crop of thistles; to this fact we could testify. It is a pity that thistles are not profitable or commercial crops, they seem so easily raised, and with them no weeding would be needful, for they effectually choke all other things when they have got a fair start.

As we drove along this elevated and lonely tract of cheerless country—though its cheerless aspect did not trouble us at all—we came to a rough and little-used bridle-way that crossed our road at right angles, and led downward to the right and left of us. Here was a sign-post with two arms extended which were thus inscribed :—

To Combroke	To Harwood's House
Foss Road	Foss Road

This now grass-grown and deserted-looking track was of old the great Roman Fossway leading through the country north and south. Times have changed since those "masters of the world" travelled this way, lords of this old England; and is the world so much superior to what it was in the days of Augustus Cæsar, for all the centuries that have passed? Has not sometimes the parrot-like cry of progress been the cry of backward, oh? What would Augustus Cæsar and the Romans of his age have thought of our Black Country, of our money-making selfishness, of the slums of our manufacturing towns, caused by the curse of cheapness and hateful competition?

Soon after leaving the ancient Foss Road we had another steep descent, which led us down into, and through, Compton Verney Park, the mansion of which is close upon, and plainly seen from, the highway. The park is beautifully timbered and pleasantly diversified by hill and dale; at the bottom of the descent the road comes to a lovely little lake (from whose sides rise wooded banks), and just where the silvery mere narrows, we crossed it by an embankment and a bridge. Then our road once more led us up hill, this time through a double avenue of bird-haunted elms growing out of grassy margins by its side. There was a delightful sense of spaciousness about that old highway; it was not close bordered by hedgerows; the land on either hand was not tilled to the uttermost yard, there were bits of wild waste grounds here and there unenclosed, sometimes with fallen timber on, but always picturesque and pleasing to look at. An English country road, remote from towns, is full of pictures; at each bend of the way a fresh one is presented to you as you journey on, and there is ever a certain sort of mild excitement, as you progress, to discover what the next turn will reveal; as with the English climate, so with the English roads, they are always doing something unexpected.

After a while we descended into the quaint and homely little town of Kineton, as sleepy and picturesque a place as any one could desire. Kineton is one of those old towns that seem neither to have grown nor diminished in size for generations; it is primitive and picturesque: by the way, I have never yet seen a town prosperous and picturesque. Kineton, I should imagine, has altered but little since the last coach took its last change at the old inn there; owing to the coming and going of post-chaises and the coaches it was erst more lively at times, and that was all. The chief feature of the place, as in most country towns, is naturally the church, round which the houses are grouped; this is built of a warm-tinted stone very agreeable to the eye. It would be interesting to know where this stone was quarried, as we have not much building material in England so pleasant to look upon.

On the top of the church tower was a large, not to say ostentatious, gilt weather-vane, that glinted in the sun in a very noticeable manner as the wind kept swaying it round a point or two, and back again. It appeared to be the most lively thing in the sleepy old town! A weather-cock and a windmill are departures from the ordinary properties of buildings in that, instead of being firm, they are in frequent movement; I have seen a dreary-looking old house made to appear quite cheerful by the simple addition of a bell-turret to the roof with a big weather-vane on the top; the latter seemed at once to give life to the place by its restlessness and golden-glistening. Anything that moves readily attracts the eye, and assumes an importance out of all proportion to its size. I hardly think that modern architects appreciate the decorative and enlivening qualities of the old-fashioned, quaintly designed weather-vane; it is useful, also, as well as a bright ornamental detail. What a lot of pains and pride the builders of the Tudor and Elizabethan period took in these trifling additions to the houses they raised. It is well-considered trifles that give a peculiar charm to a building that their grander features fail to convey. Many a modern architect can plan a convenient house, yet fails in such small accessories; he cannot, or will not, trouble about them, so he gets "such things" machine-produced from Birmingham or elsewhere, with nothing of feeling or art in their design; they are multiplied by the million and follow you all over the country till familiarity breeds dislike. Even a good thing monotonously repeated becomes distasteful in time, and a bad thing repeated is detestable!

As we were glancing at the exterior of the church a clergyman came out, and we asked him if there were anything of special interest within; he replied that there was an ancient recumbent figure in stone of a former priest, under a canopy, and a barrel-organ! "There are plenty of effigies still left," he resumed, "but I do not think in these advanced days you will easily find a church with a barrel-organ. In that I fancy we are almost, if not quite, unique." We had a good deal of church-exploring lately, and we did not feel inclined to do any more that day; but we thought that we would just have a look at the effigy and the organ. The effigy, which was a relic of the pre-Reformation days, we found a good deal the worse for age—and possibly for ill-treatment as well; it had arrived at that state when its chief interest lay in its antiquity. I am no blind worshipper of a thing merely because it is old—a fossil otherwise would appeal to me more than even the Pyramids, for it was ancient when they were not, and medieval monuments are of a mushroom existence compared to it. The chancel of the church is mostly taken up with mural tablets and tombstones to the Bentley family, several of which were surmounted with a quaint crest in the shape of a mermaid. One of these tombs is inscribed as follows:—

Frances Bentley
died feby ye 24th.
$168\tfrac{3}{4}$.

The date given $168\tfrac{3}{4}$ is worth noting: with our small antiquarian knowledge we came to the conclusion that for some cause there was an uncertainty as to whether this Mistress Frances Bentley died in the year 1683 or 1684. It may, however, bear some other explanation.

Leaving Kineton we had, for the first two or three miles, an excellent level road that led direct to Edgehill—the long and historic range of heights so called rising steeply up right in front of us. This part of England abounds in memories; on the plain we were passing through was begun the first contest between Charles I. and the Parliament. We were on historic ground—an English battle-field. The past seemed very near to us that day. Visiting the spots where great events have taken place brings those events back to us: for the moment the defeat of the Emperor of the French at Sedan appeared farther off than the defeat of King Charles of England here.

On a commanding position on the crest of Edgehill the royal forces were gathered on 23rd October 1642. The Parliamentary troops being encamped in the valley below, the latter would doubtless have seized the heights before the king's arrival; but Hampden, with most of their artillery and ammunition train, had not yet reached Kineton, as he could only make slow progress for want of horses. On the king's side a hurried council of war was held, whereon that prudent and skilful soldier, Earl Lindsay, advocated a retention of the strong position the royal forces held, and awaiting there the attack of the Parliamentarians. Prince Rupert, on the other hand, however, with his impetuous nature, advocated descending to the plain and giving immediate battle to the enemy before Hampden could arrive; the Prince's advice was taken, and the battle commenced. Rupert advancing, drove back and severely handled the Parliamentary left, whereupon he proceeded to Kineton and began his favourite occupation of plundering. If instead of this Prince Rupert had wheeled his force round and taken the Parliamentarians in the rear, as he could have done, the day might have had a different ending. But whilst Rupert's cavalry were busy plundering, Hampden was hastily advancing, being hurried forward by the distant sound of the cannon and the firing; Rupert was driven back by Hampden, and the rest of the king's army were forced to retreat, with heavy loss, to their original position on Edgehill. So far it appears to have been a drawn contest, the Parliamentarians remaining masters of the battle-field, and the king still holding Edgehill and barring the way to London.

Reaching the foot of Edgehill we had a very steep and rough ascent; the original makers of this road had no idea of gradients. How the coaches managed to get down day after day without accidents, we could not imagine; perhaps they did not. It proved to be the stiffest bit of hill work we had during the journey, and we rested twice during the ascent; and to do this we had to pull the dog-cart across the roadway, and to put a stone under the wheels. We found some big stones ready to hand there that had manifestly been used by previous drivers on this steep stage for the same purpose. Bullet Hill we noticed that this particular part of the Edgehill range was marked on our map; possibly because of the number of bullets that, with other relics of the battle, were picked up here for long after the fight.

We were glad when we came to the end of our toilsome ascent. Upon reaching the top of the hill we rested awhile to admire the extensive prospect, looking back towards Kineton, and for miles beyond that little town our eyes ranged over a vast expanse of pleasant country that stretched away to a dreamy distance of rugged hills. From where we halted we had a bird's-eye view of the old battle-ground, seeming very peaceful and uneventful now, and looking very beautiful too just then, with the golden tints of the sunlit foliage, the silvery gleam of gliding water, the blue of the far-away hills, and here and there the roof-trees of nestling farmsteads showing amongst the well-tilled fields. The day was growing old, and the sun was sinking low in the sky; a golden glow was spreading in the west. We felt that we could not linger much longer there without running the risk of being benighted on our way. The wind had dropped; there was a strange stillness in the air, unbroken even by the rustle of leaf or song of bird. Broad mysterious shadows were slowly creeping over all the landscape; the only signs of life or movement were the upward rising of thin spirals of faint blue smoke from some hidden hamlets or sequestered homes. It was one of those tranquil moments when all nature seems at rest, and the world a second paradise!

As we drove along the crest of the wooded hills we still caught charming peeps of the country below through the trees. At one point we passed near to an old weather-beaten windmill, the first we had seen for several days, and we welcomed it as we would an old friend. We had come now once more into a land where wind, and not water, is the power

THE VIEW FROM EDGEHILL.

that drives the ancient mills—all those that have not been improved away by steam, that is. From this elevated spot we had a grand and gradual run downhill of some miles all the way into Banbury. Even after their long and tiring morning's stage our horses seemed "as fresh as paint," and trotted freely on, the dog-cart following of its own accord. It was a most enjoyable experience that five miles' rapid run into Banbury in the cool of a perfect evening. We positively seemed to glide along, so excellent was the surface of the road. In the stillness of the evening the clatter, clatter of our horses' hoofs on the hard road, the crunching of the carriage wheels, the jingle of the harness and of the pole-chains sounded quite inspiriting,—sounds that are as music to the ear of those who love driving. There is something very exhilarating in making the pace sometimes on the road, especially when the way is clear, the going good, and the carriage begins that measured swing which is the most restful motion in the world.

So driving on in the quiet gloaming we reached picturesque Banbury of nursery renown, just as the light had faded from earth and sky. The very hour to arrive at a place so curiously famed; for the gathering gloom screened from our gaze all that was commonplace, and allowed us to do a good deal of innocent romancing, according to the notions of our childhood, as to what Banbury, and especially its cross, was like; aided possibly by sundry highly-coloured illustrated and faithful (?) representations of these in certain children's story books of the pre-artistic age. Here we found a comfortable old-fashioned inn of the kind that Dickens loved to describe. So happily ended a long and most enjoyable day's drive.

Banbury was well known to me by name at a very early age owing to the classical nursery rhyme—

> Ride a cock-horse to Banbury Cross,
> To see a fine lady get on a white horse;
> Rings on her fingers, and bells on her toes,
> She shall have music wherever she goes.

I used to wonder then what Banbury Cross was like; and now that I am grown up and have made a pilgrimage to Banbury, I wonder still, for the ancient cross, rendered so famous by nursery tradition, is, alas! no more, it having been destroyed with countless others at the Reformation. I do think they might have spared this one for old association's sake; but the Banbury people were stern Puritans, noted of old for "religious zeal, cakes, and ale." A curious combination, it seems to me. And was not their Puritan zeal thus satirised—

> To Banbury came I, O profane one,
> Where I saw a Puritane one,
> Hanging his cat on a Monday
> For killing a mouse on a Sunday.

On the site of the old cross a new one was erected in 1859; but this is not hallowed by romance, and had no interest for us. It is a nineteenth century structure—and looks it!

There are some interesting and rather picturesque houses scattered about Banbury, notably one in the main street. The ground story of this has been converted into shops; but above, the old house is unaltered, and has three gables projecting and supported on three rounded bays beneath. This quaint old method of building by projecting upper stories is useful as well as exceedingly picturesque; and I wish that architects who build country houses would give some consideration to this convenient and effective style of architecture, so pleasing to the eye.

Always on the outlook for curiosities wherever we went, here we unearthed an old glass with the following puzzling inscription thereon:—

>Drink your glass
>and
>Think your toast.

It struck us after some consideration that possibly this glass belonged to some cavalier, and was used in the time of the Commonwealth to drink the health of "Prince Charlie over the water." Anyhow, it points the wisdom of thinking without talking, when talking might be dangerous; or as the old proverb pithily puts it, "Speech is silvern, but silence is golden."

Opening our bedroom window next morning we looked out upon a clear blue sky, with the golden sunshine streaming down on the ancient roofs of the houses around, and glorifying everything else it shone upon. "Another simply splendid day!" we involuntarily exclaimed. "Let's make an early start." Already we felt a longing to get into the country again amongst the green fields and shady woods. The weather was too perfect to stay in a town, even in a quaint old country town like Banbury.

The first thing after rising, as our custom, we went and looked at the horses to see how they had fared overnight, and very fresh and fit they looked, so that we arranged to start immediately after breakfast. Our horses had indeed improved in condition on the journey. It may be a fanciful idea of mine, but I verily believe that the change of air and the excitement of travel are as beneficial to horses as to human beings. Certainly our horses did get excited at times, and went along in a delightfully free manner; they even became playfully frisky now and then, as though they entered into the spirit of the tour and thoroughly enjoyed it. The monotonous routine of the park wearies a horse; he may not admire scenery, but he likes a change of road; at least I have frequently observed that my horses (other conditions being equal) go with more spirit on a fresh road than on one they know well—always excepting when their heads are turned stableward on the latter. During the whole of the outing our horses were never once off their feed in spite of many hard days' work, and they arrived home looking as well as they could look—fit, if needs be, to forthwith recommence the journey. The art of driving long stages across country with the same horse, or horses, seems to be a lost one since the advent of the railways. The magic that lives along the rein, communicating subtly from horse to driver, how few understand it now! This is a mechanical age, wherein men drive mechanically, forgetful that an animal is not a machine. We always made it a point of taking our horses gently up the hills, and sparing them as much as possible on heavy roads; but when the way was level, or the gradient in our favour, we then sped on apace if we felt so inclined. We were provided with a powerful brake, so that the horses had never imposed upon them the wholly needless labour of keeping the carriage back going downhill. According to our experience of years of road travel, a good whip, with decent cattle, who looks after their welfare on the journey, may drive all Britain over and have no trouble on the way.

CHAPTER XIX

A pleasant road—A morning drive—Railways and roads—Aynho—Village stocks—A sketch—Old associations in buildings—A trysting-place—A curious dispute—A crop of Indian corn—Buckingham—The finest tonic in the world—Bell-ringing—A tramp at prayer—Sunsets—Winslow—A curious window—An amusing conversation.

On leaving Banbury we at once struck upon a capital, smooth, and pleasantly undulating road with broad fields on either side that gave a certain feeling of spaciousness to the views around. The earth, we noticed, was of a reddish tint; this, with the yellow crops of corn and the deep blue distance, made a charming combination and contrast of colour. There is an undefinable pleasure to the trained eye in looking out for colour in the landscape, irrespective of the scene; an unknown pleasure this to the majority of people, who are content to let artists see colour for them in pictures. Many a sandy waste and bleak moorland, the forms of which are dull, and their aspects dreary to depression, are rendered beautiful to the painter simply by their colour.

We were glad that we had made so early a start, for the freshness of the morning air was delightful, and its fragrance delicious; the soft southern wind was laden with the sweet scents of countless wild-flowers. Early in the summer morning and late in the summer afternoon are the perfect hours for driving; only, alas! the early morning soon wastes away into the ordinary day, and the late afternoon quickly lapses into the gloom of the gloaming.

We had not gone very far before we came to a quiet old-world village of thatched cottages and picturesque homes, some of which stood shyly back from the highway, surrounded by their walled gardens — a village that, with its surroundings of big trees, might have come out of fair Devon and been transplanted into Oxfordshire. The morning air was crisp, the road was excellent, the horses were trotting briskly on, under which circumstances we felt disinclined to call a halt; otherwise the village might have detained us, for it appeared to abound in pretty sketchable bits. Just then we felt in that deliciously dreamy mood which is the luxury of laziness. Our delight was to glide on through the lovely country, and let its quiet beauties infuse themselves into us.

Our road retained its good qualities for some miles; smooth, winding, and gently undulating it kept, so that driving on it for driving's sake became a real pleasure, the progress was so easy, and the scenery, if possible, improved as we journeyed along. By the roadside were wide grassy margins with red cattle feeding thereon. I do love to see these unenclosed spaces by the way, they so suggest to me the idea of ampleness—an awkward word, I own, but I cannot find another to express my meaning so clearly. It is pleasant to feel that even in our little England there is land enough and to spare, and that every square yard is not enclosed behind hedgerow, fence, or wall.

Then we came to a spot where our road crossed, respectively, a canal, a river, and a railway, on a series of bridges following one another in succession. The railway bridge caused the road to take a sharp pitch up and down, where it formerly was a dead level; and though it may seem a trifling point, this high-pitched railway bridge suggested to us that, as there are many such on the old main roads, they must to some appreciable extent lengthen the distance of a long journey, as given in our pre-railway travellers' handbook, the still useful *Paterson*.

Then we arrived in due course at a quaint out-of-the-world village, known by the curious name of Aynho, the houses of which are all substantial and stone-built, and most are thatched; some have little walled-in gardens full of flowers. This was another very Devonshire-looking village, and of a type rarely found so far east in England, the combination of stone and thatch being thoroughly west-country. Aynho is built on the slope of a hill, and the road winds in and out as it mounts upwards. At the first bend to the right we espied the ancient stocks still *in situ*, and apparently in good condition and fit for duty, had not their use happily passed away. We were pleased to come upon this relic of times long gone by. The village street was deserted as we drove up it, excepting that an old-fashioned gig with an old horse in it was standing at a cottage door; this, rightly or wrongly, we took to belong to the country doctor, who, we presumed, was going his rounds. The parson and the doctor seem, as a general rule, to be the principal people in an agricultural hamlet,—the two best houses therein are nearly always the rectory and the doctor's abode.

After Aynho, the country we passed through, though very lovely, had a lonely look; there were few habitations of any kind to be seen, only a series of green meadows and tilled fields bordered by tree-lined hedgerows, and rutty lanes branching from the highway that seemed to lead to nowhere in particular. There were big branching trees by the roadside of oak, elm, beech, and ash, that cast a grateful shade upon the dusty road; then for a change came a row of picturesque Scotch firs, that gave quite a character to the landscape, with their tall stately trunks, whose red bark contrasted effectively with their dark needle-like foliage high overhead. Scotch firs are very dignified trees, and a group of them is always a telling object in the country side, they are so strikingly individual; the ramification of their branches is a study, they turn and twist about in a most bewildering manner that makes them most difficult to draw.

A dip in the road now took us down to a sluggish stream, which we crossed on an old bridge, and then found ourselves in the little village of Croughton. Here we discovered a primitive inn with stabling attached, so we baited our horses there. The inn, though primitive, was not picturesque; for ourselves we elected to picnic somewhere out-of-doors, for the weather was warm and the sitting-room offered to us was small and stuffy, and we thought that we detected in it the faint smell of stale tobacco smoke, which was not very appetising. So we wandered round about outside and found a quiet and shady spot by a stream near an old mill, where in the fresh air we thoroughly enjoyed an *al fresco* meal. Then, whilst our horses were taking a well-earned rest, we proceeded to sketch an old farmhouse that made a very pretty picture. Just as we were finishing this a party came up to us—evidently to see what we were doing—whom we took to be the farmer himself, and thus he spoke: "You bees a drawing of the old place, sir, I sees. Well, I don't see much beauty in it myself; it's too old to be beautiful. Dear me, now you've gone and put in a lot of weeds! Weeds bain't beautiful, that they bain't; they's nuisances, and I don't see has how you needs to draw them. Yes, it's main like the old house; but them weeds do spoil the drawing, that they do. Now you take my advice, sir, and leave them out." And so he chatted cheerfully on; a bank of tall thistles in the foreground being the offending weeds, which doubtless were not lovely in his eyes, but which came well in the composition—for even weeds are beautiful at times. But different people see things differently. I was once painting an old rather tumble-down cottage, which I happened to call delightfully picturesque in the hearing of the tenant thereof; he, however, thought otherwise, and declared that there was nothing delightful about it in his opinion; he wanted a home to live in, not one to sit out-of-doors and look at! And there was a good deal to be said from the cottar's point of view.

As the weather was so warm we did not hurry back to our inn, as we concluded to do our last stage during the cool of the evening. So we wandered about in search of another subject to sketch, and at the further end of the village we discovered its secluded and peaceful God's acre with an ancient church standing therein, an unpretending structure whose external walls were of simple rough-cast. The venerable old edifice, so innocent of any ambitious architectural merit, somehow touched our feelings in a way that no lordly cathedral ever could. There is a certain power in humility.

We found the church door open, and entered the building,—more, I fear, for a rest within its cool walls than for any religious motive or curiosity. There was not much of special interest therein, as far as we could discover from a lazy look round, but the structure appealed to us on account of its hoary antiquity. For centuries past the old church has been the centre of the village life; its very walls seemed hallowed by the oft-repeated prayers of generations of worshippers, who mostly rest beneath grass-grown, unnoted graves without, but some under crumbling stone tombs or monuments. To repair such a building, sacred with past associations, is needful at times; to restore it—in the modern acceptation of the word—is to rob it of its special character, the priceless dower of age, and all that renders it quaint or beautiful. The weather-stained walls, the lovely tints of lichen, the rare green of moss, the creeping ivy, and the general mellowness of age that the changes and chances of a long life leave on a fabric — these alone are the gift of Time.

Thus we mused as we sat down to rest in that old village church, so full to us of poetry and picturesqueness; more impressive, in our then mood, was the mystic shade of its gentle gloom than any grand or costly architectural *tour de force*. Love of old buildings is due to sentiment; after staying for some months in a new country far away on the other side of the world, where my eyes never rested on a building that was not of yesterday, I shall never forget the inexpressible delight it gave me on my return home to visit an ancient and unaltered church dating from before the time of the Crusaders,—for there was a monument to one therein with his legs crossed orthodox fashion. An old storied church is a petrified poem, a precious possession to be jealously guarded from the professional restorer's hand. Better even than he the village mason, for the mason would probably be content simply to uphold what there was, and have no clever or ambitious ideas of his own as to how the church should be improved, even at the cost of making it look brand new; the mason at least might spare us from a floor of showy Minton tiles—better in a private house or in an hotel,—bright brass work in the modern medieval style, gaudy and meaningless stained glass, or carved oak executed in the best possible manner by contract! Art by the square foot or yard, that profits no one but the producer! And not him so greatly, owing to competition.

Glancing around the shadowy recesses of the ancient interior, our eyes, grown accustomed to the dim light, alighted upon a young man and a younger maiden sitting very close together,—a pair of lovers, evidently, who thought that they had found a safe retreat from the outer world within the church, as many learned men in another way have likewise thought, and have not found the peace they expected. The couple seemed somewhat abashed at being discovered; possibly they had been accustomed to use the open church as a trysting-place on week-days, being the most retired spot they could find free from the villager's prying eyes; for, sad to relate, though the rural churches may be open every day—as many are now, never but once during our journeys do we remember to have found a worshipper within one, and of all unlikely people that worshipper was a beggarly-looking tramp, of whom more directly, as we discovered him next day at Buckingham.

Just outside the churchyard we observed a large elm whose trunk was of great girth. This fine old tree was enclosed by iron railings, to prevent it being damaged by the village youngsters, we presumed. It is pleasant to see trees thus cared for and preserved, for the great charm of English rural scenery is due to greenful hedges and leafy trees.

Returning to our primitive inn, we found at the door thereof two men engaged in a hot dispute about a halfpenny change; one man was the driver of a waggon, the other was on foot. The man with the waggon started on, but the man on foot followed him, still arguing the important trifle; and when we overtook them some mile or so on the road they were still arguing. What struck us as specially peculiar about the matter was that the party walking declared he was going every inch out of his way to get his halfpenny, and that though the dispute was hot, no bad words were used as far as we heard, for the animated conversation was not carried on at all in a *sotto voce*, and was therefore public property; indeed I have heard worse language used at a polite game of croquet, to say nothing of golf. When we overtook the arguing couple we felt greatly inclined to pull up and end the dispute by paying the halfpenny ourselves; but we felt that it surely was more a matter of honour than of money, so we passed on and saved our halfpenny. It pleased us much, however, to hear a dispute of such a nature, by such a class of people, carried on so comparatively good-naturedly, if in a loud tone of voice.

We had an open country with the road all in our favour on to the very pretty village of Tingewick. There we met a brewer's dray with the name of Hopcraft thereon; and a very happy name we thought it for a brewer—almost as suitable as Cutwell for a tailor, which we came upon elsewhere. It always interested us when driving to note the names of the country people, as far as we could glean them from the shops, waggons, carriers' carts, local papers, and so forth. It somewhat surprised us, in these days of rapid and cheap travel, to find how certain names are localised in certain districts. Names, unfamiliar to us, we discovered to be quite common in one part of the country or even county, yet not to be discovered in another, and *vice versâ*.

On the road we passed a crop of Indian corn growing and flourishing in a cottage garden. Though this crop will not ripen in England, unless in an exceptionally hot summer, and then in a warm spot, still it will come well into ear any season; and I have often wondered why this plant is not grown thus with us as a vegetable, for green Indian corn boiled is very delicious, and is universally used in America; it would afford the housewife a change of vegetables, of which we have not too much choice.

Buckingham, as we neared it, struck us as being a picturesque town. We were agreeably surprised with the old-fashioned place, as we had expected little of it; but it certainly deserves the title I have given it. The Ouse winds round its foot, from whence the ancient houses of the town rise in delightful irregularity, at least from an artist's point of view. Those people, and there are some, who like a town laid out chess-board fashion, would probably not admire Buckingham.

We crossed the slothful Ouse on an ancient bridge, close to which was a droning mill; above us rose the sleepy old town, crowned by a church, and a very charming approach to a place we thought it, quite capable of being made the subject of an effective picture.

As we drove along and up a street called the Chewar we observed the following inn sign, showing an attempt to attract attention and customers :—

The
Robin Hood.
If Robin Hood is not at Home,
Walk in and drink with Little John.

Some way farther on we noticed an old-fashioned inn with an ancient archway leading to a long stable-yard. We liked the look of the place, and though we knew nothing about it, as usual—for we prefer our own judgment in the choice of our hotel to possibly interested recommendation,—we drove confidently in and called for the ostler, who presently emerged from some hidden recess and took charge of our horses, whilst we sought accommodation for ourselves. I believe that we were the sole occupants of that ancient hostelry that night; and it seemed as though both landlord and landlady could not do enough for us, which was a very pleasant, but, I rejoice to say, not an uncommon experience. Yet once again it appeared that because we arrived by road a special interest was taken in us,—we were not the usual every-day travellers. It is a curious thing that so much attention should be bestowed on those who elect to drive by road.

During the evening we found our way into the bar of our hotel for a last smoke, as well as for an excuse to see and listen to the talk of the town folk.

But neither the people that chance brought there that evening, nor their conversation, was of special interest; so we sought our room at an early hour, and the dreamless, restful sleep that comes to those who have spent the whole day driving in the fresh open air—Nature's harmless and almost infallible narcotic. Fresh air is the finest medicine in the world for the majority of curable ills; it is a wonderful tonic and soporific combined, it gives "iron to the blood and phosphates to the brain."

Our dreamless slumber was, however, all too effectually disturbed at 6 A.M. precisely (we looked at our watch) by the incessant and noisy clanging of a church bell,—at least we took it to be such. Nowadays when nearly everybody, poor or rich, possesses a watch, and when clocks are plentiful and cheap, I really do not see the need of this medieval church-bell ringing, doubtless necessary at a period when time-keepers were scarce and unreliable. Everybody must or should know the hour of service of their particular church; and chapels get on very well without bells. It should be remembered that in a crowded town, especially with a church having a number of daily services, the constant clang, clang, clanging of loud-tongued bells is very wearisome and even injurious to invalids; and surely it is no part of the duty of a Christian Church to annoy or cause needless suffering to others? In the country, where the church, as a rule, is not in close proximity to dwellings, matters are on a different footing, and the sound of bells mellowed by distance is restful rather than disturbing.

Wandering about the town next morning, we found our way to the church of "SS. Peter and Paul," which is built on a commanding eminence affording fine views. The tower of this is old; the rest of the edifice appears to be modern, and therefore uninteresting to the antiquary. We noticed on the floor of the porch, as we entered, a bundle of ragged old clothes, together with a pair of much-worn boots, and within the nave we found a very shabbily dressed and rough-looking man, evidently a tramp, to whom, we presumed, the unsavoury bundle and boots belonged. He was kneeling down in one of the pews, his head buried in his hands, seemingly in silent prayer. He looked up for a moment as we entered, then resumed his former position, and took no more notice of us. From the momentary glance we caught of his face it looked sadly haggard and worn, almost pathetic in its expression of hopeless trouble. Had he come there, weary of the world and his lot, to plead with Him who said, "Come unto me, all ye that labour and are heavy laden, and I will give you rest"? We were careful not to disturb this worn and wearied worshipper, and as the church was modern and of no interest to us, not even architecturally, we quietly departed. Somehow, we hardly knew why, this poor specimen of suffering humanity brought before us Tennyson's lines from " In Memoriam "—

> Man, her last work, who seem'd so fair,
> . . . .
> Who built him fanes of fruitless prayer.

We were touched by the pathos of the scene, the

sorrows of the world, the thorns that beset the path of the unsuccessful in the struggle for existence. Was this aged tramp Nature's "last work," pleading for rest and peace in a "fane of fruitless prayer"?

Buckingham is an old town that pleased us greatly, yet why it did so it would be difficult to tell, for though its position is fine, its buildings are in no manner noteworthy. However, one edifice certainly attracted our attention, from its peculiar character and prominent position in the centre of the main street. This was the Fire Station; but it was by no means an ordinary structure, being built like an old castle, though on an insignificant scale. It was doubtless intended to be picturesque; but to us it seemed a freak in building, something to wonder at rather than to admire. Even this was better than the square-box style of architecture, with no aim but to keep the weather out. It did strive to be picturesque, even if it failed; and so far this was an acknowledgment that beauty was worth striving after.

The weather looked showery on the morning we left Buckingham; there was a plentiful supply of gray rounded clouds about, manifestly charged with aqueous vapour, with only a few small patches of deep blue showing between. A wild, warm west wind was blowing, strong and sweet, that was delightfully refreshing, and a little rain we felt would be welcome rather than otherwise, for the roads were dusty, and the wind now and then blew the dust about more than was agreeable. We had an excellent road at starting, with wide grassy margins, very tempting for a trot or a canter on horseback—so much so, that for the moment we almost wished that we were riding instead of driving. There were big trees too on either side of the way, and the wind made a restful, musical rustling amongst their innumerable leaves and branches—a gentle continuous "surring," which is so grateful to the ear of the jaded town-dweller. Country sounds are as soothing as town noises are disturbing and irritating; they are as far apart from each other as melody is from discord.

The west wind made the distance seem near and darkly blue, for the air was clear and the freshening breezes kept it swept free from all impurities. Here and there the distance was blotted out for a time by a soft silvery mist that told of a transitory shower; but where we were the clouds blew by overhead and no rain fell, so the dust was master of the situation. I really do not think that a driving tour could be taken with any pleasure in a less moist climate than England, for we have ever found that dust, and not wet, was the one "fly in our ointment." Properly equipped, one can defy and even enjoy rain, but dust penetrates everywhere. Not only does rain freshen the air and all vegetation, but the clearing-up of a storm oftentimes causes a revelation of wonderful atmospheric effect; a dust storm affords no compensations.

The country we passed through was purely an agricultural one, and though very charming to look upon, with its tangled hedgerows, verdant meadows, wide fields of golden corn ripening for the harvest, green woods, with a circling distance of indigo blue, still there was nothing about it specially to describe, and I am not sure whether it was not this very fact that made it so pleasing to us. It did not (as more famous scenery oftentimes does) rouse up one's feelings; it was a gentle, natural, dreamy, unassuming landscape. One may admire grand scenery, even be in awe of it, but the gentle and unassuming is the more lovable. Almost anywhere in rural England, far from spreading towns and railways, an artist may find excellent material for a picture. There is a rare harmony and mellowness of colour and a softness of outline about the English landscape that the scenery of no other country — except perhaps Holland — possesses. Our humid atmosphere gives very artistic effects, and our clouded skies are ever varied and interesting, frequently providing us with a Turneresque sunset—or rather, should I not say, revealing gorgeous effects that Turner so loved to paint. One does not always realise the value of a thing till you have lost it; so it never occurred to me what a deprivation it would be to live without being able to see the sunset each day; one sets so little store on the familiar. It happened on a certain occasion, however, that I was staying for a month in a secluded spot in wild Wales, where the high mountains to the west hid the sunset from my view. I felt all the while that there was a something wanting, but what it was I could not for the first few days comprehend, till I suddenly discovered it was the absence of the sunset. I believe that there were

plenty of sunrise effects, only I did not see them!
An artist living there assured me that the sunrises
were pale and colourless compared to the sunsets,
and I frankly accepted his word for it. He did now
and then behold a sunset; for he would climb to the
top of the hills to view it.

The first place we came to on the way was the
little town of Winslow, where we alighted at the
clean-looking Bell Hotel, and were ushered into
a tiny and tidy sitting-room, with some freshly
gathered flowers in a vase on the table, and we
at once felt that our short stay there would be a
pleasant one. We have generally found that
flowers on the table or in the windows are the
sure sign of a good inn. There have been exceptions to the rule; but very rarely. On the other
hand, I regret to say, it by no means follows that
an hotel with Scripture texts framed and hung on
the bed-room walls is either good or reasonable.

A neat and very civil maid waited upon and
served us with our usual mid-day meal of cold roast
beef and cool, clear ale. Our lunch over, we set
out for a ramble round the town. Noting the Post
Office we entered it to purchase some stamps;
whereupon the man who handed them to us asked,
"Have you seen our church yet? There's a
curious stained-glass window in it you should see;
it is the portrait of the wife of a gentleman, and
there has been a good deal of fuss about it; for, you
see, she is represented as an angel with wings and
a halo round her head, and some people object to
it. I thought you would like to know, as you are

driving through the town." We thanked him for his information, and, as we had no special point to make for, determined to go and see the window. It did not strike us for the moment as strange that the party should know that we were driving through the town, and therefore presumably on a driving-tour; yet the fact appeared to us afterwards somewhat odd, as we had never been into Winslow in our lives till about an hour ago. Probably he had seen us drive in, and had guessed we were touring by road.

Entering the church, we soon discovered the window in question, and found it to be as we were told. A very pretty and poetic idea certainly, and one that pleased us, though perhaps it would not do to be repeated too often, as it failed to be decorative, for the modern-looking middle-aged face seemed strangely unlike the usual medieval rendering of the face of saint or angel; yet it did not sin against taste half so much as do many ugly and ostentatious monuments that frequently fail to adorn the walls of our churches. It is the ideal that is so beautiful and attractive in art, not a barren fact photographically correct.

When we were in the church the sexton was tolling the bell, and between times he was talking loudly to a poor old woman; so loudly that we could not avoid hearing all that was said. "How much will it be for an hour?" the old woman asked. We presumed she meant for the tolling of the bell during that time, but we might have been mistaken; and the conversation may have related to some other matter. In reply to the query, the sexton named a sum, which I have forgotten. "How much for half an hour?" then asked the woman. "That will be half as much," replied the sexton. "Very well," said the woman, "give me a good half-hour's worth." The conversation amused us; but, as I have remarked, we may have misunderstood its purport.

CHAPTER XX

Mist and rain—An evening effect—Aylesbury—Notice to trespassers —Exploring—Old-fashioned hospitality—The building material of the country—Wayside inns—A peaceful progress—The Chiltern Hills—Tring—Life at a country hostelry—Commercial travellers—" Nothing new under the sun "—Quaint gargoyles.

RETURNING to our inn, the long-deferred rain began to fall at last in the shape of a thick uncomfortable drizzle, which was not very inspiriting. We waited some time to give the weather a chance to clear up, but it did not avail itself of the opportunity; the ostler said he thought it was set in for wet for the rest of the day, but he kindly prophesied that it would be fine in the morning. However, we did not feel inclined to wait till then, as we expected letters at Aylesbury, at which place we proposed to spend the night; so we had the horses harnessed, donned our waterproofs, and set forth on our way.

The thick drizzle prevented us from seeing much of the country we passed through at first, for our horizon was limited by the misty state of the atmosphere. As far as we could judge, the country was a very pretty one, pleasantly diversified by gentle hill and wooded valley, but it was unfortunately just that kind of scenery that requires sunshine to do it justice. The wind blew soft and warm; and as there was no dust, we began to enjoy our drive in spite of the rain. We had the highway all to ourselves; and as it was not a day for sketching or photographing we trotted along apace, the horses showing no signs of fatigue in spite of the four hundred miles, more or less, of hard and continuous road work they had done.

After a time we came to a very picturesque village, with a charmingly quaint old house by the roadside, and an ancient church with a fine old gray tower that lorded it over the lowly dwellings around. Just then a gleam of watery sunshine broke forth, the misty rain ceased, the air cleared, and we began to have hopes of the weather. Leaving the village, we had a long descent with a fine view of the open country spread out before us, or rather, perhaps it would be more correct to say that we imagined there was a fine view ahead; for a good deal was left to the imagination, the trees and fields below us vanishing into a gray mist and looking very unsubstantial. Then the clouds lightened, the mists rolled off the land, our horizon gradually extended, gleams of sunshine came and went, till at last the sun conquered the rain-clouds and shone down on a moist world, which soon was glowing with colour. As we neared Aylesbury, even that unromantic town looked almost romantic with the golden light of the setting sun reflected in many a window, on the wet roofs of the houses, and on one or two restless weather-vanes that flashed back the light. It was not pleasant driving into Aylesbury, for it was the end of a market day, and cattle and sheep thronged the roads, to say nothing of sundry shouting drovers who only seemed to bewilder the cattle the more they shouted, and numberless farmers' carts hurrying homewards. At that moment Aylesbury struck us as the busiest place we had been into since we left London : it is fair to confess, however, that the town was very quiet next morning. These country market towns wake up into activity once or twice a week, as the case may be, and slumber on for the other days. Here we drove into the ample courtyard of the George Hotel, where there was still a goodly array of farmers' conveyances gathered around; and within the old house we found their owners discussing the bad times over their pipes and glasses, their dismal talk and jovial looks contrasting strangely. I verily believe that the English farmer positively enjoys to have a good grumble; it is one of his long-standing prerogatives.

Aylesbury offered no attractions to detain us, so we started off in good time next morning, the more especially as it turned out gloriously fine. On the first two or three miles of our stage we observed several boards in different spots with notices thereon warning people not to trespass. The sight of these did not please us, as we had almost forgotten that such things existed, not having happily seen one for many a day. During our journey, when out of the beaten track, we had felt no compunction in harmlessly trespassing here and there for the sake of a view, to make a sketch, take a photograph, or for the nearer inspection of a ruin or ancient home that appeared interesting; but with a notice-board prominently placed in front of us we felt less free to do as we would.

It is one of the many charms of getting right away into the real country, far from towns and railways, that there seems more liberty to get about. There, according to our experiences, you may wander—I prefer the word "wander" to "trespass"—wherever you are inclined almost, so long as you are careful to do no damage, and will meet with no rebuff. One day I wandered over several fields, as I could not find a path, to get a view of a quaint old home whose antique red roof, great gray gables, and substantial chimney-stacks I saw peeping above some trees. There chanced to be a five-barred gate close to the house that was locked, and as I was climbing over this, the farmer, to whom the old place belonged, made his appearance, and I quite expected he would naturally demand what I was doing there, climbing over his gate; so I at once begged his pardon for trespassing, and said that I had been attracted by a distant view of his picturesque old house, and was wishful to see it close at hand, and to make a sketch of it if he would not object. "And you be right welcome, sir," he replied. "I'm sorry as how you had to climb over the gate, but we have to keep it locked for the cattle, they rub against it so, and open the catch and get away." Then observing that I was hot—for the day was warm—he would have me come inside his old home

AN OLD ENGLISH FARMSTEAD.

with him, "Just for a glass of milk, it will refresh you." Now, I do not care to drink milk when I am hot, for it does not suit me, and I should have greatly enjoyed a glass of good ale; but I took the milk, not to hurt the feelings of my kind entertainer; and I shall not readily forget the delightfully cool and clean kitchen he took me into, with its well-scrubbed red brick floor, its brown-beamed ceiling, its genuine old ingle-nook with oak settles on either side, its curious fireplace built on the stone hearth, with a wood fire blazing therein and an iron pot hanging above suspended by chains. From the fire came the grateful fragrance of burning wood, and from the pot a most savoury odour. On the high shelf over the fire were brightly polished glowing copper and shining pewter utensils that gave a cheerful look to the room; and these articles were every whit, in their way, as decorative as the expensive oriental china and other ornaments that rich men place on their mantelpieces and walls. Nor should I omit to make mention of a deeply-recessed leaden lattice window, in the lower portion of which were flourishing geraniums in pots.

The kind-heartedness and simple hospitality of English country folk in remote corners of the land is very pleasing and very genuine. We were delighted to find that this good old-fashioned trait lingers yet in the distant shires. Let us hope that it will never quite die out. After all, "the traveller makes his own welcome." A friendly manner and pleasant words that cost nothing are an almost unfailing passport in rural England, it opens doors and begets countless little favours that money will not buy. Civility wonderfully oils the wheels of life, and it is not an expensive commodity to deal in. An American friend once told me that he had often heard of, but had never met with, a surly Britisher; but then, my friend was a very pleasant-mannered man, which may account for his happy experience,—if people will go blustering about, they have no right to complain if strangers resent it.

A few miles out of Aylesbury we passed through a very pretty village with a flint-built church, showing that we had arrived in a chalk country; for in long past days, and even in the more recent but still pre-railway times, owing to the difficulty and cost of transit, buildings were generally constructed of the materials of the neighbourhood; and in a chalk country the only enduring building material is flint. We noticed that the Bell Inn here had a fine elm in front of it on a triangular patch of grass. A spreading tree before a wayside inn, especially if there be a seat round it, is the traveller's delight, for there he may refresh himself out-of-doors in the grateful shade. On a hot summer day, how good a thing it is to drive off the glaring dusty road beneath the shelter of a leafy tree and enjoy a glass of cool foaming ale. Driving in the summer time is thirsty work. I think that being out in the open air so much has something to do with it, under which circumstances a call at a clean wayside inn for a glass of bitter ale is one of the minor pleasures of the road. The village, as I have said, was a very pretty one; but as we drove through it we did not feel sufficiently curious to stop to ask its name, or even to refer to our map for that information; we felt too delightfully lazy to trouble about trifles; and after all, as we reasoned to ourselves, what mattered it,—it was the village that pleased us, not its name.

So we drove on in a quiet, contemplative mood, dreamily noting all the varied beauties of the country we passed through. It is truly a delightfully restful way of travelling, this placid progress across country,—no haste, no worry, no noise, no fuss, no rush for tickets or places: you can only thoroughly enjoy the beauties of the country when there are no disturbing influences at work. A day's rural ramble is easily spoilt if there be any haunting anxiety as to catching—or missing—the last train home. The true Nature-lover abhors haste, or being bound by slavish time.

Presently the Chiltern Hills came into sight, the hedge-rowed fields ceased and gave place to the open down-land, sloping gently to the valley, the crests being crowned in places by clumps of beech trees, and elsewhere fringed with firs. We were still in the pleasant county of leafy Buckingham, that land of beautiful beech woods—woods that give a special charm and character to the scenery of this portion of England, and perhaps reach their greatest glory in that picturesque fragment of a former forest, the famous Burnham Beeches, near Slough.

In time we reached the foot of the Chiltern range, and had a long ascent through a chalk cutting to their low summit. Reaching the top of the hill we had a splendid prospect, looking back right over the rich and verdant vale of Aylesbury with its fertile fields lessening to a horizon of hazy blue woods. Then a short stretch of pleasant road brought us to the long one-streeted town of Tring, —a pleasant little place it struck us, sufficiently prosperous not to be dull, yet not so prosperously progressive as to have lost its old-time air in the rage for so-called modern improvements. Here we drove up to the Rose and Crown Inn, an unpretending, homely hostelry that seems to have suffered little change either outwardly or inwardly since the days of the coaches; the very antithesis this to the large and luxurious modern hotel where people congregate in crowds, and where the bill, if not unreasonable for the luxurious accommodation afforded, is not on such a scale as always to suit the man with a moderate income. It is another of the advantages of travelling leisurely by road, that coming into a town you can see and select your inn for yourself, you are not at the mercy of the first railway omnibus.

There is a good deal of quiet interest to be had in watching the life at a country town inn. The first thing that strikes you after London is the delightful absence of hurry and a sense of restfulness. You may go into the old courtyard and have a leisurely chat with the ostler, and often be well entertained thereby; for we have found that ostlers are generally characters, and not averse to gossiping. Many of the country people, and most of the farmers living around, drive over to the principal inn of their local town to bait their horses whilst they do a little shopping; and naturally they are all well known to the ostler. And if there be any little history or tradition connected with their families or homes, he will, you may be sure, retail it to you,—of course it is needful to take some of his stories *cum grano salis;* but the experienced traveller knows pretty well how much to allow in this respect: most ostlers appear to possess that royal faculty, the knack of remembering faces. Then within doors the waiter, who is an Englishman, and ten to one owns to the name of George or William, will provide you in the same way with all the latest provincial gossip, from his point of view, whilst he attends on you at table.

These homely and home-like country hostelries are never tourist-crowded, for they offer no attractions to the tourist; the people you meet in them are genuine travellers, and are generally far more sociable than the usual idlers at a fashionable watering-place hotel, who interest me not. Moreover, these country inns have no regular season, their business is much the same all the year round; so that they have no need to charge heavily in the summer time in order to make up for a long and unprofitable winter, when the fashionable watering-place hotel is probably deserted, although the landlord thereof finds his rates and taxes still going on. I like to feel at home at mine inn, and this I generally do at the rural hostelries on the way; there seems to be a friendly, good-natured feeling about them. Their landlords, or landladies as the case may be, do not disguise the fact that they are pleased to see you; and not being over-crowded and under-servanted, every one appears to have enough leisure to study your convenience, from the landlord down to the useful boots. All this is very pleasant, and adds vastly to the enjoyment of the traveller.

At the Rose and Crown we were ushered into the commercial room; why, I do not know, unless we looked like commercials, or unless there were no coffee-room; however, we were not displeased, as we thought that we might possibly learn something of the world from the commercial traveller's point of view. We found a capital cold luncheon spread there, and no one within, and we forthwith sat down and commenced to do duty to the viands. Presently a "commercial gent," as the waiters term this class of guests, came in—a stout, jolly-looking individual; he gave us a bow, and, after politely begging our pardon, sat down before the fare placed on the table, to which he did ample justice, possessing, apparently, like ourselves, a hearty and healthy appetite; and we noticed that he was most attentive in passing us anything that we required. There are possibly many gentlemen who would think it beneath their dignity to sit down to table with a commercial traveller. However this may be, it struck us that there was a certain courteousness in the manner of this "commercial" in politely begging our pardon before seating himself at our table, which was in agreeable contrast to the usual way in which strangers place themselves beside you at a fashionable *table d'hôte* without a word. There are such things as Nature's gentlemen.

Then in a few minutes the door was again opened, and another "commercial gent" of a wholly different stamp made his appearance. He was a young, thin, and active man; looking around as he entered, he exclaimed, "What, no hot dinner!" in quite an aggrieved tone of voice. Then he rang for the waiter and inquired of him why there was no hot dinner provided; and it was some time before the waiter could pacify him. Then he sat down to the cold but excellent repast, and ate his food, grumbling all the while. He hurried through his meal, and soon departed with a big bag in his hand, and we were not sorry to lose his company.

When he was gone the stout party exclaimed, "He's a young 'un at it; when he gets a little older and more experienced he'll settle down a bit and take things more quietly, as I do. He'll soon get knocked into shape. He has not got his commercial manners yet." The last sentence struck us as fraught with meaning; for I believe that there is a strict code of behaviour amongst "commercials," and he who departs therefrom is quickly "sent to Coventry" by the fraternity.

Left alone with the staid old "commercial" we thought it a good opportunity to glean from him, if possible, an insight into the *vie intime* of the commercial traveller's life; and he appeared nothing loth to give us his views on the question. It appeared that he had been a "commercial" ever since he was a young man; he rather liked the life; anyway, it was far better than being cooped up in an office all day. Then there was plenty of change of faces as well as scene; and good living was the rule. He thought he had a much better time than many a banker's clerk; but he was thinking of retiring from the "profession." The life was not so pleasant as of old. There was nowadays more competition, and the work was therefore harder. Before the railways became so common he used to drive about country from place to place, which was very pleasant: that was the heyday of the "profession." Allowing for an old man's pessimism, doubtless there was some truth in his remarks. He had three counties allotted him to travel through, he commenced at one point and ended at another, taking every place on the way in regular rotation. It took him nearly three months to do his three counties.

Then as we glanced round the room our eyes chanced to alight on a bright oblong metal box, with a handle in the middle of the top, that stood on the sideboard. We wondered what it could be. Noticing our glance the "commercial" exclaimed, "That's a penny-in-the-slot affair; they used to be very common in my younger days, forty years or so ago, in most commercial rooms, but they've gone out of fashion now almost entirely; I don't know a single house where there's one in use. There's a slit on one side at the top, and you put a penny in it, when the lid at the other side comes up, and you can, or rather could, take a pennyworth of tobacco out; that's how they worked." Whereupon we got up to inspect the machine, but found that it was out of order; it was there manifestly for an ornament, or perhaps as a curiosity. It was in fact a portable "penny-in-the-slot machine," on the same principle as the larger ones that are now in vogue, and may be found at the most important railway stations. Truly "there is nothing new under the sun," for afterwards on reaching London we chanced to notice the following paragraph in the *St. James's Gazette* which shows that the principle of the invention, instead of being new, was known and utilised even in the far-off pre-Christian days. This, then, is the paragraph—"Ancient Egypt is looking up in every way. Some of its contrivances appear to have been quite up to date. Actually they had already, more than two thousand years ago, what we call 'a penny-in-the-slot,' for the extraction of something useful, pleasant, or otherwise desirable." After this follows a description of the ancient machine, which appears to have worked in precisely the same manner as those of to-day.

Before starting on our afternoon's drive, we took a stroll round the town, and made one or two sketches of the quaint gargoyles on the church. Some of these are curious; one represented a most undesirable creature, yet had the quality that few pure inventions have, that the nondescript animal looked as though it might have existed, you were able to trace bones and muscles in the carving,—the sculptor had at any rate a knowledge of anatomy. It was the improbable made possible.

In the churchyard, amongst the numerous trite morals and commonplace inscriptions, we noted one pretty idea; it may not be original, but it was fresh to us, and, we thought, worthy of being copied. It runs as follows :—

> 'Tis sweet as year by year we lose
> Friends out of sight, in faith to muse
> How grows in Paradise our store.

CHAPTER XXI

A late drive—The hour of romance—The peace of evening—Berkhampstead—The last day of a holiday—Chance acquaintances on the road—A puzzling problem and a possible explanation—An ancient gabled house—The contrast of the old and new—A picturesque waterway—Watford—Bushey—A retrospect—Back again in London.

WE started late from Tring, just as the sun was getting low in the golden west, and the shadows were growing gray and vague. It was a charming drive we had that evening; the air was cool and soft and sweet; the country beautiful with beech-clad hills to our right, looking, doubtless, doubly so with the mellow last gleam of the sun resting on the wooded heights—for the parting rays of the sunset give an added touch of poetry to even the finest landscape.

At one point to our left we had an extensive prospect over a vast stretch of level plain; and in the mystic gloaming, with a very slight aid of fancy, this might have passed for the sea, so straight was the horizon and so little definite was there for the eye to grasp in the dark blue-gray world spread out below us. For a person of poetic temperament there is a peculiar fascination in a late evening drive, for then the imagination may have more or less of a free rein, so much of the landscape and one's immediate surroundings being mysterious and undefined in the gathering gloom.

There is a subtle charm that twilight throws over a landscape which oftentimes gives to the most prosaic subject an air of romance. I have seen an ugly modern building, a gaunt, unfinished, pumping-house to a lead mine, as beheld against the darkening sky, look like some gray, grim, feudal castle keep; and a commonplace ruined farmhouse, with its great roof-beams black and bent, appear almost spectral thus. Truly twilight is the hour for romancing!

In the half-light there is a dim uncertainty all around, except where tall trees or buildings may rise upwards and show strongly silhouetted against the sky, or where a full flowing river or still pool reflects the mellow light above into the gray-toned gloom below. With twilight there comes a hush, not an absolute silence any more than there is in the daytime, but Nature seems more restful then, and sounds that one hardly notes in the noon, such as the quiet gurgling of a river, or the soft rustling of the wind over a cornfield, gently assert themselves at that tranquil hour. With twilight, too, comes the refreshing sense of repose; for the day's work is done, the ploughman and shepherd have gone home, the just perceptible smoke steals slowly upwards from many a scattered hamlet or solitary home, and the lights begin to gleam in windows here and there as the stars above come out.

So we drove on through our quiet little bit of

world with our lamps shedding forth an uncertain light ahead, of no use to show the way, but of use to prevent any one running in to us; for we have found that country people sometimes drive rather carelessly at night.

Then we arrived at the thoroughly typical "thoroughfare" town of Berkhampstead, which appeared to us to consist mainly of one long street. Here we drove up to the King's Arms Hotel and spent the evening in our sitting-room looking over the sketches and notes of our most enjoyable outing. Generally at this time we had our maps out and studied the road ahead, and made our plans for the next day; but that night we preferred to look backwards instead of forwards, for our journey, alas! was nearing its end: at that hour on the morrow we should probably be once again in dear old smoky London. We realised the fact that we were driving back into the heart of civilisation as represented by the largest city in the world; that smoke-stained buildings and stone pavements would soon take the place of sunny old-time homes, greenful hedgerows, and lovely spreading landscapes. The last day of a holiday is not generally an inspiriting one, especially the last day of a driving tour when returning to the mighty, many-peopled metropolis. Gradually the pleasant and quiet country roads would give way to the busy and noisy city's streets; omnibuses, tram-cars, and hansom-cabs would again become familiar sights. There were no more discoveries, scenic or otherwise, probable on the last twenty-six miles that remained for us to accomplish, to give an added zest to the day's stages. It is the continued state of expectancy that renders each day on the road so mildly exciting and so abounding in interest—there is something delightful in being a discoverer in ever so small a way; to come suddenly and wholly unexpectedly upon a beauty spot, a fine prospect, a curious church, a romantic ruin, a quaint old home, a picturesque past-time hostelry with its traditions of the coaching days, or any interesting relic of former times, is one of those special pleasures that however often repeated never seems to pall. Each turn in the road is fraught with possibilities!

There is another pleasant feature about a driving tour: not only does it take you amongst fresh and constantly changing scenes, but it brings you into contact, from time to time, with stray artists in search of new painting ground, antiquaries exploring the country like yourself, enthusiastic archæologists, quiet anglers, farmers, countless old-fashioned rural folk, and the numerous uncatalogued specimens of humanity that frequent the road, to say nothing of entertaining landlords and gossiping landladies—for the latter do exist, even in these busy times.

The conversations you may have with the various people you come upon might be considered by some as dull and unprofitable, but they are characteristic of the talkers, and therefore interested us; one thus gets a glimpse of the world from a wholly new point of view. As a rule the most interesting people that we have met on the way have been antiquaries, they always seem so delighted to converse with a stranger having similar tastes, and we often learnt a great deal of their lore from our chats with them, though in such cases we could not, of course, always accept what we were told unreservedly, for if there be a person given to strong opinions upon any specially disputed point in which he holds a particular view, that man is an antiquary.

Now one of the things that has frequently puzzled us during our many wanderings in England, is the peculiarity that prevails in a number of ancient churches, namely that the chancel deviates markedly in a straight line from the nave. This fact has also, I believe, perplexed a number of learned people, for it has been manifestly intended from the first, and is neither the result of an accident nor of an after alteration, the churches being of one period. The most generally accepted explanation of this peculiar departure from the usual and natural architectural procedure is that it typifies the writhing on the cross. This explanation never quite satisfied us; but during our travels we chanced to learn the views of a certain antiquary on this point, and he professed to have solved the mystery, at any rate to his own satisfaction; and though I should not like either to accept or to reject his theory, it appears to me deserving of consideration, and I give it here for what it may be worth. It appears then that this gentleman chanced one morning, very early, to be inspecting an old church in which the chancel deviated from the straight line in question, and he observed that the first rays of the sun as it rose came through the east window and rested upon the eastern sepulchre that contained the founder's tomb.

But this was not all, for he afterwards learnt that it happened to be the Patron Saint's day; and the idea occurred to him that most probably this curious deviation of the chancel and the east window with it was purposely so arranged, so that the first rays of the rising sun of that special day might rest upon the founder's tomb. We have not had any opportunity yet of testing the truth, or otherwise, of this theory, but it certainly seems a plausible explanation of a puzzling problem, bearing in mind the poetical ideas of the medieval churchmen.

As we had a long day's drive before us, we left Berkhampstead early next morning. I am afraid, however, we were not in our usual buoyant spirits, for it was the last day of our tour; and though all good things must come to an end in this imperfect world, still the end was unwelcome.

Just beyond our inn, close to an old milestone inscribed "To London. 26 Miles"—that has been curiously preserved in the heart of the town—we noticed a charming time-mellowed old house of three gables, with stone-mullioned windows of leaden lattice lights; and this was really the last noticeable picturesque house on the journey. It seemed to us to give a grace and a dignity to the rather commonplace street. These modest old English homes that are so comfortable to live in, as well as pleasant to look at, are to the modern villa as a diamond is to paste.

Our way lay now along a wooded valley; some of the hedges we observed were of clipped beech, and chestnut trees began to make their welcome appearance in the landscape, and for a time road, railway, and canal ran close together—the railway too close indeed for the comfort of our horses. The scenery was very pretty in places, and there was plenty of life in the prospect, with the rapid rush of trains on one hand, and the slow progress of canal boats on the other. Great was the contrast between the two modes of transit; the one a sudden roar, a rush of steam, a cloud of dust, a shrill metallic shriek, and before you had hardly time to think about the matter an express train had come and gone; the other an almost noiseless and tediously slow movement of towed barges. England is a country of sharp contrasts, for in it the old and the new are so frequently thrown into close proximity, as where the railway goes beneath the feudal castle walls, or in some ancient churches the electric light glows in the medieval gloom, and lights up tombs of olden knights in their armoured effigies.

Driving on, we found that there was more traffic on the road than we had been accustomed to; we could not complain of loneliness any more; and there were a number of public-houses on the way also; one of these proclaimed itself by the title of "The Friend at Hand," another was called "The Fountain"—not a very happy title, we thought, for a house where beer rather than water flowed; still another bore the unfamiliar sign of "The Artichoke." But why the titles we noticed should all be so uncommon we could not tell.

Then as we drove slowly on, some little distance before reaching Watford, we espied a pretty bend of the canal with a lock at the end of it; the gates of this were just being opened for some barges to come through, whilst other barges were coming up in a contrary direction. We thought that this made a very pretty picture, so halted awhile in order to photograph it, whereupon the bargemen at once began to pose themselves, each one looking straight at the camera, to our disgust, for by so doing they spoilt our picture, but to their own manifest satisfaction; this innocent proceeding on our part caused a delay of the traffic of, I should judge, a good five minutes!

Some time after our return home we saw an engraving of one of Turner's pictures called "Canal, near Watford." This was evidently intended for the very spot that we had photographed, only Turner had the audacity to introduce some exceedingly high hills, if not mountains, in his distance, where there are none, and our photograph shows only trees. Some artists do, I know, boldly change the position of mountains in their pictures from the exact place they occupy in nature; they simply move mountains about to suit their composition— but Turner created them!

Then we drove along an excellent road to Watford, which old town appeared to us to be flourishing, increasing in size, and rapidly losing what little picturesqueness its prosperity has left: here we baited our horses and gave them a good rest, preparatory to taking our last stage in.

Leaving Watford we passed through the village of Bushey, where we noticed its ancient church close by the roadside, with a spreading elm and a large pond in front; we at once recognised this spot as forming the subject of a fine Academy picture some years ago, and called, if I remember aright, "Our Village." Here, too, we noticed some young ladies walking about artistically dressed—one of the party, indeed, looked as though she had stepped out of some picture; we were for a moment puzzled to account for these prettily and effectively garbed maidens, till we remembered that Professor Herkomer had a school of painting here, and we concluded that they were the outward sign of this little world of art. Anyway it was a pleasant thing, and a relief from the tyranny and monotony of uniformity, to see young women carefully carelessly attired and picturesquely clad, instead of solely fashionably, which anybody can be who has no taste but merely money. We stopped a few minutes at Bushey, and walked down a lane to get a view of Professor Herkomer's new house that he is building for himself. I do not care to criticise this, simply because I do not understand it, and it wants time to comprehend an entirely new departure in building; still I think I may say that it looks too stately and too foreign for its peaceful and essentially English surroundings—in fine, it does not "smack of the soil." It is monumental rather than homelike: but I have said that I do not care to criticise this structure, and here I am doing so.

After leaving Bushey, Edgeware was reached in due course and left behind; houses by the roadside became more and more frequent till the country ceased altogether, and we found ourselves late in the afternoon at home in Kensington, from whence we had started. Our journey was ended, and only a pleasant memory of it remained to think over and dream about in the days to come — a precious possession this. There are three delights of travel, the anticipation, the realisation, and the remembrance. We had passed through lovely landscapes that the railway traveller never catches a glimpse of even ; we had taken our ease at many a comfortable, and not a few quaintly picturesque old-fashioned inns ; we had seen ancient abbeys, storied castles, historic and haunted homes ; we had loitered in sleepy medieval market towns and primitive and pretty hamlets. Our course had lain through leafy lanes, and across wild wind-swept heaths, through rich and homelike pastoral lands, and over rugged moors and rounded downs, by winding river and tumbling stream—our journey was a perpetual picture, a feast of beauty. Each of us could say " I, too, have been in Arcadia," and sorry we were to leave it.

The chronicle of our tour is now finished. In case it may be of use to any of my readers I have given an Appendix, with an itinerary and mileage of our journey, so that they can follow in our pleasant track, wholly or in part, should they be wisely minded to try a holiday on the road ; and a more delightful tour — so abounding in beautiful and changeful scenery and interesting and romantic relics of the past—could hardly be devised or desired.

CHAPTER XXII

CONCERNING DRIVING TOURS

I AM frequently being asked personally by friends, and by letters from strangers, how we managed on the road generally, and what sort of accommodation we found at the country inns on the way. I have already, in a previous book, *A Tour in a Phaeton*, devoted a chapter to driving expeditions; but as the work is now out of print, I have thought, even at the risk of repeating myself to a certain extent, that a few words on the subject might prove of interest to any of my readers who may possibly feel inclined to follow our excellent example, and take a holiday on the road.

In the first place, those who do not keep a carriage can easily hire a horse, or a pair of horses, and a more or less suitable conveyance of a jobmaster, and, provided he be not a fashionable one, at a moderate charge. I have hired a pair of useful cobs thus for £2 (the pair) per week, taking my own dog-cart, and driving, of course, myself. The jobmaster I dealt with told me that he has frequently sent a coachman out with a horse and carriage, so that even the man unaccustomed to "handle the ribbons" is not debarred thereby from taking a driving tour.

Should you job a carriage, whether of two or four wheels, it is wise, if possible, to select one of the dog-cart pattern, as you are thereby enabled to keep your luggage locked up out of the way, and secure against dust or damp. If this be not possible, it would be well to purchase a tin uniform case, to be procured from most military outfitters at a small cost; these cases are light in weight, besides being strong, wet and dust proof—a rare combination of good qualities—they are most convenient for travelling. For those who go a-driving across country and over unknown roads, a brake is an almost indispensable adjunct to a touring conveyance, and is a great economiser of power when going down hill; for it should be borne in mind that it requires nearly as much labour to keep a carriage back when descending a steep hill as to start it on the level. Rubber brakes are by far the best kind, and a pair should last a lengthened journey; unfortunately they are expensive.

Maps are a necessity. We always take separate ones of each county; these can be had mounted on linen for one shilling each; if not so mounted they are apt to tear when opened in the wind, especially if it be raining at the time. We always provide ourselves with the reduced Ordnance Survey maps, published by Messrs. Smith and Sons, which we have found very trustworthy. A red chalk line previously traced over a road that you are likely to follow assists in distinguishing it from others when consulting the map in a hurry.

Guide books out of the beaten track of travel and tourists' haunts are of little use. We rely on our copy of Paterson for all the information we require as to the roads, the rest we have the pleasure of discovering for ourselves. This truly wonderful work, though over sixty years old, is still a most useful publication. Fancy a future traveller consulting for his present information a Bradshaw of that age!

It is advisable, before starting, to provide yourself with a supply of small silver and coppers, as change is sometimes scarce on the road, and its possession saves trouble and unnecessary expenditure in being obliged to give a shilling when a sixpence would suffice, and so forth. Also a pair of knitted worsted gloves for driving in the wet should not be forgotten, as when damp the reins do not slip through them.

It is an excellent plan to carry a spare feed of oats and a few beans in the driving-box, to be used in case of a camp-out on the road, or to fall back upon should the corn not be good at some remote country inn; the oats or beans can be replenished when passing through a town.

A waterproof apron of some kind you must have, and let it be of ample size so that the ends may be well tucked in under you at the sides. There is another advantage, too, in having the apron large, as it is the very thing to spread on the grass, cloth side uppermost, when picnicking in the country.

The best kind of a mackintosh for personal wear is one provided with a cape, so that you may be able to drive with your hands under the latter, and thus keep them comparatively dry. Some kind of a cap with a big peak is a luxury in wet and windy weather, as the peak keeps the rain out of your eyes and allows you to drive in comfort; indeed, when properly equipped, driving in the rain is by no means a disagreeable proceeding.

Be careful of your whip when entering the low archways of the old-fashioned country inns, as the top is apt to be caught. We have broken more than one whip by carelessness in this respect, and from want of experience it is at the commencement of a journey that such a provoking mishap is most likely to occur.

It is advisable to take a spare pair of *comfortable* driving-gloves with you in case of loss or damage to those in use. Let your gloves be of full size and easy; nothing is more wretched than driving in tight gloves. Candles for the lamps should not be forgotten in case of being benighted on the road, nor matches to light them with.

There is no necessity, on arriving at a country town, to put up at the first hotel you come to; we always make a point of driving slowly round about a strange place, and leisurely inspecting the different hostelries before making our choice. An old road traveller can almost invariably tell a good inn from external appearances, as readily as an artist can tell a good painting from a bad one.

Before starting on a journey, it is wise to have

the carriage wheels oiled, and the harness carefully overhauled; such a simple precaution may save trouble and even delay on the road.

These few hints may not appear separately very important, but it is just the care about such minor matters that goes a great way to enhance the enjoyments of a lengthened tour by road. It is annoying, when in remote country places, to find that there is this or that trifle wanted. In case of need the Parcel Post is very convenient in getting anything on from home, as it penetrates almost everywhere.

APPENDIX

ITINERARY OF JOURNEY

	Stages in Miles	Total distance in Miles
London to Kingston .	10	
Kingston to Guildford	$17\frac{1}{2}$	$27\frac{1}{2}$
Guildford to Liphook .	$16\frac{1}{2}$	44
Liphook to Petersfield	$8\frac{1}{4}$	$52\frac{1}{4}$
Petersfield to Winchester	18	$70\frac{1}{4}$
Winchester to Romsey	$10\frac{1}{2}$	$80\frac{3}{4}$
Romsey to Salisbury .	$16\frac{1}{4}$	97
Salisbury to Stonehenge and back	$21\frac{3}{4}$	$118\frac{3}{4}$
Salisbury to Warminster . .	$21\frac{1}{4}$	140
Warminster to Bradford-on-Avon through Norton St. Philips	$15\frac{1}{4}$	$155\frac{1}{4}$
Bradford-on-Avon to Malmesbury through Chippenham	22	$177\frac{1}{4}$
Malmesbury to Cirencester . .	11	$188\frac{1}{4}$
Cirencester to Cheltenham over the Cotswolds	$15\frac{1}{4}$	$203\frac{1}{2}$
Cheltenham to Upton-on-Severn through Tewkesbury	$16\frac{1}{2}$	220
Upton-on-Severn to Worcester .	10	230
Worcester to Bromyard	14	244

	Stages in Miles	Total distance in Miles
Bromyard to Leominster	12	256
Leominster to Ludlow	11	267
Ludlow to Craven Arms	8	275
Craven Arms to Bridgenorth through Munslow	21	296
Bridgenorth to Kidderminster	14	310
Kidderminster to Droitwich	$10\frac{1}{2}$	$320\frac{1}{2}$
Droitwich to Stratford-on-Avon through Alcester	$21\frac{1}{2}$	342
Stratford-on-Avon to Banbury over Edgehill	$21\frac{1}{2}$	$363\frac{1}{2}$
Banbury to Buckingham	18	$381\frac{1}{2}$
Buckingham to Aylesbury through Winslow	17	$398\frac{1}{2}$
Aylesbury to Berkhampstead through Tring	12	$410\frac{1}{2}$
Berkhampstead to Watford	12	$422\frac{1}{2}$
Watford to London	$14\frac{1}{2}$	437